133- DC Segregation '48
(2 x)

THE TRUMAN ERA

1945–1952

By I. F. Stone

A NONCONFORMIST HISTORY OF OUR TIMES

THE TRUMAN ERA

1945–1952

I. F. STONE

With an Introduction by Robert Sklar

LITTLE, BROWN AND COMPANY

BOSTON   TORONTO

To

ESTHER

the best of me

Originally published in 1953 by Monthly Review Press

Library of Congress Cataloging-in-Publication Data

Stone, I. F. (Isidor F.), 1907–
    The Truman era, 1945–1952 / I. F. Stone
      p. cm. — (A Nonconformist history of our times)
    Originally published: New York : Monthly Review Press, 1953.
    Includes index.
    1. United States — History — 1945–1953. 2. United States — Politics
and government — 1945–1953. 3. Truman, Harry S., 1884–1972.
I. Title. II. Series: Stone, I. F. (Isidor F.), 1907–
Nonconformist history of our times.
E813.S85   1988
973.918 — dc19   88-6791
                                              CIP

MV

*Published simultaneously in Canada
by Little, Brown & Company (Canada) Limited*

PRINTED IN THE UNITED STATES OF AMERICA

INTRODUCTION

The Truman Era was I. F. Stone's farewell to daily journalism. When it was published in 1953, Stone had already launched, in January of that year, the independent weekly newsletter that was to become over the next two decades among the clearest and most consistent voices of opposition to United States foreign and domestic Cold War policies. The founding of *I. F. Stone's Weekly* in the last months of the Truman administration, at a time when anti-Communist hysteria had made Senator Joseph McCarthy of Wisconsin the most powerful political figure in America, was for Stone an act as much of necessity as of choice. The repressive atmosphere of intolerance toward radical and even liberal opinions had gradually eroded the opportunities for newspaper reporters and columnists like Stone. One after another the radical daily papers of New York for which Stone had worked during the Truman years—Ralph Ingersoll's *PM*, Bartley Crum's New York *Star*, and Ted O. Thackrey's New York *Daily Compass*—ceased publication, the last in November, 1952. *The Truman Era* brought together the best of Stone's articles and columns from those papers, and also several from *The Nation* magazine, on which Stone served as Washington editor from 1940 to 1946. The work stands twenty years later as it did when it first appeared, as a unique expression of daily newspaper work in the United States: of accurate, witty, objective, and committed reporting that rises by its own qualities to the level of contemporary history.

Stone's articles and columns collected in *The Truman Era* combine the immediacy of the moment with the broad contextual background of social and historical structure and change. He was a newspaperman with a distinctive style and voice. He always let his readers know there was a person behind the words, someone who had actually experienced the events of which he was writing, who could convey a sense of atmosphere, the nuance of tone and expression. His prose was always simple and direct, yet it could make a point, deflate absurdities, create human portraits, with quick touches of humor and irony. His newspaper work already demonstrated the skills for which *I. F. Stone's Weekly* was to become famous, his ability to find the significant fact in a buried phrase or a back-page item, the needle of truth in a haystack of falsehood. Stone was a writer who forthrightly proclaimed what he believed in, even when his beliefs became in the atmosphere of McCarthyism more dangerous to think and say: the trend toward socialism is irreversible, freedom of thought is the basis of all other freedoms. He believed together in socialism and libertarianism at a time when the universal wisdom in America held that they were as separate as the poles.

Unquestionably it is the perspective Stone derived from his beliefs that gives *The Truman Era* its significance as a work of contemporary history. He was no slavish supporter of either of the two great power blocs that began to form in the aftermath of World War II. He was blind neither to the faults of the Soviet Union nor of the United States. From the earliest moments of the struggle for power which began even before the end of the war, Stone recognized the anti-Communist dogmas which shaped United States foreign policy and contributed to the growing hostility between the wartime allies. In a period when a bipartisan political coalition and the major organs of opinions sought to convince the public that United States postwar policies were benevolent, defensive, freedom-loving, and above reproach, Stone understood what few others were able to grasp: that the United States had worldwide economic, political, and ideological ambitions of its own; that armed conflict and the maintenance of dictators against popular will were tactics the United States was capable of employing in pursuit of its goals; and that the Cold War was as much a consequence of American aggressiveness and intransigence toward the Soviet Union, of American expansionism and drive to control other countries and areas of the world, as any similar motives on the part of the Russians.

Nowhere was Stone's perspective on the Cold War expressed more originally and effectively than in his book published the year before *The Truman Era,* in 1952, *The Hidden History of the Korean War.* In the winter of 1950–51, while he was working in Paris away from the atmosphere of official Washington and close to independent European sources of news, Stone began to question the authorized version of events surrounding the outbreak of the Korean War in June, 1950, and the subsequent American military policies, tactics, and pronouncements. He brought his evidence together in a book-length manuscript, but such was the repressed and frightful atmosphere of the times that every publisher he contacted in Great Britain and the United States rejected the book as too controversial. Finally the manuscript came to the attention of Leo Huberman and Paul Sweezy, editors of the then newly founded independent socialist magazine *Monthly Review,* now entering its third distinguished decade. Their Monthly Review Press brought out *The Hidden History of the Korean War* in 1952 and *The Truman Era* in 1953.

Stone's criticism of official United States foreign policies and the American role in Cold War hostility have in recent years been followed up by a group of historians seeking to revise and reinterpret the history of American foreign policy during the Second World War and the Truman administration. These "revisionist" historians, beginning with the work of William Appleman Williams and including later studies by Gar Alperovitz and Gabriel and Joyce Kolko, among others, have substantiated through their research many of the insights Stone developed in his newspaper reporting and investigating at the time the events were happening. Stone's *The Hidden History of the Korean War* and now *The Truman Era* thus take their place as central works among "revisionist" accounts of World War II and postwar American foreign policy aims and methods.

The Truman Era is particularly valuable for its independent view of public affairs in mid-century America from outside the narrow partisan context of two-party maneuvering. The years of

Harry S Truman's administration from 1945 to 1953 still are not firmly fixed in our historical consciousness. Textbook accounts may speak of the atomic bomb and the Berlin Airlift, the Alger Hiss case and the growth of anti-Communism, the Chinese Revolution (or "the loss of China") and the Korean War, the Marshall Plan and N.A.T.O., the "Soviet threat," containment, and the rise of the Cold War. But rarely have they been able to provide insights into the underlying order and structure of events, other than the standard historical homilies about change and anxiety, challenge and response. Stone adds to these accounts an indispensable grasp of the fundamental continuities in American public policy throughout these years of rapid transformations. From the first articles on the San Francisco conference to set up a United Nations organization he recognizes the basic American purpose to maintain a strong anti-Communist stance and to accept its corollaries, rebuilding and eventually rearming the defeated World War II enemies Germany and Japan, struggle and tension in foreign affairs, continued high taxes and increasing government expenditures for American and foreign military requirements, the creation and support of corrupt and undemocratic regimes in many parts of the world.

Historians will continue to debate whether postwar United States foreign policy was a necessary response to a real Soviet challenge, or an aggressive American ideological quest to redeem the balance of twentieth-century history, to defy and hopefully to annul the Bolshevik revolution of 1917 in Russia and the Maoist revolution of 1949 in China. But whatever the reasons for America's diplomatic, economic, and military posture toward the world, no one can deny its consequences for political, social, and intellectual life within the United States. There are few works about the postwar years that can show as clearly as Stone's *The Truman Era* how the American struggle to preserve "the free world" went hand in hand with an effort to destroy freedoms in the United States. It was not one of those paradoxes of which historians are fond of speaking; it was a calculated goal shared by both major political parties to incite fears of foreign attack and domestic subversion, to enflame passion, impose conformity, and suppress dissent, the better to pursue foreign policy objectives.

Two decades later we are still living with the results of governmental policies of the Truman years, in our domestic lives as well as in Indochina. In 1971 the New York City Board of Education announced that it was thinking about reinstating the teachers of whom Stone writes in *The Truman Era,* who were fired from their jobs twenty years earlier for refusing to tell the Board whether they were then or had ever been members of the Communist Party. We will probably never have a complete record of the number and variety of people who lost their jobs, their careers, or even their lives because of repressive policies in the Truman years. But it would be accurate to say that nearly everyone who lived through those years was diminished by the attacks against freedom of thought within the United States. Nearly everyone learned to be careful, to be anxious, to fear: not to sign a petition, not to join an organization, not to give money, not to be seen with certain books, not to speak your opinion lest someone misinterpret, accuse, inform. Americans were told every horror story of Soviet suppression of free expression, and everyone knew that Siberia was the cold and barren place where the Russians sent their dissidents for punishment. Yet all too few Americans realized they were generating their own Siberias in their own minds.

How could it be that a nation proclaiming itself the champion of freedoms everywhere was so indifferent to, and even actively engaged in, the destruction of its own? The American philosopher William James once provided a useful clue to an explanation. He said that there was a difference between feeling free, and acting as a free person. People feel most free, said James, when they respond with the least effort, reacting "unhesitatingly in a certain stereotyped way." We act as a free people when we make an effort to affirm and adopt a difficult task, to work against the lines of greatest resistance. Perhaps the true nature of the Truman years can be summed up in these very terms: Americans learned to define freedom as feeling free, escaping from difficult choices by embracing stereotypes, rather than struggling to act and think as free people.

One of the principal virtues of *The Truman Era* is that it both demonstrates and describes the acts of free people in the Truman years. The process of historical recollection too often reduces rather than builds up what we know about the past: books disappear, names are forgotten, movements and opinions fade from memory, and we are left with a historical record preserved by and for the powerful and influential. *The Truman Era* itself had become difficult to find, and even scholars specializing in recent American history had not been aware of its existence. Stone's book brings back much that we had lost from our historical consciousness of those years.

At the end of the Truman era, with the closing of the last of his newspaper outlets, Stone was forced to find a new way to keep his writings before the public. He formulated plans to publish an independent four-page weekly newsletter from Washington and solicited subscriptions at $5 a year from readers on the mailing lists of *PM*, the New York *Star,* and the New York *Daily Compass*, his former newspapers, and Monthly Review Press, which had published his last two books. Slightly more than five thousand responses came back—"a scattered tiny minority of liberals and radicals," as Stone later wrote, "unafraid in [Joseph] McCarthy's heyday to support, and go on the mailing list of, a new radical publication from Washington." The first issue of *I. F. Stone's Weekly* was published January 17, 1953.

The *Weekly* is history now. It became a bi-weekly in 1968, and then in December, 1971, after nineteen years of publication, Stone brought out the final issue; at the age of sixty-four he exchanged one fortnightly deadline for another, as a contributing editor of *The New York Review of Books.* At the end, more than seventy thousand subscribers were reading the newsletter, and finding in Stone's writing the same trenchant, meticulous pursuit of facts in his exposure of contemporary policies and events that he had brought in earlier years to the Truman, Eisenhower, Kennedy, and Johnson administrations.

Over the years between, those thousands of new readers turned to Stone when they began to sense that there was more in political events than one could learn from daily newspapers, television, and government press releases. For me, as for many others, it was the spring and summer of 1965, the first months of air war against North Vietnam and the commitment of large-scale American ground forces to South Vietnam, when Stone first became indispensable. When the United States government came forward with its lies—about the Tonkin Gulf incident, in its White Paper attempting to document Hanoi's "aggression," in what it said and didn't say about American activities in Laos—Stone came forward boldly with the truth. And who gave Stone the franchise for truth? Nobody. Building on his experience and convictions, his life-long commitments to freedom of thought and social equality and justice, he searched for the facts and determined their proper significance from the public records, Congressional committee hearings, *The Congressional Record,* the newspapers. The government's belief that it could fool the people rested (and rests) on its assumption that we have short memories, inadequate access to documents, and careless habits in reading the press. The assumptions may have been right; but they failed to take I. F. Stone into account. He served as our ideal reader.

What sort of man was this, who seemed to spend his days with newspapers, magazines, *The Congressional Record,* and tomes of Congressional hearings? On one occasion Stone came to my town to deliver a lecture, and after his talk a few people gathered to meet him. Stone began the conversation by remarking that he had that day finished reading Solzhenitsyn's novel, *The First Circle,* which had been published in English translation that season. It was a great book, he said. Had any of us read it? No, no, hadn't found the time. Our host was a scholar of Reformation history and theology who did much of his research in Latin. Talk of Latin made Stone reminisce. He had studied the language in high school and during his several years as a student at the University of Pennsylvania; he still liked to read the poets in the original when he had the chance. They discoursed learnedly on Vergil and Catullus. Stone recited from memory several of his favorite Latin verses. It had not occurred to me before that one source of Stone's perspectives on the United States lay in his knowledge of other histories and cultures, in his skills as an intellectual.

"Intellectual" may sound like an incongruous word to describe a man who has devoted a working life of half a century to daily and weekly journalism. Born in 1907, Stone began his newspaper career at the age of fourteen when he published his own paper in Haddonfield, New Jersey. As a student he worked for a country weekly, as a stringer for a local daily, then full time on the rewrite and copy desks of the Philadelphia *Inquirer*. He found liberal and radical employers on a succession of papers—the Camden *Courier-Post*, the Philadelphia *Record*, the New York *Post*, *The Nation* magazine, and the three papers he worked for during the Truman years. All nine of his books were based on his newspaper work; indeed, every word of his books from *The Truman Era* on first appeared in newspapers, magazines, or his newsletter before being collected between hard covers.

It is precisely because he is an intellectual that Stone's old articles seem to grow in value over the years. He is a historian, a philosopher, a man of letters, who decided to exercise his talents on the public affairs of his day. His articles create a sense of depth, of landscape, of historical setting, that is very rare in American journalism. So much of the news we get appears to have been made on a studio set, thrown up this morning, torn down tonight. There is no yesterday and no tomorrow. Stone is one of the few American newspapermen who knows how much the past can illuminate the present.

For too long the accepted image of the American intellectual was a man or woman with a divided self—a person with grandiose ideas in a grimy reality, head in the clouds, feet in the mud, unable in any way to relate a vision of what might be with the reality of what was. We would do well to replace the image of the divided intellectual with the reality of I. F. Stone and others like him—integrated men and women willing to think and write and act and struggle for a better world for mankind, here and now.

Ann Arbor, Michigan
March, 1972
ROBERT SKLAR

TABLE OF

CONTENTS

FOREWORD
HISTORY IS ON OUR SIDE

I feel for the moment like a ghost. I am writing this foreword in my old cubbyhole of an office at the New York *Daily Compass* in the same building where *PM* and the *New York Star* were printed before it. The *Compass* shut down a few days ago after three and a half years of publication. Only a few minutes ago a couple of prospective purchasers, being shown through the dark and abandoned city room on the third floor, looked in on me startled, as if they had suddenly found the place haunted.

Outside the snow is falling on the tiny triangular park below my window at Hudson and Duane Streets, and the traffic lights gleam like enormous gems in the wintry gloom. Here in the heart of New York's wholesale produce market, among the butter-and-egg men, over the space of a decade there were a series of experiments in independent liberal journalism which now have come to an end. I was a part of all of them: *PM* under Ralph Ingersoll and John P. Lewis, the *New York Star* under Bartley J. Crum and Joseph Barnes, the *Daily Compass* under Ted O. Thackrey. This book is made up of gleanings from the pages they edited. Thanks to them, and the readers and backers (from Marshall Field to Corliss Lamont) who kept those papers alive, I had twelve years of such freedom and opportunity for service as few American newspapermen and intellectuals in my time have enjoyed. I never had to write a word I did not believe. I was allowed to fight for whatever cause won my heart and mind. I was subject to no dictation, personal or political. I had the greatest privilege any human being can have — I was able to earn my bread doing exactly what I liked to do. I wrote as I pleased. They were turbulent years, but the turbulences were outside me. Within I was at peace. I developed no ulcers and I consulted no psychoanalysts. I was and am a happy man.

The year 1952, now coming to a close, was my thirtieth year in newspaper work. I began in 1922 when I was fourteen with a little monthly paper of my own in the country town where I grew up. It was printed at the local weekly's job shop, and it carried ads solicited on bicycle trips after school in that and neighboring towns. I was a strong League of Nations supporter and a Wilsonian, Left enough even then for the linotype operator who set my copy to predict between spurts of tobacco juice that I would come to a bad end. A year later I got my first job on a small city daily and worked on newspapers while I was at high school and college. I never took journalism courses because by the time I got to college I already considered myself a man of practical newspaper experience, with an old-timer's disdain for college professors who presumed to teach what they had never practiced. I thought for a time of teaching philosophy, but the smell of the newspaper shop proved more enticing than the rather spinsterish atmosphere of a college faculty. I was content to remain a newspaperman. "Content" is not the right word for it. When I was a boy, my picture of what a newspaperman should be was compounded of Galahad, Don Quixote, and William Randolph Hearst. I believed that a newspaperman ought to use his power on behalf of those who were getting the dirty end of the deal, that he ought not to join in those stale surrenders which are called the practical realities of the world. And that when he had something to say he ought not to be afraid to raise his voice above a decorous mumble, and to use 48-point bold.

Politically, I suppose I am what everybody right or left calls a troublemaker. I am not Euclidean in politics; I do not see how the rich complexity and exuberant contradictions of man and society can be bounded by straight lines and neat angles. I recall a congenial character of whom I read somewhere, I think in Macaulay, a certain Colonel Wentworth who got in wrong with the Cavaliers when they were in power by defending the Roundheads and in wrong with the Roundheads when they were in power by defending the Cavaliers. I salute the Colonel's memory and have sought to abide by his example. It is an ignoble saying that God fights on the side of the biggest battalions. The place to be is where the odds are against you; power breeds injustice, and to defend the underdog against the triumphant is more exhilarating than to curry favor with those on top and move safely with the mob. And so I have had my share in newspaper work of what I consider fun.

In thus casting up accounts, I try also to recall the darker side, for there was a darker side, I suppose, though at the moment I find it hard to recall. There was first of all the nature of the job itself. I must have written close to three million words in those twelve years for the dailies on which I worked (and for *The Nation* which I served so satisfyingly from Washington during most of the same period). Only other newspapermen will fully realize the agony of turning out so much copy: the perpetual gap between what one would have liked to get down on paper and what finally did get itself written and printed, the constant feeling of inadequacy. There was so much to learn and so little time; if only one had a few hours more, how much better the copy might have been!

Then there was another agony, which cropped up to make one sleepless in the early morning. I rarely had doubts about those I defended. I often had doubts about those I attacked. Had I been fair? Was I being a self-righteous prig, without charity or compassion? How little I understood about human beings, the conflicts within them, the compulsions under which they operated, the compartmentalized lives they led, the good for which they strove, the evil they were forced to do! How easy, and how shameful, to be a newspaper pundit, a petty moral magistrate sitting in judgment on others! I was guilty of much bumptiousness, ignorance, and injustice. But I awoke in the morning unregenerate and cheerful again, and can remember only once or twice when I did not pick up the papers outside the door eager to see what had happened next.

II

It is dark within, and gloomy without. The deserted city room is bleaker than any graveyard. Outside in the little park the few thin trees look bare and sickly in the snow. There is little time for retrospect on a newspaper, even on one which has closed down, and so I still find myself looking back on the past with impatience and forward to the future with zest. What brought America to the present pass and what hope is there for freedom of thought in America? These are questions to which I would like to give some tentative answer in introducing this collection of pieces which cover the years from the end of the Second World War to the end of the second Truman administration. These were the years which saw the beginnings of the Cold War and of the drive toward intellectual regimentation in America.

I might begin my attempt at an answer with an anecdote. In the spring of 1946, I was the first reporter to travel the Jewish underground from Eastern Europe through the British blockade to Palestine. When I got back to Washington, where I had been working since 1940 for *PM* and *The Nation*, I felt the change in the atmosphere of the capital. I dropped in to see the much-maligned Harry D. White, then Undersecretary of the Treasury, one of the ablest and brightest men in Washington. I asked him what had happened. His reply then may help to sum up the Truman years. When Roosevelt was alive, he said, "we'd go over to the White House for a conference on some particular policy, lose the argument, and yet walk out the door somehow thrilled and inspired to go on and do the job the way the Big Boss had ordered." Now, White said, "you go in to see Mr. Truman. He's very nice to you. He lets you do what you want to, and yet you leave feeling somehow dispirited and flat."

So Washington had begun to change. FDR had attracted to the capital a wonderful collection of idealists, liberals, and radicals, human spark plugs of various kinds. Their energy, enthusiasm, and devotion made the New Deal possible. The loyalty probe was calculated to drive such people out of the government, since there were few among them who did not have enough of a radical past to run into trouble. But even before Mr. Truman was led to issue the executive order establishing the loyalty inquiry in 1947, to head off similar legislation by the Republicans, men of this kind had begun to drift out of Washington to jobs in private business or the professions. The fizz was out of the bottle.

The top men Truman brought in were hardly inspiring. Tom Clark as Attorney General and Snyder as Secretary of the Treasury were samples of the new mediocrity that a mediocre President brought to Washington. With these changes at the top, the little name plates outside the little doors also began to change. In Justice, Treasury, Commerce, and elsewhere, the New Dealers began to be replaced by the kind of men one was accustomed to meet in county courthouses out in the country. The composite impression was of big-bellied good-natured guys who knew a lot of dirty jokes, spent as little time in their offices as possible, saw Washington as a chance to make useful "contacts," and were anxious to get what they could for themselves out of the experience. They were not unusually corrupt or especially wicked — that would have made the capital a dramatic instead of a depressing experience for a reporter. They were just trying to get along. The Truman era was the era of the moocher. The place was full of Wimpys who could be had for a hamburger.

This age of little men was confronted by big problems, and knew only too well its incapacity to wrestle with them. Their whole period of power thus takes on the aspects, on the psychological and political plane, of a breakdown in faith. Until his election in 1948 transformed a disarming humility into a ludicrous conceit, Mr. Truman was a man without faith in himself, surrounded by men without real faith in American society. Freedom requires courage, and peaceful coexistence requires confidence. They lacked both. Mr. Roosevelt had surmounted a crushing fate which left him forever with crippled limbs but the struggle had given him in compensation a stout heart. The man who said "we have nothing to fear but fear" had gone through days of terrible illness in which it must have seemed to him that he had things much more concrete than fear to fear. A whole government, a whole country, a whole era was permeated by that exuberant courage which was FDR. His successor, catapulted by tragedy into a job he never dreamt he would or could reach, was filled with real fear of his own capacity. There seeped out to the press in Mr. Truman's first days in the White House off-the-record accounts of frank sessions in which a little man bewailed the fate which had made him President. Mr. Truman's fears transmitted themselves to those around him and through him to the country, as Mr. Roosevelt's courage had done earlier. "Toughness" became a mask for weakness, and stubbornness a substitute for strength. Mr. Truman, who was really scared, launched the "get tough" policy. Mr. Roosevelt, who was really tough, did not need to proclaim that fact to the world.

III

The deceptive quality of the Truman toughness was soon apparent. The two big problems of the Truman years were to maintain full employment and to reach a settlement with the Russians. The "get tough" policy offered a means of appearing to solve both. Armament production was to prime the pump at home and frighten the Russians abroad. To have tried to maintain employment at home by peaceful means would have brought the administration into frontal collision with Big Business. To have tried to create a new stable balance of power abroad by negotiation with the Russians would have opened Mr. Truman to a charge of "appeasement." A toughness beyond his capacity would have been essential to buck private interest at home with a program of peaceful expansion for full employment, and to face the uproar in Congress from elements which opposed any settlement with the Russians. The course chosen by Mr. Truman also made possible the easy alternative of government by crisis and alarum. While the civilian branches of the government were in the hands of mediocre politicians, the military more and more set the pace of the administration. They naturally began to think in terms of the next war before they had even finished the one at hand.

At home and abroad, faith was needed and faith was lacking. Coexistence with Russia and Communism required faith: faith in capitalism, faith in free institutions, faith in their capacity to meet new problems and to compete successfully for men's loyalty against a revolutionary one-party dictatorship, faith in their ability to survive in a world which must henceforth be largely Communist and socialist. Such faith was beyond these fearful men, who governed by instilling fear rather than confidence. And the inevitable casualties were the philosophical assumptions which had lain for almost two centuries at the foundations of American life. These were secular, skeptical, democratic, and optimistic. They had bred distrust for the priest and contempt for the bureaucrat. They had developed a healthy suspicion of government and a lively irreverence about all dogma. They were reflected in separation of Church and State, and respect for individual belief and conscience. They implied belief in the efficacy of reason, the essential goodness of man, and the ultimate victory of truth. The First Amendment, the cornerstone of the American constitutional system, rested on the assumption that since men were reasonable and good they could be trusted to choose among freely competing ideas. American optimism and belief in social reform drew their strength from the happy conviction that men were made evil, rebellious, violent, or criminal only by the miseries of material circumstance, not by some mysterious and innate quality predestining them to damnation. To improve man one had only to improve his conditions. The corollaries affirmed the futility of force against human aspiration and new ideas, and asserted the indispensability of social amelioration and free discussion to a healthy and progressive society. In this the American shared the modern Western tradition shaped by the Dutch, English, French, and American Revolutions, by the rise of modern science and the successful revolt against clerical authoritarianism.

All these faiths began to be shaken, then more and more

openly assailed as the momentum moved America further on the road toward the garrison state and war. Secular education was attacked. The Roman Catholic Church became more powerful. Its traditional inquisitorial methods were utilized ever more extensively by Congressional committees delving for political heresy. Communist renegades shifting over from a revolutionary to a counter-revolutionary authoritarianism found comfort, protection, shelter, and patronage in the Catholic Church. Not only the politicians but the generals were constantly invoking God; forgotten was the derision with which, only a generation before, Americans had greeted Kaiser Wilhelm's *"Gott mit uns."* The young were taught to distrust ideas which had been the gospel of the Founding Fathers. Propositions which had been McGuffey Reader platitudes for generations suddenly began to seem alive and precious again to the besieged minority fighting for traditional freedoms, while a new crop of intellectuals won applause and cash by deriding these same traditions. A Whittaker Chambers rehashed and refurbished the obscurantist nonsense with which reactionary Catholic intellectuals had long attacked not only the Russian but the French Revolutions. An ex-Communist teacher, returned to the bosom of the Church, told the McCarran Committee she had been wrong in teaching her students to have an open mind.

Those who had spoken out most strongly against regimentation during the New Deal were the foremost proponents of the new regimentation which began with the Truman era. Those who objected most to the regimentation of property were the first to encourage the regimentation of mind; and the reader will see (in one of the pieces below) how much of what happened in the sphere of thought control was forecast and blueprinted in advance by the United States Chamber of Commerce. The 1946 report of its Committee on Socialism and Communism charts a program to drive out of opinion-forming agencies — schools, radio, movies, television, newspapers, and libraries — all Reds, pinks, and liberals. Socialists were considered as dangerous potentially as Communists, though the Socialist *New Leader* was recommended highly. Liberals were damned for protecting the freedom of speech of both, and the report took exception to those who thought revolutionary ideas could be "appeased by improvements in the standard of living of the people." While Truman and his advisers feared to "plan" for full employment in peacetime (the horrid word "planning" is notably absent from the collected reports of the President's Council of Economic Advisers), Big Business planned to establish a glacial conformity, a chrome-plated American version of what George Orwell saw ahead for mankind.

In this respect the postwar period merely brought to dominance tendencies already apparent, though held in check, during the Roosevelt period and before. The developments exposed by Upton Sinclair in *The Brass Check*, which showed the *"Gleichschaltung"* of the pre-World War I journalistic muckrakers, had continued. Life was already precarious during the '20s for liberal and radical writers and journalists. There had always been a strongly anti-democratic tendency in American life from Hamilton on. The old Whig spirit, the belief in government by the rich and well-born, had never died out, though it was no longer politic to express it frankly. In the pre-World War II period, the extensive if forgotten volumes of the La Follette Committee hearings showed how widespread, well organized, and well heeled were the tendencies toward a native kind of fascism. These un-American tendencies paraded in the name of Americanism and soon found an effective vehicle. The Dickstein-McCormack Committee, set up to investigate purveyors of racist and fascist views, was converted in the hands of Martin Dies into a means of attacking the New Deal and the left-of-center.

The House Un-American Activities Committee showed its real direction by making its debut in the 1938 campaign with the defeat of Frank Murphy for reelection as Governor of Michigan. The governor who refused to expel the sitdown strikers from the auto plants with blackjack and bullet was to be punished for his temerity in failing to do the bidding of what Henry Demarest Lloyd once called The Lords of Industry. Out of the same context grew the long attempt to deport Harry Bridges, an attempt which led to the passage, over FDR's veto in 1940, of an alien registration bill, the Smith Act, which also embodied the first peacetime sedition provisions in American history since the days of John Adams. The prosecution of the Minneapolis Trotskyites under this law in 1940 as a kind of cheap political favor to the Teamsters Union foreshadowed the postwar Communist prosecutions. Similarly the Dodd-Watson-Lovett case and the FBI screenings of federal employees during the war under the Hatch Act were the forerunners of the postwar loyalty purge. I wrote about the dangers of the Minneapolis case in *The Nation* at the time. And during the war I did a series of articles for *PM* analyzing several dozen transcripts of FBI hearings which showed the kind of neighborhood gossip, anti-Negro prejudice, and politically illiterate snooping which were even then used to decide "loyalty."

IV

The red menace in our history is older than the Reds. No small part of the Constitution was dictated by fear of legislation in the interest of the poorer classes, fear of such debtor uprisings as had occurred under Shays in Massachusetts. "My opinion," New York's great conservative jurist Chancellor Kent had declared in the 1830s during the fight to enable non-property-owners to vote, "is that the admission of universal suffrage and a licentious press are incompatible with government and security to property." In the 1890s the first federal income tax law was attacked before the Supreme Court as communistic. The American Liberty League in the 1936 campaign carried on in the same tradition against the New Deal, and John W. Davis, one of the leading personalities in the League, also helped to father the Un-American Activities Committee, as Mundt of South Dakota revealed in 1946. What the cry of the red menace was unable to accomplish in Roosevelt's day, it succeeded in doing in Truman's. The laborer, white-collar worker, or farmer could not be deterred by the red bogey from demanding higher wages and better social security; these were bread-and-butter issues he understood too well. But in a postwar America of high living standards and full employment, in which worker and farmer enjoyed the fruits of the New Deal, it was easy to put over the same campaign in the distant field of foreign policy. The average man knew little of Russia, China, or Reds. He shared the general fear of that strange new thing in the world, socialism. He felt impelled by patriotic impulse in a struggle for world mastery between his own country and the only other great power left. The Church, which had been unable to swing the urban Roman Catholic workers against the New Deal, was able to swing them against the menace of Communism abroad.

Though the apparent purposes lay in the field of foreign policy, the new crusade against Communism was shot through with ✓ domestic considerations. In an America being mobilized emotionally for war against Russia, it was easy to drive radicals and liberals of all kinds out of positions of influence and thus make a new successful period of peaceful reform impossible. The Republicans fought Russia in order to prevent a New Deal, while the Democrats fought Russia as a kind of rearguard action against the Republicans. As long as Truman made faces at Stalin, it was more difficult to accuse the Democrats of being communistic. Few seemed to notice and even fewer dared to say that, in the process, America and American law were being distorted into the image of that against which both parties claimed to be crusading. In the sphere of civil liberties, America began to conform far more closely to Vishinsky than to Jefferson. The ideas expounded by Vishinsky in his famous treatise on Soviet law, his naive conception that of course one does not grant the basic freedoms to those who oppose the regime in power, were followed faithfully if unconsciously by American anti-Communists. The notion that the security of the state outweighs justice to the individual began to be accepted by the Circuit and Supreme Courts in the House Un-American contempt cases and in the cases growing out of the loyalty purge. A legless veteran earning $45 a week in a nonsensitive position was discharged though he had access to no secrets and as a Trotskyist would hardly have slipped them to Stalin if he could. Dorothy Bailey, an anti-Communist leader of a federal workers' union, was branded disloyal for life, though everything on the record of the proceedings against her was in her favor. She was condemned on the basis of unfavorable anonymous testimony kept secret from her, so that she had no chance to rebut it. Her judges admitted they themselves did not know the source of the accusations and therefore could not evaluate their reliability. This was American jurisprudence in the Truman era.

There was a steady deterioration in American policy under the impact of what the reader will find described in some of these selections as the bogeyman theory of history. In the Smith Act prosecutions of the Communists, the government exhumed from the darkest and worst days of Anglo-American law those doctrines of "conspiracy" which had been used before against radicals and new ideas. There was increased reliance at home and abroad on suppression by force, and an increasingly arrogant determination to "go it alone" in the world. UNRRA, which was international, gave way to the Marshall Plan, under which we dispensed our bounty alone and for a political price. The Marshall Plan, which stressed reconstruction and economic betterment as a weapon against Communism, gave way in turn to the Atlantic Pact and the mutual security program, which stressed the importance of providing adequate military force against "internal aggression" — meaning internal discontent. The UN increasingly became a vermiform appendix of American policy, frowned upon when it threatened to act for peace, petted absent-mindedly when it could be mobilized for support as in the Korean War. From the promulgation of the Truman Doctrine in March, 1947, America declared its intention to police the world against new ideas. The country which a century before had fought the reactionary Holy Alliance with the Monroe Doctrine now set up a Holy Alliance of its own under the Truman Doctrine. We aimed to be the organizers of a world counter-revolutionary crusade, and with the slogan of "total diplomacy" to obtain at home by more velvety means some of the same kind of conformity in foreign policy the Russians also enforced at home. Washington was becoming more and more like Moscow in rigidity, suspicion, and imposed conformity. The difference lay in purpose: there to achieve socialism, here to prevent it.

The outlook is dark as these pages are being written. History warns us that the Russo-American quarrel will not be easily resolved, unless submerged again by recurrent dangers from a resurgent Germany and Japan profiting now as in the past from East-West tension. There are moments, looking backward, when these wars seem as inevitable and as irrational as the crashing of the waves upon the turbulent sea. There are moments when the traditions of liberty seem to exercise very little real hold upon the American mind. Shall we then despair? I do not think so. This is an age of birth, and birth is painful always and bloody. We independent intellectuals of the Left represent ideas whose value is attested and survival assured by all we know of men and history. The socialism in which we believe is coming everywhere; the main characteristic of our times is the erosion everywhere of property rights, the increased power of the state over the economy. Government like industry is becoming collectivized, and collective control must follow. The Chamber of Commerce is bucking a tide which cannot be held back, and history is on our side.

The same is true of the libertarian ideal. Though threatened by authoritarianism everywhere, on the Left as on the Right, by Communist as well as by Catholic, this also is an ideal of which we need not despair. Intellectual freedom must be the constant struggle and the constant aspiration of mankind; only in combination with intellectual freedom can socialism build the good society. Whatever the distortions of this terrible period, this is a truth which will survive and command the allegiance of the best in men and among them. New truths must always struggle against established orders, and room must be found for them to grow despite monarchs, priests, bureaucrats, or commissars, or that often most intolerant of despotisms, the majority itself.

I. F. STONE

December 8, 1952

"When a correspondent from one of the big New York papers persisted in his questioning at State Department, there was a stage whisper from the rear of the press conference, 'Who does that fellow think he is? The rich man's Izzy Stone?'"

PM, *March 31, 1948*

THE
TRUMAN
ERA
1945–1952

PROLOGUE
THE END OF THE WAR

Washington, August 12, 1945

More terrifying than the atomic bomb is the casual way we all seem to be taking the end of the war. It has been clear since Friday morning that there would be a Japanese surrender within a matter of a few days, if not a few hours. But the news seemed to stir extraordinarily little excitement. The finish of a World Series evokes more talk at the lunch counters.

In part this is because, as before V-E Day, there was no clear-cut announcement. Victory, expected and discounted, is no longer news. In part, this phlegmatic response may reflect the fact that people are punch-drunk on horror and sensation. Imagination has been dulled by the demands made upon it.

The cables indicate that this is not true in those countries where the war has been experienced directly. In London, Paris, and Chungking, news of the Japanese surrender offer sent rejoicing crowds pouring into the streets. There the end of the war was the end of something people had themselves felt, seen, heard, and suffered — not a distant drama played out in the headlines.

I do not feel like writing the standard editorial today in the face of all the agony the last few years have seen. Terrible things have been done to human bodies and to human minds. I think of the picture of the Chinese baby crying alone in the ruins of Nanking. I think of the German woman who said all this would not have happened if those damned British had only surrendered in 1940. And I think of the American airman who came back from dropping an atomic bomb over Nagasaki to report that the results were "good."

I am worried by the casualness with which we in America are greeting the peace, because this failure of the imagination does not bode well for the future. I wrote down "The most terrible war in human history is coming to an end," and scratched it out because I felt that to most people who read it the words would have but a pallid reality, and seem only another editorial cliché.

This is terrifying because the task of preventing another world war is a difficult one. If people do not achieve some vivid conception of what hell has reigned in parts of Europe and Asia during the past decade or so, how can one expect them to think hard enough and act firmly enough to prevent it from happening again?

Since 1931, when peace began to crumble in Manchuria, there has been war, civil war and world war, at an increasingly furious tempo: from those first shootings in Mukden and the first beatings in Dachau to the bombing of Shanghai and the civil war in Spain, from the first blitz on Poland to the use of the atomic bomb over Hiroshima and Nagasaki. What a vista of blood and cruelty!

But not blood and cruelty alone. As in some gigantic symphony played on human hearts for the delectation of a mightier race, agony has blended with a beaten-down but irrepressible, mounting, and finally victorious heroism and aspiration. These are only gaudy words to us. We and our orators have rung the changes on democracy and freedom until the words have grown shabby and nauseating. But to certain men the war's ending comes as the end of a struggle against fascism begun long before war was declared, fought in the underground hideaways of Japan, Italy, and Germany, in occupied China and in Spain, in the Vienna working-class suburbs and in the Warsaw ghetto, humbly and obscurely but as bitterly as on the broader battlefields.

Those who understand that this was in truth, for all its contradictions and compromises, a war against fascism, a successful war against fascism, a war that is slowly but surely letting loose the forces of freedom the world over, cannot take the end of the war casually. One of the reasons for the apathetic reaction to victory in our own country is that so few felt and understand this. To too many of us the war was a kind of horrible accident, disrupting families and lives for no good reason; a distant quarrel, into which we were somehow drawn.

One cannot understand what one has not suffered. How many of us are thankful that our own country was spared, that our children did not jump from their beds as the warning air-raid sirens screamed in the nights, that we did not huddle with our families in the subways, that our daughters were not shipped into slavery and our mothers sealed into death cars for the extermination camps, that our cities are not gutted by bombs, our children's faces pinched by hunger?

I know that if a Gallup poll taker came among us tomorrow 99 percent of us would vote for a permanent peace. And I know that this feeling is not to be lightly dismissed; it has already had its effect in concrete steps toward peace such as the ratification by the Senate of the United Nations Charter. But preventing war is not that easy.

Some of the causes of this war went deeper than any enemy men or movements. They were not removed by the death of Hitler and they will not be removed by the execution of Japanese generals. Some of these causes lie in our own minds and hearts as well as in those of our defeated enemies.

A small group of scientists can unlock the secrets of uranium and leap into the future. But it is harder to break a prejudice than an atom. Hundreds of millions of men the world over must take thought, must take time off from workday cares to perform a far more difficult task than that involved in the mastery of U 235 if peace is to be preserved, if the new horizons of science are not merely to provide a new and immense stage for destruction. They must shake loose from ancient nationalist egotisms; the world has grown too small for them. They must grope forward past cherished preconceptions to a better-organized society in which all men may be assured of their daily bread; the world cannot afford a renewal of the economic insecurity in which war and fascism grew, and can grow again.

I wish it were possible to throw on some gigantic screen for all to see some fraction of the suffering, the treachery, the sacrifice, and the courage of the past decade. For how are we in America to fulfill our responsibility to the dead and to the future, to our less fortunate allies and to our children's children, if we do not feel a little of this so deeply in our bones that we will be unswervingly determined that it shall never happen again?

1 | NEW WORLD ORDER OR NEW WORLD WAR?

The Curtain Rises on the UN at San Francisco

San Francisco, April 26, 1945

The United Nations Conference on International Organization opened here last night. The mediocrity of utterance provided a depressing contrast to the gravity of the occasion.

The delegates of forty-six nations gathered in the gilt, red plush, and stainless steel interior of the San Francisco Opera House. The huge crowds outside, the floodlights within, the popping of camera flashlights recalled an opening night in Hollywood.

This was the second time in a generation that representatives of most of mankind, the victorious powers in a world war against Germany and its allies, had met to establish an organization that might maintain peace and prevent aggression.

But there was here no Wilson, no Clémenceau, no Lloyd George, as at Versailles; no Metternich or Talleyrand, as at the Congress of Vienna which met in 1815 to re-establish peace amid the ruins left by Napoleon; no commanding figure, except in spirit — Franklin D. Roosevelt's.

The conference directory covers a vast and diverse conglomeration of men. It begins with Abaza, Fikri Bey, of Egypt, and ends with Zuloaga, Pedro, Venezuela. But there was little of the exotic about this gathering. Except for a scattering of uniforms and the white headdress and brown robes of the Saudi Arabians, the spectacle from the triple-tiered galleries differed in appearance

from any theater audience only in the absence of fashionably
dressed women and formal clothes. The delegates of the United
Nations looked like any assemblage of balding, elderly, well-to-do
business and professional men.

In that assembly were many of the men who had failed so badly
at the League of Nations in Geneva. A striking characteristic of the
conference for this new peace organization is the extent to which
the cast of characters remains unchanged.

The French delegation includes Joseph Paul Boncour, a leading
figure in the league. The Dutch is headed by Elco N. van Kleffens,
who was a minor figure in the secretariat.

The leading figures in the British delegation, Eden and Halifax,
were also leading figures at Geneva; the latter wholly associated
with the appeasement that broke down the League, the former a
man who never fully made up his mind whether he was for or
against the retreats, the evasions, and the subterfuges that paved
the way to war.

One relic of a great past is here. Another is remembered in
absence. Field Marshal Jan Christiaan Smuts, who was associated
with Woodrow Wilson in the writing of the Covenant, leads the
South African delegation, the one man of stature and insight to
emerge from the ultra-reactionary political life of the Boer Do-
minion.

Missing and missed from the Soviet delegation is Litvinov, another man unique in his political context, the one great-power
statesman at Geneva whose cry, "Peace is indivisible," went un-
heard, but is not unremembered.

In his place, as head of the USSR delegation, is Stalin's Foreign
Minister, Molotov, a genial, rotund little man, a wheel horse of
the Russian Revolution whose unhappy task it was to put his name
to one of the documents which proved that peace was not divisible,
the Ribbentrop-Molotov Nazi-Soviet pact of nonaggression.

Represented here, too, are the nations which pleaded in vain
for help at Geneva; some by the same men. Wellington Koo is here
from China and Jan Masaryk from Czechoslovakia. And there
are five black men of Semitic name and Caucasian feature to speak

for Ethiopia, whose king rose in humiliation that terrible day in Geneva to prophesy with majestic indignation the world consequences of his country's betrayal to Mussolini.

Far up in the galleries, among the press, was another who pleaded in vain at Geneva, Julio Alvarez del Vayo, once Foreign Minister of the Spanish republic, which "nonintervention" sent to its doom.

Absent, unrepresented, haunting the conference is Poland, which first took its pound of flesh, Czechoslovakia's Teschen, as Hitler's partner in the Munich settlement-by-amputation, and then itself was engulfed by Nazi aggression, setting off World War II.

Poland was still the center of a covert tug of war which threatened the unity of the Big Three. Clerical and reactionary forces outside and within the conference have made it the focus of anti-Soviet agitation, which is reflected in turn in Moscow's stubborn hostility to the Polish government-in-exile, its pact with the pro-Soviet regime at Lublin. Solution of this problem is the No. 1 concern of this conference.

As striking as the presence here of so many men from what might be called the Geneva cast of characters is the presence of but few from the new forces which welled up in Europe and the Far East to fight Axis aggression from underground. Most of those who speak for the once-occupied countries spoke for them during the war from London.

Only the French delegation is headed by a man who fought in the underground resistance. The dapper Georges Bidault, the M. "X" who was chairman of the National Committee of Resistance in France, heads its delegation to San Francisco. Ivan Subasic leads the men who speak for Tito's Yugoslavia.

And one man, carefully chaperoned by the Kuomintang secret police, speaks here for heroic Red China.

Here, too, are gathered spokesmen for countries which are part of the United Nations only by courtesy, last-minute changes of tune, their expediency, and our hopeful self-deception.

The Arab states, led by Saudi Arabia, which had an inflow of Axis funds when the Axis star rose high, treacherous in World

War II and unreliable in World War I, now sit at the table of the United Nations — largely by courtesy of the Standard Oil Company of California and its partner, the Texas Company, which have struck oil in Arabian deserts.

Turkey is another of the late arrivals, but Argentina, which signalized its belated and formal accession to the democratic cause by further antidemocratic measures at home, was not yet in the opening assemblage here at San Francisco, though its admission may be imminent.

Here also were three delegates for one great captive power, India, whose spokesmen were chosen for her by the British raj without consultation with her parties or her political leaders, most of them still in jail, including the far-seeing Nehru, who would have shone even in a gathering of giants, still more among the small men who are prominent at San Francisco.

The top cream of San Francisco society, in nurselike uniforms, ushered delegates and press to their seats, a hidden orchestra or phonograph played popular melodies until that moment at 7:30 P.M. when Stettinius rapped his gavel and said: "Ladies and gentlemen, the President of the United States. . ."

With Stettinius on the platform were youthful Alger Hiss of the State Department, who will be secretary general of the conference, Governor Warren of California, and Mayor Lapham of San Francisco, both gray-haired.

One longed, as one listened to their speeches and to the speech from the White House, for a memorable utterance, for a world Second Inaugural, or for that frank admission of difficulties and grim political necessities which commands confidence.

What one got was moralizing and the clichés of expression and thought all too familiar in such circumstances. Behind these phrases one did not doubt that there was sincerity; the press (this correspondent included) is overwhelmingly of the opinion that both President Truman and Secretary Stettinius are deeply and genuinely anxious to succeed in the great task before them at San Francisco.

The silent row of slim young servicemen and servicewomen who stood as a guard of honor on the platform were a flesh-and-blood reminder of the price again to be paid if they and the leaders of the other United Nations fail.

Organization for Peace ... Or Against the Soviet Union?

San Francisco, May 4, 1945

It is very difficult at a conference of this kind to see the forest for the trees, to disentangle the realities from the rhetoric, but I think I am beginning to get my bearings.

I am inclined to believe that what is going on here becomes a good deal clearer if one keeps in mind that action is proceeding on two planes. On one, the formal and public plane, a final draft is being prepared for a world security organization. On the other, the informal and private plane, quite a different tendency is at work.

That tendency, which is very strong, if not dominant, in the American delegation, is to regard the United Nations Conference on International Organization as a conference for the organization of an anti-Soviet bloc.

This is not my own opinion alone. It is the opinion privately held by some of the most astute newspapermen here, irrespective of their own political orientation. In my own case, this opinion is the net product of my own estimate of the basic forces at work, of conference gossip, and of an attempt to find some pattern into which all the diverse pieces will fit.

But I did not set this down on paper until I found confirmation in trustworthy official American quarters I may not here identify. I can only say that among the younger and more progressive men attached to the American delegation there is increasing apprehension over the extent to which the conference begins to take on the aspects of an attempt by our delegation to build an anti-Soviet world coalition.

The maintenance of the unity of the powers as a first essential of world peace is a principle to which everyone agrees. But whenever one sets out to explore some specific problem, the future of Germany, the fate of the Rhineland and Ruhr, the course of the Far Eastern war and the settlement which will emerge from it, one finds this principle forgotten.

One finds, instead, that the main question in the minds of many State, War, and Navy Department officials, and too many members of the American delegation, is the balance of forces between the USA and the USSR, an implied assumption that war between them is inevitable and that it is our job to maneuver for as strong a position as possible in anticipation of that conflict.

This dangerous belief that war between the two remaining great powers of the earth, the USA and the USSR, is inevitable — a belief which can make it so — has diverse roots.

The defeat of Germany has upset the world balance of power. The strength of the Soviet Union has both surprised and frightened many leading figures in the War and Navy Departments; the bureaucracy of both tends to be either politically naive or socially reactionary.

The divergencies of outlook between a great Communist power, dominated by a one-party dictatorship and a still revolutionary mentality, and a capitalist democracy like our own are very great, and it will take much forbearance and good will to bridge them. There is less forbearance and good will visible since Roosevelt's death.

I think we must also recognize that there is no alternative between the achievement of full employment in America by peaceful means and new imperialist adventures and war. This is recognized by the progressives among the technical staffs and consultants of the American delegation, who fear a tendency — an almost unconscious and organic tendency — to find a way out of a new postwar unemployment crisis by armed conflict instead of the peaceful, but painful, process of adjusting our economy to full employment.

American progressives must keep in mind that however "correct" the attitude of the Soviets and however conservative the policies Moscow may impose on Communist parties abroad to conciliate capitalist opinion, the contrast between full employment in the USSR and a new unemployment crisis after the war in the USA would be explosive. Many people fear the impact of so socially dangerous a contrast, but, while some of us conclude from it the necessity of a full-employment program, others may think the contrast would best be avoided by an attempt to destroy the USSR. I do not believe that anyone would advocate this publicly, and very few would even admit it to themselves. Yet there is a natural drift in that direction in some circles.

I do not set this down to be alarmist; I do not think such a conflict is at all inevitable. But I think it time that people became aware of this dangerous undertow and took steps to counteract it lest we wake up one day to find that we have permitted our representatives here to lay the foundations for a third world war — a war against the Soviet Union — while going through the motions of establishing a stable peace.

That is a rough way to put it. It by no means does justice either to the motives or the actions of many members of the American delegation, but I am convinced that it provides a true picture of what is developing here.

As early as April 26, Walter Lippmann noted a tendency to assume "that because Germany is prostrate, the German problem is no longer the paramount problem of the world." He found this reflected in "the fact that the main preoccupation of so many here has been not Germany, but the Soviet Union." And he warned that our relations with the USSR would become hopeless "if we yield at all to those who, to say it flatly, are thinking of the international organization as a means of policing the Soviet Union."

I think it is no exaggeration to say that since last week, when Lippmann wrote what I have quoted, the anti-Soviet atmosphere has grown. It is no longer a question of not "yielding" to the men Lippmann has in mind. They are, if not running the show, at least playing the dominant part in the American delegation and in the conference.

Some of them have been very open and very indiscreet in voicing their anti-Soviet views at the social functions in which celebrity-dazed San Francisco has been lionizing them. They have been equally open in spreading anti-Soviet propaganda "off the record" to correspondents who are their confidants or mouthpieces.

One correspondent, on a conservative paper with more access to these circles than I, says the only two members of the American delegation who have not been spreading an anti-Soviet line are Commander Stassen and Dean Gildersleeve. I cannot vouch for that information and it may be unfair to one or two others, but I do not think it is far wrong.

In an atmosphere of this kind one may be sure that the realistic Russians, who understand perfectly well what is going on, will make few concessions on Poland and other areas important to the security of the USSR. They are no more willing than are the French to rely for their security solely on a new world organization, especially one born in such circumstances.

If this seems wicked of them, it may well be kept in mind that the United States Navy, on the question of international trusteeship, is equally unwilling to accept the new organization as a substitute for effective American control of the Pacific islands and perhaps some of the African territories where it considers bases necessary to our own security.

Whether President Truman is aware of, and supports, the kind of maneuvering in which the American delegation is engaged I do not know. Since the death of Roosevelt, the leadership of the American delegation seems to have fallen to Senator Vandenberg.

Truman's own attitude is not clear. It is noted that the day after the Nazi attack on the Soviet Union he issued a particularly unfortunate statement that is now being recalled with perhaps unjustified apprehension.

The *New York Times* of June 24, 1941, carried a story by Turner Catledge in which he said Congressional reaction to "the newest turn of the European war was reserved except among isolationists . . ." I do not think that term was fairly applied to Truman, but Catledge went on to quote Truman as one of those isolationists.

"If we see that Germany is winning," Catledge quoted then

Senator Truman as saying, "we ought to help Russia and if Russia is winning we ought to help Germany and that way let them kill as many as possible, although I don't want to see Hitler victorious under any circumstances. Neither of them think anything of their pledged word."

What Truman said in 1941 may be no index of his ideas in 1945, but what he said in 1941 reflects the kind of thinking which has a strong hold on too many of the members of our delegation in San Francisco.

2 | MOLDING THE NEW JAPAN

How Soon We Began to Forget

Washington, June 15, 1945

Last Friday, in his thrice-weekly Washington column, Frank Kent published a piece called "A Way Out for Japan." Kent said that if the Japanese surrendered now they might be able to keep Korea and Formosa.

Kent warned that if the Japanese did not surrender soon, the Russians would come into the war. He declared that if the Russians entered the war the terms imposed on Japan and especially on Japanese industry would be very harsh.

Kent hinted that the USA and its enemy, Japan, had a common interest in opposing the Soviet Union. He said that if the USSR entered the war the Russians would demand Manchuria. He predicted that this would mean the communization of east Asia and he indicated that we were as strongly opposed to that as the Japanese are.

It may be that this column of Kent's was of no significance except to illustrate the lengths to which a Washington commentator will go on a hot afternoon. But I am not inclined to dismiss it so easily. Kent is an old-timer in the business. (I remember his famous book, *The Great Game of Politics,* as one of the eye-openers of my youth.) He is a responsible, conservative journalist and I doubt whether he would write in this way unless there was substantial basis for such speculation in official circles.

As a matter of fact, the views advanced by Kent with approval are remarkably like those exposed with disapproval in recent issues of *Amerasia.* The Amerasia Case involves a group of people in government and in journalism who have been very critical of just such trends in our Far Eastern policy, and are accused, justly or unjustly, of "leaking" confidential information to combat them.

I believe Kent's views must be taken seriously, and that they are held in influential circles. I think they are very dangerous, for a number of reasons.

The Japanese are playing a double game, much like the double game played by the Nazis in 1939. The Nazis used the red bogey in London and Paris and the capitalist bogey in Moscow to prevent the formation of a grand alliance against them.

A similar process is taking place in connection with the Far Eastern war. Our government knows that the Japanese are using such views as those expressed by Kent to convince the Russians that they ought to remain neutral in the Far East.

The Japanese are hoping that fear of Communism will lead us to go easy on Japan. They are also hoping that distrust of anti-Soviet undercurrents in Washington will lead the Russians to stay out of the Far Eastern war.

There is a second source of danger in the kind of thinking reflected by Kent. There is a faction in the State Department which is friendly to the zaibatsu, the handful of great family-monopolies which dominate Japanese industry and finance.

This faction would like to defeat the Japanese military, but to leave the emperor and the zaibatsu in power. But the emperor and the zaibatsu are the twin peaks of Japanese society as now constituted. They represent the development of a highly monopolistic capitalism on top of a feudal society.

Capitalism did not develop there as here, from the bottom up. It was not accompanied, as in the USA, by a steady rise in living standards and a constant expansion of the domestic market. Nor did it develop from the restless efforts and irresistible energies of a wide mass of enterprising men with ideas and capital.

Capitalism in Japan was imposed from the top, ready-made as it were, by a few families. It was imposed on a society in which the land was largely held by great feudal lords. Feudalism kept the mass of the Japanese people landless, impoverished, and ignorant. It provided a huge reservoir of cheap labor for the highly developed industries Japan copied from the West.

But this cheap labor also meant a poor home market. Japan's industries could undercut those of the West. But they had to find a market abroad because they did not have an adequate market at home. The intensified drive for foreign markets, the intensified competition with American, British, and French industry, the imperialist drive to control whole market areas, fascism within Japan, were the inevitable result. They will be the inevitable result again if we restore a Japan dominated by the emperor and the zaibatsu. A new generation of Americans will have to spill its blood in a new struggle if the only result of the war is to restore the same old Japan.

The people who fear Russian entrance into the Far Eastern war and favor the zaibatsu in Japan are also the same people who would give the Kuomintang a blank check to wage civil war on the Chinese Reds instead of uniting China to help us defeat Japan. Should these people succeed in converting their obsessions into accepted policy, the cost in American lives would be a very heavy one.

Washington, August 13, 1945

Our government was prepared to wage total war, but is reluctant to make a total peace. The atomic bomb was the logic of war carried to an extreme which many people (the writer included) felt abhorrent. But no such remorseless logic is visible in the current surrender negotiations with Japan.

We can spend two billion dollars and marshal the best brains of science the world over to solve the problem of the atomic bomb. But we stand on the threshold of victory with no program for Japan, and little more than the vaguest notions of what to do with our victory except to preserve "order" and get rid of Japanese "militarists."

This is but another, though major, example of the disparity between our technological efficiency and our political capacity. We fight war with atomic bombs but make peace with diplomatic duds. Technologically, we have surpassed the wildest dreams of Jules Verne. Politically we are somewhere back in the early nineteenth century.

The price may some day be another Pearl Harbor. We were caught asleep then. Will we wake in time now?

3 | GERMANY: REPEAT PERFORMANCE

The Nazi Industrial Plot for the Next War

Washington, March 18, 1945

This is the story of a secret meeting held in Strasbourg, France, last August 10. Its source cannot be disclosed at this time, but full details are known to the War Department. The meeting was attended by a group of Nazi officials and industrialists and it was concerned with preparations for World War III.

An Associated Press correspondent with the United States forces in Belgium seems to have obtained some knowledge of the facts here to be disclosed. For in the *New York Times* of January 7 one may find an obscure five-paragraph dispatch, datelined *"With*

American Forces in Belgium" and headed, "Nazis bind industry
in 'next war' plans."

The account in the *New York Times*, buried on an inside page in
an inconspicuous position, refers to policies by which the Nazi
Party hopes to support itself underground after defeat and to pre-
pare for another attempt at world conquest.

But the dispatch to the *Times* makes no mention of the meeting
where these plans were outlined nor does it name the men who attended. Most important of all, it contains no reference to the fact
that, in the discussions at Strasbourg, United States big business
firms were mentioned and plans outlined once more to draw them
into collaboration with German industry.

The Strasbourg meeting to lay plans for World War III deserves
study for several reasons:

(1) It indicates the need for treating Hitler's industrial collaborators as war criminals.

(2) It focuses attention on the flight of German capital abroad.

(3) And it shows the danger of leaving future American policy
toward German industry to be molded by men drawn from concerns which were cartel partners and financial collaborators of
German industry before the war.

The meeting in Strasbourg was presided over by a man who is
both an SS official and an industrialist. He is Dr. Scheid, a director
of Hermadorff und Schonberg, and an SS *Obergruppenführer*.

The men to whom he spoke were mostly representatives of the
same great Rhineland and Ruhr industries which secretly financed
Hitler's rise to power.

A smaller and more private meeting followed this one. It was
presided over by Dr. Bosse, representing the German armaments
industry, and was attended only by spokesmen for the three big
firms, Krupp, Roechling, and Hermadorff und Schonberg.

At both the main meeting and the more private one which followed, the industrialists were told that Germany had lost the war
and that it therefore became necessary to take steps preparatory
to defeat.

The industrialists were told that the Nazi Party planned to operate underground at home and abroad, and that in return for government aid in exporting capital they were secretly to provide the Nazi underground with funds.

They were given the Nazi Party's promise that when it felt strong enough to come out into the open after the war all such "loans" to the underground would be repaid.

The German industrialists were informed that the Nazi Party expected some of its more prominent leaders to be caught and put to death but that many lesser men would survive and these were to be given hideouts as engineers and technicians in industrial plants under conditions which would permit them to work with the party underground.

Industrialists also were instructed at Strasbourg to plan to establish small secret armament research laboratories at which work could begin on new weapons for World War III.

These laboratories were to be established in large cities and in out-of-the-way towns, to be known to very few people in the party, and to have a liaison man with party higher-ups.

Use of patent pools and cartel agreements was cited at Strasbourg as a means of making funds available abroad which could be diverted secretly to Nazi purposes and as a means of re-establishing German industrial power, especially in Latin American markets.

The Strasbourg affair shows that after this war, as before, German industry may again seek to operate on a political as well as a purely business basis, that efforts will be made again to correlate it closely with German plans for renewed aggression, and that United Nations industrialists who resume their old ties with German industry may find themselves indirectly and unwittingly involved in dangerous relationships.

One thing is clear from the account of the Strasbourg meeting: not to punish German industrial and financial collaborators with the Nazis is to encourage their renewed participation in similar adventures after this war, and to leave secret nuclei of opposition and conspiracy both in Germany and abroad.

American Big Business and the Future of the Reich

Washington, March 19, 1945

To a large extent, the personnel chosen by the State Department, the Army, OSS (Office of Strategic Services), and FEA (Foreign Economic Administration) to plan the future of Germany is being drawn from those circles in Big Business, finance, and the corporate bar which did a great deal of business with the Reich before the war.

Here are a few hitherto undisclosed examples. Allen W. Dulles of Sullivan & Cromwell is in Switzerland, where we have been trying to stop the leak of German capital abroad. Important agencies are depending on Dulles to advise them on facts and policies in connection with German finance and industry. Sullivan & Cromwell is our leading corporation law firm and before the war served many corporations and banks dealing with the Reich.

Dulles is also a director of the J. Henry Schroder Banking Corporation of New York, the American branch of an old British banking house of German origin, whose operations helped Hitler obtain raw materials and foreign exchange before the war.

Another director of the Schroder bank, Samarkand-born V. Lada-Mocarski, has just been appointed vice-consul in Zurich by the State Department after many months in the supersecret OSS, where he was an adviser on German matters.

In Paris there is a group of American bankers and Big Business men in uniform, dealing with questions of German policy. Among them are Paul Mellon and his brother-in-law, David K. E. Bruce, both of the Aluminum Company of America; Alfred duPont, of E. I. duPont de Nemours & Company; Junius Spencer Morgan, of J. P. Morgan & Company; Lester Armour, of the meat-packing Armours; Edward Bigelow, of the State Street Trust Company of Boston; Lloyd Cabot Briggs, of Abbott, Proctor & Paine, and a number of other upper-bracket socialites and Big Business figures.

Three men, Allen Dulles, David Bruce, and Irving Sherman,

vice-president of A. G. Becker & Company, Chicago, are doing a considerable share of the military and intelligence masterminding in connection with the coming occupation of the Reich. Sherman was once head of the Becker firm's Berlin office.

The reason given for leaning so heavily for German intelligence on upper-crust business, finance, and law is that these circles alone had contact with the Reich before the war and can alone provide information we need in planning the future of the Reich.

But anyone who reads the story of the Strasbourg meeting may well doubt whether men from firms which had close and profitable relations with German business before the war can be relied upon for the policies necessary to make the Strasbourg plans impossible.

Very few American businessmen dealt with Germany before the war because they favored Nazism. They dealt with it on a business-is-business basis. But there were very few German businessmen who dealt with the USA on the same basis. There were very few whose economic transactions were not geared into the political program of the Third Reich, who did not help in economic warfare, in the financing of propaganda, and in espionage.

Let us look at the Strasbourg meeting in the light of the past. It shows, first, that German Big Business is again preparing to play a political role, that unless stopped it will secretly help the Nazi underground in preparation for World War III.

This makes it essential to treat as war criminals those German businessmen and financiers who collaborated in the rise of Nazism and are prepared to provide the money for its rebirth. Can their old associates on this side of the water, most of them politically naive, be expected to deal ruthlessly with the men they knew only as cultivated gentlemen, jolly *gemütlich* burghers, able architects of business policy?

The Strasbourg meeting makes it clear, secondly, that the Germans hope to resume their old cartel and patent ties abroad and use these as sources of funds and influence with which to rebuild Germany's power to fight again.

These cartel and patent agreements were weapons of German imperial policy. But they looked different from this side of the water. Here they were regarded as profitable means of dividing markets, stabilizing prices, eliminating competition. Can the American firms which were linked with German agreements of this kind in the past be relied upon to support rigorous treatment of these cartel and patent ties in the future?

The third important point brought to light by the Strasbourg meeting is the fact that the German government is now encouraging the flight of German capital abroad to provide funds and centers of action for the future, especially in Latin America. But from this side, this export of capital is often a means of making profit, of recovering on German assets, of helping old friends and business associates of the prewar period. Can we depend on American Big Business and financial firms to help block this flow of funds?

Security agencies in Washington know that there have been communications between American and German firms in recent months arranging for transactions that enabled Reich businessmen to get their funds out of Germany. Such transactions obviously can be mutually profitable.

Security agencies in Washington also know that conferences between representatives of Axis and Allied firms have been held in Lisbon during the past year.

Evidence of this may be reflected in Attorney General Biddle's able and outspoken annual report to Congress. The Attorney General warns, "many international agreements allocating world territories are merely in abeyance during the war . . . *in numerous instances negotiations have already been carried on for their resumption.*" (My italics).

The French underground press called attention to one meeting in Lisbon last December, which is reported to have been attended by representatives of both I. G. Farben and Anglo-American chemical concerns. There was a meeting there last May, attended by representatives of several big German, English, and American firms.

We know that such meetings as those in Lisbon could be held only with the knowledge of the State Department, and that any companies taking part in them must have had permission to obtain passports and traveling facilities. From a business point of view, such meetings are understandable. Most of the big banks and big business firms are planning and thinking about the role German industry will play in the future, and what their own relations with it may be.

But it seems to us that all this behind-scenes activity is advisable only if carried on within the framework of United Nations policy toward Germany. Otherwise we leave events to drift, and the drift from this side of the water is back toward revival of the ties that helped the Germans before and may again.

We think the time has come to bring this whole subject into the open and to discuss it; to hear frankly from the businessmen and bankers as well as the experts. To let a policy of drift continue, to let strategic posts be captured by the Big Business crowd without public knowledge, is to risk the danger that ordinary business considerations on this side of the water will lead to our inadvertent collaboration with such plans as those outlined at Strasbourg for nurturing Nazism underground and preparing for German revival.

Potsdam and the Conscience of Mankind

New York, August 3, 1945

The Potsdam conference should stir the imagination and satisfy the conscience of mankind. The palace whence the Kaiser launched Germany's first attempt at world domination was an apt and salutary setting in which to hammer out the peace terms which mark its crushing defeat in the second. These terms, first shaped at Yalta and carried further at Potsdam, still are incomplete. They are, if anything, kinder than the German people deserve, designed not so much to punish aggression as to prevent its recurrence.

The terms themselves mark the acceptance, though with some modification, of the idea embodied in the so-called Morgenthau Plan which was also Franklin D. Roosevelt's plan — the idea that the safest and wisest course for the victorious powers is permanently to reduce the industrial and therefore the warmaking potential of the Reich. The agreement of the Big Three on this fundamental premise for a permanent peace finds its most striking embodiment in the clauses on reparations. The Soviet Union, though a socialist state capable of absorbing reparations in the form of manufactured goods, has agreed with the USA and with the new Labor government of Britain that reparations shall be taken in industrial machinery and equipment. A contrary decision would not only have permitted, but stimulated, the reconstruction of German industry to turn out goods for reparations.

The lengthy communiqué issued after the three-week conference at Potsdam discloses decisions covering all of Europe, and the list of high military and naval men who accompanied the heads of state indicates that the Far East may also have been discussed. But the most dramatic decision of the conference, and the one which gives most hope of extirpating the roots of fascism everywhere, is its statement vigorously shutting the door of the United Nations against Franco Spain as the product and the accomplice of the Axis. So strong a declaration from the powers that dominate the world today should itself be of great value to the Spanish people in ending the Franco dictatorship. One hopes, however, that the Big Three, especially since the change of government in England, will follow with economic sanctions to end fascist tyranny in Spain.

In the position taken on Franco, as in the welcome statement offering a place in the United Nations to a democratic Italy, one is tempted, perhaps incorrectly, to suspect the effect of Churchill's defeat. For he was long Franco's friend and the stubborn foe of popular forces in Italy. One hopes that we shall some day have a full account of what happened in Potsdam after Attlee and Bevin replaced Churchill and Eden; one wonders just what was the attitude taken by the American delegation on the Spanish question, since among them were State Department officials, like James Clement Dunn, long known as patrons and protectors of fascist Spain.

The decisions on Germany, though perhaps less obviously than that on Franco, mark a decisive defeat for those financial and in-

dustrial circles in the USA and Britain with prewar leanings toward
fascism and postwar hopes of resurrecting the great German com-
bines which were Hitler's backers and their partners in world
monopoly. The Potsdam agreement calls for the decentralization
of the German economy in order to eliminate "concentration of
economic power as exemplified in particular by cartels, syndicates,
trusts, and other monopolistic arrangements."

This is more than a blow at the industrial and financial circles
which twice supported and profited by German aggression. It is also
a blow at scarcity economics, at restrictive agreements, the world
over. For in Britain and in the USA and in Latin America, monopoly in drugs and chemicals and high-grade steels and electrical
equipment was made possible largely by agreements with the big
German cartels for division of markets and the elimination of competition. To end monopoly in Germany is to weaken it everywhere.

The problem of the treatment of German industry was the primary stumbling block to Allied cooperation within the Reich, and
it was on the hope of irreconcilable differences in approaching the
problem that shrewd German political strategists surely counted
for the first permanent rift among the Big Three. The Churchill
government, reflecting the views of the City, London's Wall Street,
was pretty much for reconstituting the status quo of cartel and
combine. Opinion in this country was split. The Soviet Union's
position had not been made entirely clear. The joint decisions at
Potsdam to reduce the Reich's industrial potential and break up
monopoly control of what was left represent perhaps the greatest
achievement of this historic conference.

But the conference did more than agree on these negative,
though essential, propositions. It also opened the door on the
positive side to the democratic and anti-fascist reorientation of German politics. President Truman and Prime Minister Attlee have
agreed to follow the example set by the Red Army in its own zone
of occupation and to lift the ban on political activity within the
Reich. The effect of this ban, within the British and American
zones of occupation, often seemed rather to stifle democratic and

popular stirrings than to prevent the return to influence of forces friendly to Nazism or undemocratic in their own fashion.

Equally encouraging on the positive side was the decision to treat Germany, during the period of occupation, as a single economic unit and to seek uniform administrative policies in the different Allied zones. The alternative policy would ostensibly have split the Reich, but its actual effect would have been to split the Allies. For differences in regulation, policy, and treatment of the various zones would make it easier for the Germans to resume their old game of splitting the victors and playing one off against the other.

It is in maintaining and perfecting a unified Allied policy toward the Reich that the safety of the world lies. For no terms, short of a Carthaginian peace, can prevent the most populous European country west of the Russian border, the Continent's most advanced country technologically, the most militaristic people in Europe, from making another attempt at Continental supremacy if the victorious powers fall out among themselves.

It is in the Reich that Allied unity will be tested, the possibility of a third world war decided. Potsdam indicates that so far the Big Three are meeting that test. Only by a continuation of the newly adopted policies and the unity demonstrated again at Berlin can the world hope to control Germany long enough and effectively enough to bring into being a new generation, to break and remold the German national pattern of arrogance, callousness, and aggression that has twice cost us and the world so dearly.

It Begins to Happen Again

New York, July 17, 1946

The new instructions sent General Lucius D. Clay, United States military commander in Germany, not only turn their backs on Potsdam, but are designed to make German industrial revival our first consideration in Europe.

The new instructions may be utilized to submerge the Marshall

Plan in the Hoover Plan. It was Hoover's contention, in the report he made to the President last March, that we need do little more for European recovery than to scrap the Potsdam pact and permit the revival of German industry. His thesis was that this would "do infinitely more for Europe than American loans and charity." This is a thesis the present Congress will find more attractive than a new program of foreign lending.

"Start every plant," Hoover recommended, " 'heavy' as well as 'light,' which can produce non-arms goods." This would mean the abandonment of the program to reduce Germany's war potential, and the new instructions do just that. General Clay is instructed "to eliminate industry used *solely* to manufacture arms," but he is called upon only "to *reduce* industry used *chiefly* to support the production of arms, ammunition and implements of war." (My italics.)

What this may mean in practice can be seen from a dispatch from Berlin which was published in last Sunday's *New York Times*. It said General Clay was not only negotiating a higher level of industry agreement with the British, but pressing them to permit production of vanadium, which is necessary to high-grade military steel, and of aluminum, essential to aircraft. The Potsdam agreement expressly forbade the production of both these essential war materials.

To make German revival the prime consideration of American economic policy in Europe is not the same as fitting Germany into an overall plan for European recovery. This may graphically be seen in the case of two basic commodities, coal and steel. Coal is in short supply. How shall it be allocated? It is needed to revive German industry and it is needed to revive French industry. The French have complained that they were not getting their fair share of German coal; they are likely to get less, not more, as the new program gets under way.

To re-establish German hegemony in the economy of western and central Europe is not unwillingly to recognize unalterable economic fact. It is to permit Germany to move back into a dominating position obtained by political and economic planning for aggression.

The British and the Americans are determined further to raise German steel capacity to 12,000,000 tons a year. But Germany has virtually no iron ore. Its iron comes principally from Lorraine. The French, according to a Harold Callender dispatch from Paris in the *New York Times* of June 22, complain that they have gotten nowhere with their proposal to expand French steel output instead of German, to bring the coal and coke of the Ruhr to Lorraine instead of sending the iron ore of Lorraine to the Ruhr. It is true that Germany can earn more on finished steel than on coal and coke, but it is also true that France earns less. The over riding consideration is that the Anglo-American decision is thus limiting the potential of France while increasing that of Germany.

A careful reading of recent dispatches from abroad will show that Britain as well as France is getting stepchild treatment in our new emphasis on German revival. This was apparent from the chilled reaction of London to some frank off-the-record talks by visiting American officials recently, notably Secretary of Commerce Harriman, who let the British know they could expect no preferential treatment in new lending plans.

The anti-British tinge creeping into current discussions is more apparent in the negotiations by which American authorities are now pressing the British for a moratorium on socialization plans for the coal and steel industries. Our position, according to an Associated Press dispatch from Berlin on July 12, is that with such a moratorium "American private capital would be willing to make necessary dollar loans to revitalize these industries."

There is money to be made in the Reich, and many big American corporations content in the past to be junior partners in cartel arrangements with the Germans now hope to assume a senior position. The new instructions, while reiterating opposition to cartels, open the door to "monopolies subject to government regulation in fields where competition is impracticable." Couple this with the fact that one of the few major export industries in the United States zone is chemicals, and you can see that the rebirth of I. G. Farben is just around the corner.

Behind the scenes we are high-pressuring the British to give up socialization plans which, under Allied control, offer far better guarantees against a rebirth of militarism than in letting the old Stinnes-Krupp crowd take over. On paper we are still neutral on the subject, though the instructions exempt foreign-owned property and insist there shall be no public ownership without free choice "through the normal processes of democratic government." In the meantime, it is General Clay's "duty to give the German people an opportunity to learn of the principles and advantages of free enterprise" — no doubt à la Standard Oil and duPont, with their German opposite numbers.

We are moving steadily in the direction of finding a social base for ourselves in those very elements in Germany which twice provided the sinews of German aggression. And with it (*Herald Tribune* dispatch yesterday from Frankfurt-am-Main) goes new indoctrination for our troops. A new orientation course explains that, while Germans like military pomp, they also have a finer side. They love "nature, fine music, good paintings and home comforts." A year more and crematoriums will be dismissed as red propaganda. So rapidly is Germany winning the peace.

4 THE COLD WAR
IS LAUNCHED . . .

Unnoticed News Bulletin

Washington, December 31, 1946

The press generally seems to have overlooked two salient points in the so-called "progress report" on "economic reconstruction in Europe" made public here over the weekend by the influential House Special Committee on Postwar Economic Policy and Planning.

One is that the committee not only proposes to raise the level of industry allowed Germany under the Potsdam agreements but suggests the wisdom of permitting the Reich to retain its two key war industries, synthetic oil and synthetic rubber.

The other is that the committee at the same time not only proposes to restrict private American sales to the Soviet Union but to institute a world-wide trade war under American leadership against the USSR.

One extraordinary parenthetical reference in this report would seem to indicate that the committee would even allow the Germans to do research in atomic and bacteriological warfare, so long as they were subject to "inspection." Reports of the Allied Control Commission after the last war showed that inspection was circumvented and thwarted even under a Social Democratic regime in the Reich.

The report urges the State Department to initiate steps to prevent other nations, as well as ourselves, from supplying the Soviet Union with the materials needed for the reconstruction of its war-ravaged industries.

"Merely to refuse a loan to Russia," the report says, "is not enough."

The report proposes that all sales to Russia be subject to export license control by the Department of Commerce "under conditions set by the Department of State," with a special view to preventing the Russians from obtaining "American know-how and some of the most secret processes in fields of radar, electronics, communications, catalytic chemistry, etc., basic in the superiority of American defense."

That the influential House committee is thinking not merely of defense secrets but of blocking industrial development in the USSR is to be seen in its further recommendation:

The committee "urges upon the State Department the exercise of the maximum pressure upon other systems to follow this lead, and calls specific attention to the danger of having Britain, Sweden, Switzerland and France operate along these lines, to supply Russia with an industrial development that can only be deleterious to the interests of a secure and peaceful world under present Russian policies."

The committee objects in particular to the arrangement by which Sweden will supply a large part of its billion-kroner trade credit to the USSR in electrical equipment. It urges the Civilian Production Administration not to wait for Congressional authorization but to use its export licensing powers to shut off shipment of these and other "capital goods items" to Russia.

While objecting to industrialization of Russia, the committee throws doubt on the necessity of forbidding Germany in the future to operate two of the key synthetic war industries built up by I. G. Farben between the two first world wars. These are the synthetic petroleum and synthetic rubber industries. The Reich has been most susceptible to blockade in rubber and oil in the past and the Wehrmacht could not have fought as long as it did without synthetics at its disposal.

The report is critical not only of the Russians but of the British and the French as well for alleged unfair treatment of the Germans, and says: "Germany is the special responsibility of the Western powers, and on its fate mainly depends the future of Europe in relation to Communism."

Thus the old familiar Nazi line of the need to strengthen the Reich as a bulwark against Bolshevism reappears in a Congressional report, less than two years after the second World War ended, and it reappears in a context suggesting that America's principal postwar concern is preparation for a third world war, this time against the USSR.

What Is Really Going On Behind the Iron Curtain?

Washington, November 23, 1947

It is important for American public opinion to understand the basic assumption which makes so many makers of American foreign policy ready to accept an intensified East-West split. The assumption is that Russian control in Eastern Europe, as within the USSR itself, is based merely on ruthless terror, and that, even if this regime does not collapse from within, there are millions living under it who would be drawn to our side in a crusade for freedom.

The hope of collapse from within is not a sound basis for policy, since this hope has existed in the West for thirty years, and the USSR hasn't collapsed. The fact that it hasn't collapsed should indicate that there are other factors than ruthless terror responsible for its survival. Once this is recognized we may be able to see the situation in Eastern Europe more clearly.

These other factors include a planned economy, a fanatically devoted Communist Party, and substantial advantages for the peasantry and working class as compared, not with Western freedom and standards of living, but with past regimes.

This aspect of life in Eastern Europe west of the Soviet border is as poorly covered by the American press as was the same aspect of life in the Soviet Union before the war. The British press, however, which is being edited in a quite different atmosphere, has been devoting considerable attention to this other side of the East European picture.

In Germany itself, to judge from two leading articles on "Divided Germany" in the London *Times* for October 20 and 21, the Russians seem to be doing a better job in their zone than we in ours. In ours — according to the *Times* report — there has been little land reform, "nothing decisive" has been done about the German steel trust, and the promised transfer of heavy industry to public ownership is "still a matter of words."

Beyond the so-called "Iron Curtain," the London *Times* correspondent found that "the picture . . . bore little resemblance to the ugly silhouette so often imagined in the West." Land reform has been "an outstanding political success" and the Soviets have given the peasant the incentive to produce by allowing him to dispose as he pleases of all food raised above his quota. In the Anglo-American zones, he must theoretically hand over all he produces above his own food and seed requirements; the result is to discourage expansion and encourage hoarding.

In Hungary a London *Times* correspondent (September 22 and October 10) found sweeping land reforms successfully accomplished, industrial expansion under way to provide for landless laborers, new opportunities for education opened to working-class students, and considerable political freedom. "Correspondents can go where they please, except for a few restricted areas."

The London *Spectator,* an independent conservative weekly, in its issue of September 26 carried an article, "Poland Revisited," by F. Elwyn Jones, a Laborite M.P. who traveled extensively in central Europe and the Balkans before the war. Mr. Jones pictures a terribly devastated country making great strides toward recovery in industry and agriculture.

The London *Observer,* a conservative organ, in its issue of September 21 offers a vivid example of how America defeats itself in the "get tough" policy with these new Eastern regimes. The *Observer* correspondent in Warsaw cited the cancellation of an American credit to buy cotton for Polish textile mills. The Poles then applied to Moscow, "received 50,000 tons of cotton on favorable terms at less than the world market price," but in return had to "pledge to send their entire bumper sugar crop to Russia." Much of this sugar, the *Observer* reported, "would otherwise have gone to Britain and western Europe."

The *Manchester Guardian Weekly* for August 14 carried an interesting analysis of the various Two, Three, Four, and Five-Year Plans now being put into effect in the countries of the Russian sphere of influence. While the Communists have played a leading role, the writer says, "In east central Europe such planning responds to a genuine need," the need of a backward agricultural area to develop its industrial resources as the only means of raising living standards and absorbing its surplus population.

"In the sense of an isolationist trading system," says a writer in the London *New Statesman and Nation* for November 8, "there is nothing that can be called a Molotov plan. But what eastern Europe clearly has got, and what the West has not, is a plan in the genuine sense of a positive conception of its own regional development."

These are not lands of liberty in the Western sense, but they are not one-party states, either, in the Russian manner. Opposition groups exist, though the Petkov execution in Bulgaria vividly illustrates the limitations on their freedom. Petkov's whole life and record make the charges against him difficult to believe, even if one is aware of the "cloak-and-dagger" efforts being made to stir up civil strife in the Soviet satellite countries.

With the exception of Czechoslovakia, these countries knew little freedom before the war. Rightist repression and feudal exploitation were the rule. It is in such a context that "revolutionary methods," for all their dreadful abuses, are almost inevitable.

The London *Economist* (August 16), in an article on the dilemma facing the socialists of Eastern Europe, indicates the kind of elements we are apt to rally to any "crusade for freedom" in that part of the world. "Opposition to the Communists" in Eastern Europe, the *Economist* says, "is increasingly monopolized by those who, under a thin varnish of 'western liberalism,' remain chauvinists, clericals, anti-Semites, and fascists, and fundamentally hate any form of democracy."

To sharpen the split in Europe is political and economic folly. Western Europe can live under such a split only if the United States is willing permanently to supply much of its food and to open its markets wide to West European goods.

Eastern Europe, on the other hand, has a surplus of food and labor. Basic reforms have created considerable support among the masses for its new regimes. If necessity requires, regional economic planning could create a new industrial power in Europe with Polish coal, Romanian oil, Czechoslovakian factories, Yugoslav ores and timber, Hungarian wheat.

It is quite true that a program of this kind would be enormously difficult without machinery from the West; the split is economic and political folly for them as well as us. The split is one which the suffering peoples of Europe can ill afford, East or West. It would add to shortage and strain on both sides. But the East can stand it better than the West. That is the basic weakness of the whole "get tough" policy.

5 | WHICH WAY AMERICA?

Remolding the Public Mind

Washington, August 1, 1947

Three simple ideas are being hammered into the American consciousness; repeated like a musical motif in a thousand variations; reappearing daily in new headlines, Congressional "investigations," and UN wrangles. One is that we will have to fight Russia. The second is that we must rebuild Germany. The third is that FDR was no good. The average American, bewildered by this barrage, helpless amid the complexities of international politics, parliamentary procedure, and supposedly expert opinion, may yet find certain rough-and-ready yardsticks for judgment. He can judge the first two propositions by the third. He may know little about Russia or Germany, but he can judge FDR for himself. The three propositions are not as distinct as they may seem; they are part of one package, neatly tied with a bright red ribbon, by the old hate-Roosevelt brigade.

Blessed Land: Blind People

Washington, September 14, 1947

As I read the stories on the growing food crisis, I recall my feelings on returning home from abroad last spring.

When my plane circled over Washington, I saw first the broad

36

blue Potomac and then the green fields along its banks, and what had been a commonplace seemed a revelation. Here was plentiful water and fertile earth. One no longer took these for granted after seeing the parched desert lands and the eroded mountains of Palestine.

As we swung down over the city, I saw the wide familiar avenues, the great dome of the Capitol, the pleasant lawns of the White House, the traffic swarming antlike in the streets. Here were sweet evidences of peace one no longer took for granted after seeing the devastated acres around St. Paul's in London and catching the sickish smell that betrays still unburied bodies in the nightmarish ruins around the Bahnhofplatz in Munich.

The country seemed blessed, but its people seemed blind. To talk with people, to hear the debates in Congress, to read the papers again, to listen in on the constant tidal roar of yammer and complaint that is politics in America, was a sour experience.

I felt that America had never been less worthy of its past, more small-minded; that America was unappreciative of its blessings and heedless of its responsibilities, the responsibility of the more fortunate for the less, the duty of the strong toward the weak, the obligation of the rich toward the poor.

Everywhere in the huge mass of Eurasia, from England to China, human beings were struggling with real and terrible problems. I had seen the one-inch square of butter that is an Englishman's ration for a week. I had heard of the dank cellars from which the indomitable Poles were emerging to rebuild their country. I had been humbled by the courage among the ragged Jews of the illegal immigration. I had seen how thin the people are on the boulevards of Paris.

Here no one seemed to appreciate what it meant to have a roof over one's head, a job, a secure life for one's children, food ample by any reasonable standard, cities untouched by war, a home, a country. America seemed like one of those idle, dissatisfied rich women with no babies to mind and no dishes to wash and lots of time to nurture neuroses.

I recall these feelings now because this food crisis is more than a problem in food supply. It is, in a very real sense, a moral crisis and a political crisis, a test of the intelligence of the average American, the measure of his heart as well as his head.

In any system of society, it is safer, more tactful, more expedient, to criticize the ruler by indirection, to find scapegoats, to blame advisers. The ruler here is *demos,* the people, and it is customary when things go wrong to blame politicians, the wicked "interests," reactionaries, and so forth.

But this is a free country. The people have power, when they want to use it. When they want something deeply, they can and do get it, despite the obstacles and the weight of wealth in the scales of ordinary politics. And when things go wrong, the people must share their part of the blame; they are adults, they have voices — they are neither gagged nor children.

Why did we get rid of price control and rationing so much earlier than we should have? Basically because that's what people wanted; they were tired of wartime restrictions. And, as the mail to Congress during the OPA fight indicated, people were far more interested in getting *theirs* as farmers, producers, and workers than in stabilizing prices as consumers.

The politicians in Washington deserve their due occasionally. They've been afraid to tell the truth about the world situation, about the special session of Congress needed to meet it, about the necessity for reimposing some kind of rationing and controls at home. They've been afraid to tell the truth because ordinary Americans don't want to face up to unpleasant facts and don't want to make even minor sacrifices to help the less fortunate elsewhere, to help those who suffered in the war from which we profited.

We need to ration meat to save grain, but meat rationing is unpopular. We need to darken our bread in order to save wheat, but gray bread is unpopular. We need to reimpose price and wage controls, but people only want to control the other fellow's price or wage, not their own. We need to forget political prejudice and recognize that loans to get more Polish coal and Romanian wheat are at least as necessary to stem world shortages as loans to rehabilitate industry and agriculture in our own sphere of influence, but it's unpopular to say a sane word about the "Reds."

Our failure to meet the crisis is fundamentally the failure of average Americans to face up to their responsibilities in a free country and a devastated world.

The lag in European recovery, the growing food shortage abroad, the failure to take steps in time to conserve food here and control its price, the unwillingness to plan production for reconstruction needs are destroying the hope that we could escape with a quick price recession from the war's impact on our economy. Inflation is spreading as surely as a plague; the food on our own tables grows dearer, the price spiral dizzier. We may pay with a really severe crash for having answered as Cain answered: "Am I my brother's keeper?"

The Kind of "Containment" We Need

Washington, October 5, 1947

Quite a dispute has been going on here about "containment." Mr. X in *Foreign Affairs* outlined a policy for "containing" the Soviet Union. Mr. Walter Lippmann in a brilliant rejoinder came to the rather wistful conclusion that the real problem was to "re-contain" the Red Army. I want to add my own modest penny's worth to the containment controversy. I want to deal with another kind of containment necessary to the maintenance of peace: I mean the need to get the average American capitalist to contain himself — or, in vulgar language, to keep his shirt on.

What Mr. Vishinsky, I suspect, genuinely does not understand is that the average American capitalist is frightened, despite our monopoly of the atom bomb and our enormous and undamaged industrial potential. He is scared of socialism, and in a way he has a right to be scared: ideas are more powerful even than atom bombs. And the idea of socialism, of social ownership and control of the means of production, an idea older than Marx, an idea at least as old as Jesus and his first followers (see Acts, 2:44-45), has become the most potent idea of modern times.

Not only the parties of the Left abroad, but those of the Center and Right have taken on the color of socialism. There is a Catholic "socialism" derived from the encyclicals of Leo XIII and Pius XI. Fascism came to Germany in the guise of National "Socialism." These — from the common man's point of view — are phony socialisms, but in politics, as in society, imitation is a form of flattery. As an Italian antifascist exile once said to me: "No one bothers to counterfeit bad coin."

The dominant characteristic of the '30s was that everywhere in the world, in one guise or another, private property rights were weakened and the right of the state to control economic life was strengthened. This was true wherever one looked, whether in the USSR under Communism, in central Europe under fascism, in France under the popular front, in England under a "National" Tory government, or in the USA under the New Deal.

Most of the major currents of our time seem to force government in this direction. The impelling motives range from the necessities of war to the popular desire for security. Every interest, the farmer, the worker, the capitalist, seeks by legislation or organization to shield itself from the rigors of the free market.

American conservatives as well-meaning as Harold Stassen have been talking nonsense about nationalization in Western Europe and Britain, as if "free enterprise" were the sacred cow there that it is here. The British Conservative Party in its annual conference at Brighton has just overwhelmingly pledged itself to retain nationalization of the Bank of England, the coal mines, and the railroads, if re-elected. It opposes further nationalization, but it does advocate central economic planning. This is a portent that deserves meditation.

I would suggest that the one way to allay the almost hysterical fears current in the American capitalist class is to recognize — and force the neurotic patient, as it were, to recognize — an essential fact about the modern world: socialism is coming everywhere. War cannot stop it; a third world war against the Soviet Union may overturn the Stalin regime, but its cost will end free enterprise in America. The first step in ending the neurosis that is driving American capitalism to its own destruction in a new war is to face up to this fact.

Once faced, its full impact may be softened and recovery from hysteria aided by two other observations. One is that, given a little good sense and a period of peace, socialism will come in each country in its own way, in its own tempo, as determined by the character and traditions of its people and by the state of its industry and education. Socialism in France, the country of 1789, will not be the kind of socialism determined for Russia by its backwardness and its tradition of reform from above. The world is not going Communist, Russian model, unless American policy is so incredibly stupid as to leave the masses abroad no middle road.

The second observation is that the capitalist who is shrewd enough to move with the tide can still make money in the next generation or two. There are fundamental businesses like coal, railroads, and farm machinery which remain a sound basis for investment under any system. Money loaned to Polish government mines or Yugoslav government farm credit banks would be more safely invested by far than the funds we extended in the '20s to Peruvian dictators and decadent Romanian politicians.

The wise American capitalist — there are a few — will also recognize that the USA is not immune to the world trend. Two generations of change, from the first income tax to the TVA and public ownership of atomic energy, attest the growing power of the American state over economic processes. The failure of the business community to prevent the current inflation after the glowing promises made when the OPA was scuttled is another signpost: we are heading for another bust which will see the government forced into economic planning (or war) to maintain full employment.

The wise businessman will not seek to buck these trends. He will seek instead to make a place for himself in a "mixed" system, partly socialist, partly capitalist. The evils of communism on the economic plane are overcentralization and bureaucracy; both have a deadening influence. If we face the future without hysteria we can, in so big and individualistic a country as the USA, seek to prevent these evils by maintaining as much individual business enterprise as possible within the framework of economic planning.

But the trend toward socialism is irresistible, though atom bombs level everything from Moscow to Vladivostok, though the palest pinks of Washington are immured in Alaskan hoosegows. This is the handwriting on the twentieth-century skies. This is the future. The American capitalist would be wise to recognize it and contain himself. This is the "containment" we need for world peace.

The Fear That Haunts Washington

Washington, October 31, 1947

American politics and American thinking are haunted by the continued rise in prices.

If American society could be placed on a couch in a psychoanalyst's office and the shades drawn, it would soon become evident that there is a relationship between the consciousness of uncontrolled inflation on the one hand and the hysterical babble about Reds on the other.

Much of what is happening in Washington becomes clearer if one recognizes a deep-seated insecurity, a fear that, despite all the oratory about free enterprise, the so-called free enterprise system is drifting rapidly toward another of its periodic collapses.

The past year or so has seen the complete failure of the mechanisms — if you want to give them a more concrete term than they deserve — on which the Right relied for the achievement of postwar stability.

One was supply and demand; it was said that if only OPA were abolished, supply would soon fill demand and the price rise level off. The other is voluntary self-regulation, as espoused both by Republicans and by the Truman administration; it was hoped that this idea would lead businessmen to keep prices and profits down, out of enlightened self-interest. Both of these hopes have been disappointed.

One need only read the business pages and the business papers day after day to see that this is well understood by thoughtful men in the business world, that most of them believe only a sharp drop in business can stop inflation, and that such a bust sooner or later is in the cards.

A "bust" will, however, have political consequences, and the historian may see the current antics of the Un-American Activities Committee and similar bodies as an attempt, in advance, by a cold war against leftists and intellectuals to prevent those consequences.

The consequences envisaged are not, of course, revolutionary; American society is much too healthy and wealthy for that. The consequences lie in a renewed desire by the mass of voters to use democratic processes to achieve greater economic stability and security. This is what the Un-American Activities Committee stigmatized as "red" during the Roosevelt period.

That the Rooseveltian spirit is still alive in the Democratic Party may be seen from the militant resolution on price control drafted by the Democratic National Committee during the past week. That the Truman administration still hesitates to take a Rooseveltian approach is indicated by the fact that the new national chairman, McGrath, succeeded in shelving the resolution.

Current hysteria is not unrelated to this dangerous combination of indecision with a secret loss of confidence; FDR's courage is lacking, coupled with a subconscious fear that maybe the Reds are right. FDR was haunted by no such doubts; in an age of dictatorship, he proved how much could be done by democratic means.

To return to the psychoanalytic metaphor with which I began, I would say that, to understand the atmosphere of Washington, one must understand that the alternatives for the American economy are a manly attempt at control and reform, or the suicidal drive to a new world war.

War preparations or war have an insidious appeal because they provide an acceptable reason for renewed controls, and a new market and source of profit with which to delay depression. This is the path of least resistance, like another binge for an alcoholic. But in this sphere a lost weekend may mean a lost world.

The ABC of an Effective Foreign Policy

Washington, August 27, 1947

You cannot kill an idea. You cannot substitute bullets for bread. You cannot make misery more palatable by putting it under guard. You cannot build a stable society on exploitation and corruption. When Mr. Truman understands this as fully as Mr. Roosevelt did, American foreign policy will begin to look like something more than a futile attempt to build bulwarks against Soviet expansion on the quicksands of bankrupt ruling classes.

6 | SOME DEAD AMERICANS AND WHAT DIED WITH THEM

LaGuardia and UNRRA

New York, September 22, 1947

That long and lonely fight in the Bronx is ended. We have lost a great New Yorker and a great American. It is sad that the passing of Fiorello LaGuardia should have been pitiful. He was a man to provoke violent reactions — anger, hatred, enthusiasm, love, exasperation, devotion, anything but pity. He who loved combat, crowds, five-alarm fires, rough-and-tumble debate on street corners and on the floor of Congress, tumult and crisis, with all the ardor of a mischievous and exhibitionistic small boy, should not have had to wrestle unseen with a stealthy death. He should have died splendidly in battle, not slowly shrinking into skin and bone on a sickbed, restless, impatient, and frustrated, a giant spirit in a shrunken child's body, watching with dismay as the world moved through misery he had tried to alleviate toward a new tragedy his unheeded warnings foresaw. This, for the Little Flower, the Mayor, Butch, the Hat, was a cruel end.

LaGuardia's background was of that richly composite and polyglot kind that is America's glory, however much it may depress the anemic D.A.R. He was half Italian, half Jewish, and wholly American. He was born in New York but spent his childhood and youth in Arizona. From the Southwest he brought more than a fondness for sombrero-brimmed hats so broad they made the stout little fellow look like a perambulating mushroom; he brought something of the breezy independence of the frontier. No figure in American politics ever thumbed his nose so brashly at party regularity and got away with it. In the midst of the smug Coolidge era, when the party bosses tried to get rid of this maverick Republican, he defied them and was re-elected to Congress as a Socialist. He was a New Dealer before the New Deal; the leader of a rebel Republican faction which rode herd on the Hooverites in the early '30s, fought hard for relief, blocked the sales tax, and in 1932 triumphantly put through Congress the Norris-LaGuardia anti-injunction act, forerunner of the Wagner Act and LaGuardia's greatest legislative achievement.

What were the qualities and circumstances which enabled La-Guardia to serve fourteen years in Congress, to be elected Mayor of New York for three consecutive terms, to become a national and international figure, without that loyalty to party machine which is ordinarily an essential to success in American politics? He survived in Congress because his base was on the East Side, among the poor and the politically advanced. He succeeded without a

machine in New York because Tammany mismanagement, a left-
ward tide, and a sense of civic responsibility made it possible for
LaGuardia to muster a coalition which ranged from Wall Street
bankers to Union Square labor leaders. He gave the city competent,
honest, and reasonably progressive government for twelve years —
the best mayor New York ever had. Though he was as temper-
amental as an operatic tenor, and as flamboyant as a prima donna,
LaGuardia was a tireless and capable administrator. He was a
natural-born popular leader for a democratic people: straightfor-
ward in speech, free from cant and hypocrisy, shrewdly and dis-
armingly candid in tight spots, with a flair for the direct and the
dramatic.

To protest against Prohibition, LaGuardia brewed beer in his
own office in Washington. To illustrate a speech on the high cost
of living after World War I, he waved a lamb chop before a
startled House of Representatives. To show his contempt for
Hoover during the '30s, he gave his own White House invitations
to street urchins. To make Midwestern farmers realize the need
abroad, LaGuardia went on a personal tour as head of UNRRA;
at one rally, in Minnesota, he mounted a farm wagon, held aloft a
loaf of bread, and ripped off six slices to show assembled farmers
an entire day's food allowance in some European countries —
"And mark you, there's no gravy goes with it." This was not
demagogy. LaGuardia was not a demagogue; he was not one to
mouth irresponsible nonsense to inflame a crowd. But he knew
how to capture popular imagination. He knew how to translate
abstractions into concrete and vivid realities. He could talk the
ordinary man's language as no ordinary man could talk it — he
had the gift of plain, direct, and salty speech. Fiorello was no
ivory-tower intellectual.

LaGuardia was never more earnest or more farsighted than in
the efforts he made during the last year of his life to prevent the
drift toward a new war. His proposal for a United Nations
emergency food fund, last November, and his testimony against
the Truman Doctrine, last March, were a plea for the continuance

of international cooperation, a warning against the consequences if America tried to use its food and its money as instruments of political domination. "It is reminiscent," he told a United Nations Assembly committee last November, "of the old days of politics here in my town, when the poor in the district were given a basket of food on Christmas and during the winter a bag of coal or two. Along came election time, and they were . . . taken in hordes to vote the ticket." Before the Senate Foreign Relations Committee, last March, on the Truman Doctrine, he pleaded, "Let us not do anything that will create the impression that we want to rule the whole world, that any government that does not please us will be put out of business."

He urged another approach: "We can lick Communism in this world by making democracy work, by proving to the world that people can live properly and decently."

The Truman administration and the State Department had decided otherwise. They had decided to abandon UNRRA for a system under which we proposed to exact a political *quid pro quo* for feeding hungry people; it was to be — starve, or else. "You cannot find the theory or purpose of UNRRA in the revised statutes or in the treaties," LaGuardia told the Senate committee, "but if you will go across the street to the library and ask for a book called the New Testament, there you will find the spirit of UNRRA, and you will find the purpose of it, and you will find the way it was administered."

LaGuardia spoke to no purpose. It was a bitter spectacle for the dying man to see, as he predicted, that the United Nations would begin to break down once we abandoned international principles in the handling of the food problem. He died an unhappy man; in Washington the kind of men and policies he fought in the '20s were back in power; abroad he saw the old mistakes and a new war coming. The few who saw him toward the last knew that sorrow stood at his bedside. The peace death promised was unwelcome to one whose joy it had always been to war for the good.

Harry D. White and Internationalism

Washington, August 18, 1948

I would not demean the memory of Harry D. White nor pander to the men who helped to kill him by saying that he was not a Communist. If he was one, Communists have reason to be proud. For he was a man of brilliant mind and understanding spirit.

But I think I know more about Communists and Communism than do the backwoods bird-brains of the House Un-American Activities Committee. I certainly knew Harry White better than the inquisitorial bigots who put the final unbearable strain on his ailing heart. And I do not think Harry White was a Communist, if the word is to be used correctly and without quotation marks.

Harry White was the product of a free society, and too independent in his thinking to tread anybody's line. He knew his history. He was aware of the fact that there is more to historical processes than is dreamed of by the simplistic. He was not afraid to look at the world about him objectively and he could, I suppose, say the word "revolution" without wincing.

But White was no parlor bolshevik or dilettante theoretician. He was a hard-working and very practical economist who went to the Treasury in June, 1934, and stayed on for no mysterious reason. He was attracted to the New Deal like many other intellectuals of progressive outlook because he saw in it an opportunity to be useful, to hammer out necessary social changes on the clamorous but firm anvil of democratic processes.

I don't want to use hackneyed words or paint a saccharine picture. I have heard the New Dealers gripe plenty in the old days about FDR, but it is true that Roosevelt inspired them. He gave them a sense of accomplishment and purpose. He made it seem worth-while to work all hours — and the United States never had more devoted servants than men of White's kind. Their lights burned late and their ulcers ached early.

History will record, even if current hysteria forgets, that it was men of White's kind who restored faith in orderly government, who proved it could work in the USA at a time when elsewhere in the world free government broke down in disillusion, and dictators rose to power on mob violence.

Think back to the bonus marchers and foreclosure riots and Huey Long and realize what might have happened in America on a large scale if there had been no Roosevelt and no New Deal, no Harry Whites and no "Communists" to give back to ordinary Americans faith that the traditional ways of free government were fully capable of satisfying their aspiration for greater security.

These men hated fascism, as all decent men must. They were friendly to the Soviet Union, for they understood the dreadful circumstances out of which the Russian Revolution sprang. They hoped that in time the Soviet dictatorship, given peaceful conditions, would swing back toward democratic methods. They wanted to build a new and better world after the war.

In this sense, White had an internationalist outlook, as must every intelligent man in our time. But those who had the privilege of talking with him off the record during some of his most difficult postwar negotiations knew that White was no softy, that under the surface he had an unexpected vein of American nationalism, and that in dealing with the Russians as with the British he was not at all disposed to let them, as the *Chicago Tribune* might say, take the shirt off Uncle Sam's back.

The history of White's role at Bretton Woods, where he and the late Lord Keynes were the principal architects of the World Bank and the International Monetary Fund, will show how skillfully he worked to protect American interest — and primacy — within the framework of a new world monetary order. The difference between the original Keynes proposals and those of White is the difference between proposals tailor-made to British needs and those framed to suit American purposes.

White worked toward a vision of a more stable world. He felt he had helped to lay one of its cornerstones at Bretton Woods, whereby world resources were to be pooled for reconstruction and monetary stability. He tried to lay another cornerstone in the

Morgenthau Plan. This did not, as its critics alleged, seek to "turn the Reich into a goat pasture." It sought permanently to end the danger of German military revival by placing the Ruhr under international control, reducing the warmaking potential of the Reich, and turning the country toward light rather than heavy industry.

White was not naive about the difficulties of dealing with the Russians. But he also saw that the inevitable corollary of a breakdown in good relations between the West and the Soviet Union would be the rebirth of the German menace against which America had twice been forced to fight, and a new war. But this is a view which invites reprisal from powerful sources with a vested interest in world hate and tension. Secondhand hearsay gossip, unsuccessfully retailed to a grand jury by two ex-Communist agents, provided the opportunity to smear White and destroy him. Events may yet prove in blood and fire just where in this picture treason to America's best interests really lay.

Events will show it does not lie on the name of Harry White. He fought for his country overseas in World War I as a lieutenant of infantry. He worked for it as faithfully and honorably in World War II and after. His crime was that he belonged to a group of men who helped to make democracy work at home and hoped to make international collaboration work abroad.

That is why the Rankins, the Hearsts, the Peglers, the peddlers of poison, and the paid hounds of slander, leaped on him in hate. Killing White was but an incident in the war being waged to kill the free America which bred him.

Frank Murphy: The Quality of Mercy

Washington, July 22, 1949

There is an old Latin chestnut — *"de mortuis nil nisi bonum."* It may be translated as "Say nothing but good of the dead." The saying invokes a common charity in a common fate. Thanks to it, crooks and stuffed shirts without number have been lowered to their graves with reverence. Who would grudge all but the few innately evil the last kindness of a little hypocrisy?

This ultimate comfort that we accord to scoundrels does not seem to be forthcoming here when a tribune of the people passes. I use the old-fashioned phrase because Supreme Court Justice Frank Murphy was in so many ways like those tribunes the plebs of Rome elected to wield the veto in their protection.

We are not accustomed to seeing the veto power of the Supreme Court wielded in that way. Traditionally, the Court has been the tribune of the big property owner, his final bulwark against reforms.

Perhaps this explains the curious disparagement with which the respectable press of the capital — the *Post, Star,* and *News* — treated the passing of Mr. Justice Murphy. But then he was always offending respectables. He successfully defended Maurice Sugar when the latter was disbarred as a radical in the backwash of World War I. He was the first mayor (Detroit) to call for federal aid to the jobless when Mr. Hoover's rugged individualism was still the American gospel.

Mr. Justice Murphy's unforgivable offense in some people's eyes was his refusal to drive out the Flint sitdown strikers with the National Guard. How few remember not only what he did but its wisdom. A little patience prevented grave disorder. How different if he had treated the auto workers as Hoover and MacArthur treated the bonus marchers!

This was never forgiven Murphy. The money powers of Michigan made sure Murphy never ran for public office again. He was the first victim of those pre-election smearings in which the Dies Committee specialized, and it cost him re-election in 1938. Had his name not been Murphy, had he not been a Roman Catholic, had he been a Jewish left-winger like his lifelong friend Sugar, the smear treatment would have gone so far as to make it impossible for FDR to appoint him Attorney General and then Supreme Court Justice. These accidents of his Irish origin saved him.

FDR put Murphy on the Court because he wanted a judge who

could not be tied into knots by Sullivan & Cromwell or Cravath, de Gersdorff, Swaine & Wood. He wanted a judge who could not be convinced that the Founding Fathers wrote the Constitution especially to protect Amalgamated Can from having to pay its charladies a living wage.

But Mr. Justice Murphy was more than a wise bit of "court packing" by FDR. (No one called it that when the Court was kept well packed with corporation lawyers like Murphy's predecessor, Pierce Butler.) Mr. Justice Murphy was no rubber stamp. He was a man of warm heart and saintly spirit, who cared deeply about justice and about liberty. This did not, as the local editorials imply, dim his vision; it sharpened his insight. None saw more truly than he the terrible racistic implications of what was done to the West Coast Japanese. None was readier to speak for the hated and the hunted, whether it was the anti-Catholic Jehovah's Witnesses or the fugitive Eisler.

I hope some publisher will give us a collected edition of his opinions. There is much in them that is nobly thought and uttered. The main complaint against him is a curious one. The editorials in the *Post, Star,* and *News* all lament his "disposition to show mercy, even at the expense of law and order."

Mercy needs no justification beyond itself, but it is often wisdom. A story may be told in Mr. Justice Murphy's defense.

Scholars have noted that, in the Hebrew text of Genesis, in the beginning God is referred to as "Elohim" but later as "Jahveh," which the orthodox, forbearing to invoke the sacred name, called "Adonai."

Modern scholars believe this indicates that two different versions have been put together, but the medieval rabbis, who pondered the text long and lovingly, had another explanation. The great Rashi said that "Elohim" denotes God under the aspect of justice while "Adonai" is his designation as the God of mercy.

Rashi's interpretation was that the Torah first uses "Elohim" alone "because at first He created the world strictly on the principle of justice." Later "Adonai" appears because God saw that "the world could not endure on that basis alone" and "added thereto the principle of mercy."

I offer the story in tribute to a Justice whose death makes many of us feel a sense of personal loss.

Jo Davidson: The New Exiles

New York, January 6, 1952

I saw a lot of Jo Davidson in Paris last year. He was lonesome. He had an insatiable appetite for people, and an enormous need for talk; he talked with genius; it was gusty talk shot through with devastatingly acute perceptions; he talked in a booming voice that matched his vitality; it was like visiting with the Jehovah of the Old Testament, except that this old man with the graying beard had a zest and an exuberance that makes it strange to write down the words "old man" about him at all.

People always seem to be saying of some celebrity or other that he has been everywhere and known everybody. Jo Davidson really had. As a sculptor he had covered all the major events of his time from World War I and the Russian Revolution to the birth of Israel and done most of its "heads." To listen to Jo Davidson would have been overwhelming (how could any ordinary mortal ever hope to know and see so much again?) if it were not so enjoyable.

His social life (what a colorless phrase for Jo's!) had been ruined by the Cold War. He was a man unafraid to be himself, and a man unafraid to be himself can face almost anything, but he was as sensitive as a baby about a snub. He loved people, people of all kinds, and he felt terribly hurt when suddenly he found people (as they used to say in Victorian novels) cutting him dead — all kinds of people.

His recently published autobiography, *Between Sittings* (really a collaboration with his devoted wife), an utter success in portraying this most lovable of all his subjects, tells how he was first

drawn into politics. Mrs. Charles Poletti asked him to go on the
air for Roosevelt in 1940. "I demurred," Davidson writes, "saying
I was doing the job my way: wining and dining and weekending
with conservative friends, I would always bring the conversation
around to Roosevelt, explaining why I was for him and reminding
them of his achievements." Davidson adds, "I may not have convinced them, but I certainly succeeded in spoiling many a dinner
party."

It is impossible to imagine Jo spoiling any dinner party; even the
stuffiest of dinner partners could hardly resist him. It was not
merely his urbanity, energy, wit, and charm, but his genuine good
will, warmth, and interest. But this was what Jo liked, "wining and
dining and weekending." He liked good food, good clothes, good
talk, and good people, but preferably amusing ones, not the kind
who mistake spiritual anemia for good breeding.

First Jo found some of his old-time friends and drinking and
dining companions antagonized by his work for Roosevelt, and
then some of his old-time liberal friends antagonized because in
1948 he worked for Wallace. I don't know whether "antagonized"
is really the right word for it. It is difficult to believe that Jo ever
antagonized anybody. It is just that as political lines tightened
people began to huddle with one herd or another for security.

Some of his friends were afraid to associate with somebody who
had worked with "Reds." Later most of his old-time friends among
the Communist intellectuals and artists of France avoided Jo because they were afraid to associate with someone who had paid a
friendly visit to Tito. (The Left, like the Right, has its Babbitts, con-
formists, and lickspittles.) So Jo more and more found himself
isolated, caught in the cross fires of the Cold War, as every artist
must be who cares more for the rich, complex, unpredictable, endlessly exasperating and wonderful vagaries of humanity than for
two-dimensional political yardsticks.

At the same time, like almost every great artist, Jo was sym-
pathetic with all the revolutionary strivings of his time. He did the
Bolshevik leaders when they were still pariahs at Rapallo. He went

to Spain during the Civil War, a gesture of solidarity with the Republic. He never soured, but he hated to lose old friendships.

Jo Davidson was American through and through; a go-getter as well as a great artist, with the kind of energy and eye for an opportunity that is supposed to be typical of American business. He was American, too, in his utter lack of cant or "side," his rich friendliness and his informality; the West European does not give himself quite so easily. But I am glad he died in France and will be buried there. For France was his second home, as it has been the second and spiritual home of so many civilized men. For Jo, as for others in the Cold War years, France was still a congenial place where one could live as a man of good will without having to win a certificate of respectability by anti-Communist claptrap, current American style. Paris nurtured him as an artist in his youth, and gave him a home in the quasi-exile of his age. Something of Jo will be forever there among the great shades which haunt its beloved quays and streets.

I read Jo's book all through at one sitting last night. It was like another great evening with him. I recommend it to all his friends. I want to end with a suggestion. Jo was hurt because no one would buy the magnificent head of Roosevelt in his Paris studio. It moved me to tears when I first saw it, for it is not only the greatest American of our time done in all his gallant courage but it is also that better America we also saw in our lifetime, an America which was not afraid and did not go around scaring itself to death. Davidson's Roosevelt was in exile with him. It ought to be brought back home.

Jo had a few rich high-placed friends much too civilized ever to worry about his politics and much too understanding not to go on loving him. Some of them also loved Roosevelt. Can't they with help from the rest of us get up a fund to buy Davidson's Roosevelt and present it to the United Nations headquarters here? It belongs there, for the darker moments when some delegates may wonder about the United States. It is the spirit of another America not yet dead. It is Roosevelt and it is Jo Davidson, and it is a message of love and faith from both.

7 | TRUMAN AND THE TRUMAN ERA

The Imponderable of Leadership: It Just Wasn't There

Washington, January 8, 1948

The reading by the President of his annual message to Congress is the closest that Washington comes to Rome's gladiatorial fiestas. The perennial wrangle between White House and Capitol Hill opens with a touch of ceremony. The President, like a gladiator, enters to make his *morituri te salutamus* and is granted a round of applause before being set upon by the hungry lions.

Yesterday, windy but sunny, drew a crowd to the Capitol. An hour before the President's address, police with freshly laundered white gloves formed a narrow lane from the entrance, through Statuary Hall and the majestic rotunda, to the Speaker's office on the House floor. Up above it, under the naked girders erected to support the ceiling against bombing during the war, the galleries filled early.

The first faint whiff of blood from the still-sedate arena came up at 1:18 P.M. when press gallery attendants distributed a statement by House Majority Leader Charles A. Halleck (R., Ind.) describing the coming message as "designed to out-Wallace Wallace." While the reporters were reading this, Speaker Martin (R., Mass.) rapped on the bright green baize of the double-tiered rostrum and announced the names of the committee to escort the President. Halleck's name led the list: the victim was to be in secure hands.

56

Members of the House, a few with children on their knees or beside them, were crowded back into the rear seats. The Senators, older, slower, and heavier, filed in two abreast and took the front seats. Conspicuous among them was Taft, whose slight build and undistinguished bearing give him the appearance of an elderly boy, and Connally, with his ham-actor haircut.

Visiting ambassadors and ministers followed. They drew polite applause. At 1:26 P.M. the members of the cabinet walked in and filled a front row of cane-bottomed chairs. They looked ill at ease, like men who feel themselves in territory which might turn hostile at any minute. Secretary Marshall came in late, through a side door. He was received with applause and cheers, and took the chair on the aisle.

At 1:30 P.M. sharp, the Speaker struck his desk with the gavel, and cried out in a loud voice: "The President of the United States." Down the aisle came the reception committee in pairs and in the middle of them, hemmed in as if to cut off all hope of escape, was Mr. Truman, dapperly self-conscious and significantly small.

On the lower tier of the rostrum, the President drank nervously from a glass of water while the members rose and cheered. He had his speech open before him in a loose-leaf notebook. Camera flashlights popped from the galleries. He began by departing from text. "I sincerely hope," he said, "that all of you have had a pleasant holiday season and that you won't have too much work to do." The members took this deadpan, unplacated, despite some polite applause.

The annual message took forty-five minutes to read. The President, rocking back and forth on his toes, read slowly, with studied emphasis, but without force. His invocation of American idealism brought no reaction from that rather hard-boiled audience in which middle-class businessmen and lawyers predominate. He was almost two thirds of the way through the prepared speech before he drew applause.

That was at his pledge faithfully to carry out the Taft-Hartley Act. This, and his reference to maintaining "strong armed forces," were the only passages that stirred enthusiasm. There was some

light applause on the tax program, but the scattered hand clapping
for higher corporate taxes was set off by the man who may be
Wallace's running mate, Senator Glen H. Taylor (D., Ida.).

Into the climax of his passage on the Marshall Plan the President
put all the fervor he could command. He called it "a decisive contribution to world peace" and paused a moment for applause. It
did not materialize. This key passage was as warmly received as a
sermon on benevolence to a convention of bill collectors.

The Democrats seemed as cold as the Republicans, and gave no
response of party loyalty to those portions of the message reiterating
the anti-inflation program and carrying on the New Deal.

The failure was in part, at least, Mr. Truman's. One felt, not
lack of sincerity, but lack of conviction, as he plodded along in the
path laid out by Roosevelt. The manner was that of a dutiful
schoolboy, repeating a lesson letter-perfect but only half understood. Where FDR would have said "we can and must" with
magnetic fire, Mr. Truman said it with a rehearsed lilt. That subtle
emanation of the spirit, the quality of leadership, just wasn't there.

With Malice Toward None — Except Half Mankind

Washington, January 21, 1949

I still believe sheer economic necessity must move us toward an
end of the Cold War. But I must say that my belief was badly
shaken by Mr. Truman's inaugural address, which left me sick at
heart. It was shallow, naive, childishly arrogant, and self-righteous,
a call for war thinly masked as a pledge of peace.

Mr. Truman started by saying that "the supreme need of our
time is for men to learn to live together in peace." He said the
American people wanted a world in which "all peoples are free to
govern themselves as they see fit."

But these sentiments were soon canceled out by the statement
that the United States and other like-minded nations "find themselves directly opposed by a regime with contrary aims and a

totally different concept of life," a regime which "adheres to a false philosophy."

The only conclusion one can draw is that Mr. Truman believes other people should be "free to govern themselves as they see fit" — so long as they see fit to see as we see fit.

This is a dangerous doctrine. It would mean that we set ourselves up to police the world. The USA is rich and strong but not rich and strong enough for that.

Nor are its moral forces great enough for the fask. Only naivete and ignorance can accept Mr. Truman's pharisaical self-portrait of American policy. A government which constantly bypasses the UN, curries favor with Peron, does business with any number of military dictators in Latin America, deals under the table with Franco, interferes in Italian elections, and supports reactionaries in Greece has too many motes in its own eye to preach a dubious freedom in Eastern Europe and China.

I call it dubious because the Western powers during the past generation have never offered and do not offer now to either area any kind of constructive program suitable to the needs of the peoples in these backward areas. Historically, the Eastern countries are where England was in the days of the Plantagenets and France in those of the Bourbons, and revolutionary methods may now, as then, prove historically justifiable in dealing with their problems. The transition from feudalism has nowhere been made without profound social struggle.

It was the complete absence of any perspective that made the Truman inaugural address so appalling. This is not the first period in world history when the victors in a great struggle faced each other in uneasy fear, nor the first in which it was necessary for men of sharply differing belief to reconcile themselves to life together on the same planet.

The comparable periods of religious warfare between Moslem and Christian, and later between Catholic and Protestant, over issues which seemed as irreconcilable as those between Communist and capitalist societies, demonstrate that the bloodiest struggles have only postponed at terrible price the inevitable coexistence of vastly different basic beliefs. Must mankind again wait for a peace of exhaustion?

The most disturbing aspect of the Truman inaugural is that if this is what the President believes he must modify his domestic program. If this is an irreconcilable conflict, then how can he put sharp limits on military spending? And how can he protect traditional liberties against a fierce terror designed to root out and cow not only Communists but anyone who thinks peace possible? Can there be a New Deal in such an atmosphere? I do not think so.

To paraphrase Lincoln's Second Inaugural, Mr. Truman spoke with malice toward none except half of mankind (Russia and China), and with charity toward all willing to give us military bases.

Mr. Smith Pleads for Peace

Washington, January 24, 1949

In taking over the high office to which I have been elected as head of the Smith family, I want to pledge myself to peace.

We Smiths, unlike the Joneses, are peaceful people. A new war would ruin us. There are three mortgages on the old house already. We couldn't afford another scrap in this neighborhood. That's why I'm going to do all I can for peace.

So far as I can see, the prospects for peace would be excellent, were it not for the Joneses over in the next alley. They lie, cheat, steal, pick their noses in public, and forget to put the top on their garbage can.

As everybody knows, Smiths are righteous folk. We meet the interest on our mortgages, shovel the snow off our sidewalks, and we're in our pew at church every Sunday morning. We stand foursquare with God and we have reason to believe that God stands foursquare with us.

We're Presbyterians. The Joneses are different. They're Baptists. We have statistics to prove that 6,349,742 Baptists every year die from total immersion. That's the kind of people we Smiths are up against in trying to make this neighborhood a safe one.

We Smiths believe every man should be free to worship God as he pleases, so long as he doesn't turn Baptist, or spread total immersion. We're prepared to lend money to anyone on the verge of becoming a Baptist if only he'll desist from damnation.

One of the troubles with the Joneses is they're too darned suspicious. They keep insisting that we are getting ready to attack them. I have no hesitation in saying that this is a complete fabrication, highly exaggerated, only partly true, and something of a misconception.

It is true that in return for friendly loans to neighbors of the Joneses we have arranged to set up sandbag emplacements in all the backyards adjoining theirs, and are ready at a moment's notice to let loose with a new gadget of which we Smiths are right proud, the addled egg.

These eggs, as prepared by a secret process of our own, are so hard when thrown and so gaseous when broken that a fusillade of them is guaranteed within ten minutes to break every window in the Jones home, kill Mr. Jones, drive Mrs. Jones out of her head, and asphyxiate all the Jones children. But these preparations of ours are purely defensive. The refusal of the Joneses to believe this is another example of that stubborn wickedness to which Joneses are predestined.

Far from plotting war, we are anxious for peace. The front door of our home is always open to Old Man Jones. He's a crooked old scoundrel, with a nose like a tomato and a breath that would knock over a horse. Everybody knows he's an embezzler, chicken thief, bigamist, and prevaricator, but any time he wants to crawl over to my door on that dirty belly of his *I'll* talk peace with him.

We're going ahead on our own peace plans regardless. We're going to erect a ten-foot-high picket fence around the Jones house. We're building up the biggest stockpile of addled eggs in the history of our neighborhood. And we're negotiating with little Willie Jones, who's just crazy about lollipops, to supply him with all-day suckers for life, if he'll set fire to the Jones place next time his old man's sleeping off a bender.

We Smiths want peace so bad we're prepared to kill every one of the Joneses to get it.

Mr. President: The Literary Hoax of 1952

New York, March 21, 1952

It is impossible to read *Mr. President* without chuckling. The book is as fascinating as a Sears-Roebuck catalogue. As a book on the Presidency and its problems it is the great literary hoax of 1952. But as a campaign document it is superb. This is Mr. Truman's book about himself, disingenuous in its self-glorification, "folksy" in its appeal, as irrefutable as kissing babies.

The book is built for easy reading. Its 250 pages are wide-spaced. The type is large enough to be read by Grandma even if she can't find her glasses. It is as much picture as text, and most of the pictures are of Truman and Trumans. There are — by actual count — twenty-eight pictures of Mr. Truman alone and twenty-seven pictures of Mr. Truman with others. There are pictures of Ma and Pa, both sets of Grandma and Grandpa, three pictures of Sister Mary Jane Truman, three of Brother Vivian and family, one aunt, four nieces, three nephews, and Miss Ethel Noland, a cousin.

The weak spot in the book is that, for all its proclaimed devotion to Mrs. Truman and Margaret, women readers are going to ask themselves why in a book with fifty-five pictures of Truman there is only one picture each of Mrs. Truman and Margaret, though both in full color.

There are two pictures of Truman at the piano. There is one at the age of thirteen, one as a small boy with his brother Vivian, two in uniform. The only thing missing — I wonder what happened to it — is the picture of Harry S. Truman at six months bottoms up on a bearskin.

There is a full-page photo showing all Mr. Truman's honorary degrees and a full page showing his Masonic insignia. There are photostats of his favorite musical scores, including a page from *Floradora* and two compositions by Rubinstein and Chopin respectively, both bearing as posthumous honors the autograph "Harry S. Truman."

For the folks back home the book will be as good as a visit to Washington and less tiring. There are daguerreotypes of the old city. There are pictures of the Washington, Lincoln, Jefferson, and Adams Memorials. There are reproductions in full colors of such art treasures as "George Washington's Family," "Lincoln and His Generals," and "The Descent from the Cross," but not (an oversight on which the Republicans may unfairly capitalize) of "Washington Crossing the Delaware." There is also a picture of the Independence, Missouri, courthouse.

There are photostatic reproductions of the Declaration of Independence (and of the famous frieze showing the signers), the Constitution (with the original signatures), and the Emancipation Proclamation. There are pictures of half a dozen past Presidents, including John Tyler and Grover Cleveland, but no Republicans except Lincoln. There are limits to magnanimity in a campaign year.

For those who want to indulge in broader, less political, more cultural vistas there are pictures of Shakespeare, Moses with the Ten Tablets, Henry IV of France, Mark Twain, Alexander the Great, and Julius Caesar. Just why the last two were included is not clear, except possibly as a warning to J. Stalin.

This book may safely be placed in the hands of children. It does have two sexy passages, but only the old-fashioned will object to their frankness, and the message in both cases is wholesome. "In reading the lives of great men," Mr. Truman says in a sketch of his younger days, "I found that the first victory they won was over themselves and their carnal urges." This early training served him in good stead. He tells of visiting Paris after the Armistice in World War I with brother officers, and attending — every man has a right to his wild oats — the Folies Bergères. He found it "a disgusting performance."

There is a heart-warming solidity about the opinions expressed in *Mr. President,* whether on morals, politics, or the arts. In music, Mr. Truman's tastes are strongly classical: Mozart, Beethoven, and Chopin. "He does not understand Shostakovitch," his Boswell assures us, "and no political reason is involved, but he does like

Debussy." Mr. Truman puts it bluntly, "I don't like noise that passes for music today. Maybe I'm old-fashioned." Such frank confessions will lose him few votes in Oshkosh or Chillicothe.

In painting, Mr. Truman's tastes are as unexceptionable. His favorites are Holbein, Franz Hals, Rubens, and da Vinci. He also likes Gilbert Stuart. He takes issue with the so-called realists, for he believes "we see enough of squalor" and thinks art "is intended to lift the ideals of the people, not to pull them down." Of course, he has no use for "the lazy, nutty moderns. It is like comparing Christ with Lenin." (That "nut" Picasso may take this for a compliment.)

"Never," says the blurb for this book, "has a President allowed such a personal revelation while still in office." After thinking "long and hard," Mr. Truman said, he decided to make available his "private notes and papers," imposing no restrictions other than those of "the Nation's security, public interest and good taste."

The risk was well taken. Mr. Truman need not blush for what these private papers reveal. In religion, as he emphasizes several times, he is strong for the Sermon on the Mount. As an old soldier, he agrees with Sherman. In one intimate passage he wrote of his leave-taking in World War I with his mother: "She smiled at me all the time and told me to do my best for the country. But she cried all the way home and when I came back from France she gained ten or fifteen pounds in weight. That's the real horror of war."

The political aphorisms made available from his private papers show strong convictions. "It is much better," he wrote, "to go down fighting for what is right than to compromise your principles." How true. There are jottings which betray dark moments. "I rather think," he once wrote, "there is an immense shortage of Christian charity among so-called Christians."

The burdens of high office bring new insight: "No President," he wrote, "can tell what the best approach to world affairs is. He has to use his best judgment and try to keep things on an even keel . . ." That will bear pondering.

Mr. Truman has time to share the benefits of his political experience with others. "Don't spend a lot of money on advertising," he advises. "Political advertising just doesn't bring in the votes. Handshakes before Election Day and precinct workers on that day to see that the voters come to the polls win elections." The case for the handshake has never been put more succinctly.

Mr. Truman's Boswell, in one of the heart-to-heart talks recorded in this book, boldly asked him about political bosses: "Bosses," in Mr. Truman's opinion, "are usually men who are interested in the political game." They are "willing to put themselves out and do everything possible for the people." Mr. Truman went on to warn, however, that "when a political boss stays too long and gets too much power, then he is no longer benevolent. He is a danger." This is difficult to refute.

Mr. Truman confesses himself a liberal. He thinks there should be "a real liberal party." He invites "the opponents to liberalism and progress" to "join together in the party of the opposition." Mr. Truman is prepared to fight it out with those who are against progress, any time they are prepared to make that their platform.

At the same time, in speaking of a liberal party, Mr. Truman says, "I don't mean a crackpot professional liberal one." He considers "professional" liberals "a low form of politician." As early as September, 1946, he began to feel that "The Reds, phonies and the 'parlor pinks' seem to be banded together and are becoming a national danger." The Hearst papers will have trouble finding anything wrong with that sentiment.

In discussing four men, Stalin, Wallace, Baruch, and John L. Lewis, Mr. Truman lets the chips fall where they may. This outspokenness may well cost him three votes in the election. Otherwise he says nothing which should offend anybody, even Dixiecrats and Republicans. If the President has strong views on inflation, lynchings, Taft-Hartleyism, the Un-American Activities Committee, McCarthy, civil liberties, taxes, or other such dull subjects impervious to color illustration, the views are kept well hidden.

As for foreign policy, Mr. Truman and William Hillman between them managed to do a book on Truman without once mentioning the Truman Doctrine or how it came to be promulgated.

There is only a six-line noncommittal diary item on the historic Potsdam conference with Stalin — their one meeting — but nineteen lines on a luncheon with the late King George VI on Mr. Truman's way back from Potsdam. He and the King examined a sword which had once belonged to Sir Francis Drake "but the King said it was not properly balanced." Afterward, Mr. Truman discloses, "We had a nice and appetizing lunch — soup, fish, lamb chops, peas, potatoes and ice cream with chocolate sauce."

As every reader knows who has ever tried ice cream with chocolate sauce, some experiences are unforgettable.

8 | CONFESSIONS OF A DUPE: WHY I WAS FOR WALLACE

New York, August 25, 1948

I yield to no man in the variety and number of my objections to Henry Wallace's Progressive Party. I don't like yogis and I don't like commissars. I condemn the way Stalin combs his hair and I disapprove the way Molotov blows his nose. I can't help cheering for Tito, and when socialism comes I'll fight for the right to spit in the nearest bureaucrat's eye. I own a house in Washington and I don't want proletarians trampling my petunias on their way downtown to overthrow the government by force and violence. I wouldn't want my sister to marry a Communist, and force me to maldigest my Sunday morning bagel arguing dialectics with a sectarian brother-in-law.

I can pick flaws thick as flies in the Progressive Party platform. In thirty minutes, cross-legged, saying "Oom" with alternate exhalations, I can conjure up a better third-party movement than Wallace's. I can visualize a new party so pure nobody else might vote for it this year, but just wait till the elections of 2052! Oh, I'm as good as the next intellectual in a navel-meditating contest, and I can split hairs with the best of them. (Will the ushers please toss out the fellow who just yelled "How about a hair-splitter for President?") Yet with only about seventy shopping days left until election, I find I'm still for Henry Wallace.

I know I'm a dupe, or worse, and ought to have my ideological tires checked at the nearest FBI service station. I know that if the Communists came to power I'd soon find myself eating cold *kasha* in a concentration camp in Kansas *gubernya*. But I don't think I'm quite as big a dupe as those who are going to vote for Truman and the bipartisan Cold War, and expect to get peace, housing, and better prices. And I know I'm not as big a dupe as those who will stay home on Election Day and suck their politically pasteurized thumbs.

I find that Wallace's opponents supply the best sales talks in his favor. I turned timidly to the text of his Bridgeport speech after I saw a *New York Herald Tribune* editorial on it which charged him with "a talent for evasion." Aside from being a little too clever in spots, as if a Broadway smarty had been hired to juice up the writing, it seemed a whopping good speech, which could best be answered by changing the subject. The speech evaded very little, though it may not have been able to recruit Westbrook Pegler for the Bronx Concourse branch of the Communist Party.

"What people want to know," the editors of the *Herald Tribune* opined darkly, "is how Henry Wallace feels about the Communist domination of the newborn Progressive Party?" I'm prepared to brush aside Wallace's own attempt to answer this loaded question at Bridgeport, but I'm not sure that this is really the burning question of the day for most Americans, though a lot of people are trying hard to make it so.

A good many people are still misguided enough to want to know if there's going to be another war and whether everything possible is being done to avoid it; when they can find a decent place to live and whether the cost of living can be brought down without another depression.

I wasn't born yesterday. I'm not a candidate for dogcatcher. Turn off the white lights and lay off the hotfoot. I admit everything. The Communists are doing a major part of the work of the Wallace movement, from ringing doorbells to framing platforms. Okay if

you want it that way, so they "dominate" the party. So what? I'm
just a poor dupe who can't take either Dewey or Truman, and is
looking for an effective way to cast a protest vote against cold war,
high prices, and hysteria. Wallace has had his effect on both parties
already, and a big vote for peace in November might have its
effect, too. More effect, anyway, than staying home and playing
charades.

9 | FROM MARSHALL PLAN TO MILITARY AID

The Decline and Fall of Western Europe

Washington, September 29, 1947

The text of the sixteen-nation Paris proposals under the Marshall
Plan is a document to stir the imagination of a Gibbon. Soberly and
lucidly its neatly numbered paragraphs spell out the decline and
perhaps foreshadow the fall of Western Europe. To understand the
full import of Western Europe's crisis one must understand that we
are confronted with more than difficulties created by the devastation
of war and the bad weather which followed it. We are confronted
with a fundamental change in the relationship between Western
Europe and the rest of the world.

The nature of that change and of the "dollar shortage" is indicated by two observations in the Paris report. One is that before
the war Western Europe was able to pay for nearly one-fourth of its
imports of food and raw materials with its income from foreign
investments; much of this has been liquidated to meet the cost of
the war. The second is that before the war Western Europe paid in
part for its imports from America with exports to America from the
British, Dutch, and French possessions in Asia; the war has weakened their hold on these possessions.

The cost of the war is to be measured in these liquidated investments and liquidated empires. In India, Malaya, Indo-China, and Indonesia, the coolie is no longer willing to shoulder the burdens of Western Europe by providing cheap raw materials for its economy. The dollars Western Europe needs to pay for supplies can no longer be obtained from interest on past investments and the profits of colonial imperialism. This is the real nature of the "dollar shortage."

This explains why a country like Britain cannot rest content merely with restoring production to prewar levels. It must produce and sell more than ever before to make up for the loss of investments and of empire. This is generally true of all Western Europe, considered as a bloc. Its populations can be supported only if the expansion of industry and of trade is sufficient to make up for the money formerly earned as interest on past investments and as profit on cheap labor in backward areas. To express this in another way, the war has destroyed a large part of the capital of Western Europe. This capital must be restored if it is to be able again to support its present population.

This may represent the end of a major era. The primacy of Western Europe in the affairs of the world began with the opening of India and America to the exploitation of its merchants and conquistadores; the influx of precious metals from Indian hoards and American mines provided the funds with which modern capitalism had its start, and this capitalism was Western European. From this point of view, the first and second world wars represent the liquidation of Western European capitalism and imperialism, under the impact of the failure to resolve the national rivalries among the Western European powers. Western Europe has wasted its substance on its feuds — feuds which shook and devastated the world.

How is its capital to be restored? That is the No. 1 question propounded by the Paris conference. There are several ways to obtain capital. One is to steal it; that's a harsh term, but much of modern capitalism's capital was stolen in one way or another. Spaniards stole silver from the Indians; Englishmen stole the silver from Spanish galleons taking it from the New World. The hideous exploitation of labor in early-Victorian England and just yesterday in Malaya are only slightly less obvious examples of the accumulation of capital by stealing from someone else.

A second method of obtaining capital is by borrowing it. American capitalism got its start on loans and credits from Europe. American capitalism can, if it chooses, furnish the money Western Europe needs to rebuild its industries and trade to the point where it can support its peoples. Why should America lend the money? For one thing, because before the war half the exports of the world went to Western Europe, and two-fifths of the world's imports came from Western Europe; so huge a gap in world trade must be fully restored to maintain America's own prosperity.

Capital is amassed by suffering, either other people's or one's own. One takes part of the fruit of one's own labor or of someone else's in order to build improvements — factories, machines, ships, roads — that will ultimately raise the standard of living. Someone must give up something today in order to have more tomorrow: that is the logic of capital accumulation. Whether under capitalism or socialism, there is no painless way to create capital.

The third method for creating capital is to take it out of one's own hide. This is what Bolshevik Russia has been engaged in doing for a generation. The Russians under Communism have been building up their own capital, not by borrowing but by suffering, the suffering of Russia's own people. The Five Year Plans are giant demonstrations of how capital can be built up, without foreign loans or foreign exploitation, under a system harsh, ruthless, and single-minded enough to underfeed and underclothe a whole generation for the sake of the future.

If Western Europe, with much of its investments and empire gone, cannot borrow capital from America, it must either decay and lose population or adopt a regime, like Communism, Draconian enough to marshal all national resources and to harness all national energies under a system of virtual forced labor. Only so can it rebuild factories, farms, workshops, railroads, and shipping fleets without outside help.

This is not much of an alternative, because the USA will almost certainly go to war with the USSR if Western Europe should turn

Communist. Men of good will have no choice but to try to work out something like the Marshall Plan for the financing of European reconstruction by American capital.

There are many obstacles to the success of the Marshall Plan. One, hinted at by the Paris conferees, lies in American tariff policy: the higher exports necessary to make up for lost investments and empire cannot be achieved so long as the United States lives behind a Chinese Wall of tariffs. Another lies in the constant effort here to transform the Marshall Plan into a Hoover plan, which would give German reconstruction No. 1 priority. The greater economic cooperation Western Europe needs will be possible only if fears of renewed German aggression are allayed and the industrial means of renewed German aggression are restricted.

A more formidable obstacle lies in growing tension between the USA and the USSR. Western Europe's industry cannot live without Eastern Europe's food and raw materials. The Paris program assumes an easing of tension and an increase in this natural and necessary trade; if this assumption proves false, the Marshall Plan will fail.

The worst obstacles of all lie in a kind of cantankerous impatience with Europe among the American people and in the absence of leadership gifted enough and courageous enough to make ordinary Americans understand their stake in European revival. The consequent pressure on the Paris conferees to reduce their estimates is so strong that the Marshall Plan may easily degenerate into a meager famine handout, not a program for reconstruction at all capable of meeting the needs of an historic hour.

The Real Story of Point Four

Washington, June 27, 1949

The Truman inaugural address was drafted in the State Department, largely by "Chip" Bohlen, and reflected the views of the Cold War clique. The prose was bad, the political analysis puerile, and the effect poisonous. The White House staff thought the speech needed a constructive side that would make headlines, and Clark Clifford dug up an old memorandum of Donald Nelson's on American aid in developing backward areas abroad. Mr. Truman liked the idea and so Point Four was added to the inaugural message and the "BNP," the "Bold New Program," was born.

It gave liberal supporters of the administration something to cheer about. This was its political purpose. But, though intended to be not much more than a rhetorical flourish, it provided a cue for the British government. As in the case of the Marshall Harvard speech, vague generalizations were at once transformed by London into a definite program for loans abroad. A quick-witted girl moved with alacrity to say "yes" when all the young man did was express some general views on marriage.

That the Truman administration did not mean to go so far and so fast is indicated by (1) the fact that no start had then been made in Washington on the drafting of a concrete program; (2) the amount asked, $45,000,000, is paltry rather than "bold"; and (3) the message to Congress last Friday about "BNP" came five months after the inaugural and so late in the session as to make its approval dubious.

The British have lost their grip on Asia and want to develop Africa as a new source of cheap raw materials. They see that the mineral wealth of the Congo enabled Belgium to emerge rich from the war. By developing the wealth of their African territories they could then obtain for sterling and more cheaply in Africa much they must now purchase for dollars and at a high price in the United States and the dollar area. Belgium, France, Holland, and Portugal would also like "BNP" funds for similar use in what is left of their colonial empires.

Mr. Truman speaks of the "BNP" as a means of raising the productivity of backward areas so that their peoples can buy more and thus expand world trade. This is what Nelson had in mind and this is what Wallace was derided for in his famous speech about TVAs for the Danube and milk for the Hottentots. But the whole drift and pattern of events is against this. American business is grumbling that Western Europe's productive capacity has already been expanded too far by the Marshall Plan. If American capital resists full recovery of Western Europe, for fear of competition, will it support expansion of productive capacity elsewhere?

Nor does Western Europe want to build up new competitors. It cannot afford long-range planning of that kind. What it needs urgently are new sources of cheap raw materials. And these can be obtained only if native living conditions remain at a low level. They can remain at a low level only if education, nationalist feeling, trade-union organization, and the democratic means of protest are limited. This means repression of the natives, and an attempt to do in Africa what can no longer be done in most of Asia. This is the dollar-and-cents reality that must negative Mr. Truman's idealistic phrases.

What American capital wants abroad is large profit at little risk. Where raw materials can be obtained cheaply in backward regions, it is interested, as in the Arabian oil development. But where the native peoples have begun to awaken, as in Mexico — a rich potential market for goods, a safe and secure source for oil in war — American capital not only refuses to invest but uses all its influence to prevent the United States government from investing.

Hostility to foreign aid is rising with the unemployment figures. United States industry is tired of helping competitors abroad. It will try to channel any "BNP" into support of American private industry in colonial areas. But Western Europe's dollar problem is not eased when American firms, as in Middle Eastern oil, develop these new sources of supply; Western Europe in the long run must pay for these supplies in dollars. This will seem poor return for what Mr. Truman asks: an open door for American capital in Western Europe's remaining colonies. On this basis West Europe would be ceding its colonial empire to the United States. But if Western Europe loses interest in "BNP" little will come of the program. For "Wall Street" as a whole is not interested in it — even with guarantees.

ECA's experience with guarantees of private investments is illustrative. It started with a $300,000,000 fund to guarantee payment in dollars on earnings of American private investments abroad, but after a year only $4,000,000 of this fund has been obligated. Investors today seem interested only in the "sure thing": they buy annuities; the insurance companies load up with government bonds. American capitalism is becoming institutionalized. It has middle-aged spread. The kind of adventurous pioneering in economic development the world needs is beyond its capacity. How get a bold new program when most American capitalists are wary of "programs," suspicious of the "new," and fear above all the "bold"?

From Butter to Guns

Washington, July 31, 1949

It is difficult to believe that only eighteen months have elapsed between the launching of the Marshall Plan and the new military assistance program. To glance back and compare Secretary Acheson's opening statement on military assistance with Secretary Marshall's opening statement on the European Recovery Program is to see a sinister shift in first premises.

When Secretary Marshall went before the Senate Foreign Relations Committee on January 8, 1948, his premise was that of liberalism. "The foundation of political vitality," he said, "is economic recovery." Unless we extended aid to Western Europe, there would be "social discontents so violent, political confusion so widespread," as to upset the peace of the world and threaten our own security. The alternative was either to finance West European recovery or to withdraw into "an armed camp, regulated and controlled." Either we spend money for reconstruction and peace or we would be forced to spend it on rearmament and war.

In this, Secretary Marshall echoed the views that Acheson, then Undersecretary of State, had advanced in his famous speech on "The Requirements of Reconstruction." That speech at Cleveland, Mississippi, on May 8, 1947, foreshadowed the "Marshall Plan." In it Acheson said American self-interest and security demanded that we help other nations to their feet because, "without outside aid, the process of recovery . . . would take so long as to give rise to hopelessness and despair. . . . Hungry people often resort to desperate measures. The war will not be over until the people of the world can again feed and clothe themselves."

This is no longer the note being struck by Acheson. The emphasis has shifted from bread to arms. Amid the contradictions, *non sequiturs,* and fruity double talk of the Acheson statement on military assistance before the House Foreign Affairs Committee, a new premise makes its appearance.

Two years ago Acheson was arguing that political and social stability could only be assured by wiping out the economic want that bred revolution and war.

The argument now is that political and social stability can be assured only by providing sufficient military strength with which to put down discontent by force.

This shift in emphasis is made clearer in the official statement on the military assistance program by the interdepartmental foreign military assistance coordinating committee. This explains the "two-fold objective" of the Atlantic Pact as, "first, to protect the free North Atlantic Pact countries against internal aggression inspired from abroad," and secondly to "deter aggression." It is significant that protection against "internal aggression" is put first. Thus the primary purpose is to muster sufficient military strength to cope with popular discontent.

The earlier premise is that of free government; its starting point lies in the welfare of the people. The new premise is the premise of arbitrary rule, whether by feudal monarchs, clerical dictatorships, or fascist regimes; their starting point lies in the safety of the possessing classes to exploit the people with impunity. This does require military force.

Acheson's own statement admits that "the danger from Communist elements reached its peak before the moderate governments proved themselves capable of overcoming internal threats to their security. Communist strength and influence in Western Europe have been steadily reduced." But neither in Italy nor France was discontent met by force. The growth of revolutionary movements was abated by economic recovery.

Acheson does not stop to consider why and how "moderate governments" proved their strength. He hastens on to a dubious proposition. "Military assistance from the United States," he continues, "would further strengthen the hand of the democratic governments in dealing with either internal disorders or repelling aggression if it should come." But this is not true if military assistance diverts manpower and materials from economic reconstruction and encourages ruling classes to meet discontent with repression instead of reform.

"It is anticipated," the interdepartmental statement on the military assistance program discloses, "that additional military production [in Western Europe] will result in some curtailment in the production of consumer goods, both for local consumption and for export." The countries to which we will give a billion dollars in military assistance are already spending — according to the President's own arms message — more than five billion dollars a year on armament, or more than their current ERP allotments. Each new dollar from the United States will be matched several times over. Part of the program is to give them the machines with which to make their own arms. The interdepartmental statement says that $155,000,000 in United States aid in this category is expected to make possible about $700,000,000 in arms production by the European Atlantic Pact countries. This will take men and materials.

We seem to be picking up where Goering left off. Western Europe is to have more guns at the expense of less butter. If this creates discontent, there will be arms to combat it. The shift in policy reflects a shift in economic conditions. In the postwar seller's market, European capital could satisfy labor at little cost to itself. With the return of the buyer's market, labor's demands must be beaten down by force if capital's profits and prerogatives are to be preserved.

The new policy is really a very old policy — the policy of repression which stifled all possibility of developing mass-production markets in Europe, which held back industrial technology (why buy labor-saving machines when labor is so cheap?) and built up a huge backlog of revolutionary unrest.

This is the kind of program that will appeal to businessmen who wish to invest under conditions which will allow high rates of profit at the expense of low living standards, the mentality which adored Mussolini because he made the trains run on time. But what speaks through Acheson is no longer the free American spirit but something old, wrinkled, crafty, and cruel, which stinks from centuries of corruption.

10 | THE CHINESE GIANT REAWAKENS

Washington, January 4, 1950

The China policy debate on which the curtain is rising with the new Congress may easily prove to be the Great Debate of this century. The success of the Communists in China has united the most populous country on earth under young and vigorous leadership; a corrupt ruling class has been swept away. Russian experience has shown what a Communist dictatorship can do in industrializing a backward peasant country, and in giving it effective defense forces. The failure to adopt a sober, adult, sophisticated, and magnanimous policy toward this newly awakened giant may prove the ruination of American capitalism long before it has passed its inner prime.

The debate is between one set of men blinded by their preconceptions and another set of men too fearful politically to look at truths they would otherwise recognize. The former, in the context of American politics, are as politically bankrupt as Chiang and the Kuomintang. Mr. Hoover and General MacArthur, the leaders of the interventionist forces, are, like Chiang, believers in the efficacy of force against popular aspirations. It was MacArthur's armed

attack on the ragged bonus marchers in 1932 which dramatized for
the whole country the inevitable results of the Hoover policies. It
was necessary either to shoot the hungry or to feed them, and the
country, in voting then for Mr. Roosevelt and ever since for his
successors, has shown its preference. Essentially these blind old
men, frightened of change and incapable of sympathy, are asking
the United States to enforce with money and ultimately with lives
the same kind of policy it has rejected since 1932.

Were it not so much easier to hide the truth at a distance than
at home, these men could never exercise on foreign policy the
influence they long ago lost on domestic policy. Unfortunately the
constant drumming up of the red scare has made prisoners of their
Democratic opponents, who dare not be put in the position of
being any less fervent in their hatred of Communism. It is fear of
this minority in Congress and in the country, it is the constant
inflation of the red bogey by the administration itself, which makes
Truman and Acheson afraid to tell the country that the Kuomintang is a corpse and recognition of the new regime an inescapable
necessity.

The situation is not comparable to that which confronted England after 1789 or America after 1917. England fattened com-
mercially on the constant warfare against the French Revolution
and Napoleon because there were others to do the bulk of the fighting for her, and British soil remained unscathed. America could
adopt a "touch-me-not" attitude toward the Russian Revolution
after 1917 because there were others to take the brunt of what
nonrecognition and economic blockade cost. Today it is not only
American money but American manpower which would be necessary to wage war against the Chinese Revolution; Indian recognition of the Chinese Reds destroyed the hope that the other great
Asian manpower reservoir might be available. And economic blockade cannot be carried on without hurting our own satellites in the
Far East, especially Japan, more than it hurts the Chinese.

An adult policy must recognize that trade is a necessity between
nations irrespective of ideology. Once the ECA is curtailed, East-
West trade in Europe will revive despite ideological differences.

Japan and China must trade, whatever their regimes. To place political obstacles in the way of that trade in the Far East, as we have already done in Europe, would be to hamper world recovery by removing close to a billion people from the world market. If Germany cannot trade with the Russians, and Japan with the Chinese, then Germany and Japan will cut so far into the dwindling West European market as to make its recovery a hopeless task for the West Europeans and a costly one for the Americans.

If the present policy persists, we ought to take down the Statue of Liberty and substitute a statue of Canute. A sober policy, recognizing the necessities of trade, would seek, as the British are doing, to make a virtue of a necessity. Albeit under Communist control, the industrialization of Eastern Europe and Asia, if permitted peacefully to continue, will enormously raise the level of world trade. Sovietism could in this way do far more for American capitalism than Point Four. But none are so blind as those who will not see.

The historic moment is one that calls for magnanimity. That the hounded survivors of Chiang's blood purge of 1927 should emerge two decades later as masters of China was possible only because the great mass of its people were disgusted with the Kuomintang. In Formosa, in miniature, in the past year — as every correspondent, right or left, attests — the same rhythm of official corruption and public disgust has taken place. The victory of the Chinese Communists was as good as a plebiscite, and if we believe in self-determination we ought to accept it, to offer friendship, and to invite trade.

It is at this point that the wisest of the big American commentators falters. Even Walter Lippmann, for all the welcome good sense of his recent columns on the China question, thinks in terms of alliances against the Chinese Reds. This is still a negative policy. If there is to be peace in the world, if the UN is to grow in importance, the United States must do more than recognize the Chinese regime *de jure*. It must recognize that China has a right to rule its own destiny, that Communist regimes of various kinds are in the world to stay, and that no world order can survive that does not permit the coexistence of different social economic systems.

To take such an attitude, to vote for the new China's admission to the UN Security Council, would be to take a step that would do much to revive China's older friendly feeling for America. The friendship of 450,000,000 people is not lightly to be brushed aside; its cultivation may prove fateful for the future. And if we fear a solid Russo-Chinese bloc, the best way to preserve Chinese independence is to give it our friendship. The Manchurian question may prove the Achilles' heel of Sino-Soviet relations even under Communism. But dabbling in intervention, economic blockade, and hostility can only cement the solid bloc we fear, and set in motion a course that may ruin America in the next fifty years.

11 | TOWARD AN AMERICAN POLICE STATE

The Master Plan for American Thought Control

New York, March 13, 1952

The new report on Communism issued to its members by the United States Chamber of Commerce is a carefully worked out master plan for the extension of thought control in America. It would bar Communists, fellow travelers, and "dupes" from all agencies and professions affecting public opinion "such as newspapers, radio, television, book and magazine publishing, and research institutions." It would bar them as "teachers or librarians," and from posts in "any school or university." It would forbid their employment in "any field which gives prestige and high salaries" such as "the entertainment field." It also says they should not be employed in "any plant large enough to have a labor union."

These proposals would impose on every agency of public education and discussion the same "sterile conformity" foreshadowed in the schools by the Supreme Court decision upholding the Feinberg Law. It would subject renowned artists and scientists to ideological snooping.

While making a clean sweep of the left intellectuals, it would also make it difficult for any radical workingman to make a living. To bar Communists and fellow travelers from employment "in any plant large enough to have a labor union" would be to put industrial workers on notice to be careful what opinions they express in the shop or the union meeting lest these be considered "communistic" and grounds for loss of employment.

The United States Chamber of Commerce proposals would ring down a Big Business iron curtain on the thinking of America.

The source and the past record show that these proposals need to be taken very seriously. The Chamber of Commerce does not speak for a lunatic fringe of the Right. Its members and directors make up a veritable Social Register of American Big Business.

General Mills, Standard Oil of New Jersey, Monsanto Chemical, General Motors, New York Telephone, First National of Chicago are a few names picked at random from one of its "brain trust" committees.

Except for the National Association of Manufacturers, there is no business group in this country which has so well and widely organized a network for influencing legislation and opinion. The Chamber is in some ways more powerful and more responsible than the NAM since the Chamber speaks for American finance as well as American industry.

To read the five reports on Communism which the Chamber of Commerce has issued since 1946 is to see that behind the antics of Congressional witch-hunters, responsible businessmen have been working in an intelligent and organized fashion. The 1946 report suggested the loyalty purge in the government and an investigation of Communist influence in Hollywood, a year before the President issued his executive order for the discharge of disloyal employees and a year before the House Un-American Activities Committee launched its Hollywood inquiry.

In January, 1947, the Chamber of Commerce issued a second report proposing among other things that the Department of Justice publish "at least twice-a-year a certified list of Communist-controlled front organizations and labor unions." In December, 1947, the Department of Justice began the practice of making public at regular intervals a list of "subversive" organizations which had formerly been utilized only for the private guidance of federal officials.

A separate report early that year on "Communists within the Labor Movement" carried a modest footnote saying, "It is probable that the 80th Congress will modify the Wagner Act so that employers can work more effectively and without fear of law violation, with American-minded employees in opposing Communists within the labor movement." It did.

In June, 1947, Congress passed the Taft-Hartley Law over President Truman's veto. This deprived unions of the privileges of the National Labor Relations Act unless their officers took a non-Communist oath. It also weakened provisions of the Wagner Act designed to prevent employers from interfering with their employees in their choice of representatives for collective bargaining.

The 1948 report called for action to bar Communists as teachers, librarians, social workers, and book reviewers. It gave examples of "community action" for the guidance and inspiration of its affiliates. Among these were the banning of "pro-Communist commentators" from the radio, the discharge of Stephen Fritchman as editor of the *Christian Register,* the official Unitarian monthly, and the successful campaign initiated by *Counterattack* to get then Secretary of State George Marshall to refuse an award by *The Churchman. Counterattack* has been endorsed by the Chamber of Commerce ever since that sheet was founded. In addition, every anti-Communist report by the Chamber of Commerce has recommended the right-wing Socialist *New Leader,* along with the pro-China Lobby *Plain Talk,* to its members.

The new report proposes to bar fellow travelers and "dupes" as well as Communists from opinion-making fields. The wide orbit of the net cast by the Chamber is indicated by its attack on critics of the Smith Act and on those who criticize such informers as Louis

Budenz. "Many liberals," the report says, "including one prominent industrialist, have fallen for the Communist bait of attacking former Communists as unreliable. Such converts are abused as 'professional informers.' . . . Abuse leveled against such persons discourages prospective converts from leaving the party, much less assisting our government in prosecuting traitors. In this matter again certain 'liberals' are giving aid and comfort to communism."

The CIO and the Americans for Democratic Action are criticized for opposing the Smith Act, and the report implies that the latter at least may be itself involved in a Communist plot. "As early as 1948," the report says, "when the Communist Party feared that it would be driven underground, its instructions to its members were to concentrate in the 'civil liberties' field." The Chamber of Commerce report then asks, "Is it merely a coincidence that today we have thousands of so-called 'liberals,' for example, Americans for Democratic Action, who are fighting the Communist battle precisely in this field?"

The Chamber suggests an organized investigation of all former Communists, which would study their records and make possible their use as informers.

"It cannot be ignored," the report says, "that we have in our midst several hundred thousand former Communist Party members." It says that only "a minority of these are known to have made a complete switch and are thoroughly loyal and in a few cases strong anti-Communist fighters."

The report says "we have research funds and programs to investigate everything under the sun, but little attempt has been made to study these former Communist Party members: why they joined, educational level, age, I.Q., what they did, how deeply they were involved, why and when they left the party, what they are now doing, etc."

An investigation of this kind would put all former Communists under surveillance, registering them with the FBI and requiring active anti-Communist action to prove their loyalty. The proposal may sound extreme at the moment but it is unwise to treat the proposals of this powerful Big Business body lightly.

Long before McCarthy and McCarran went to work on the State

Department, the United States Chamber of Commerce in its 1947 report called for "exhaustive study" by Congressional committees into foreign policies "which appear to be more pro-Soviet than pro-American." The Chamber said such a Congressional investigation "could go into the influences which entered into such important decisions as the Potsdam agreement, the Argentine policy and the China policy." Long before the "China Lobby" became a familiar phrase the Chamber in these reports on Communism had begun to reflect on the loyalty of public officials hostile to Chiang Kai-shek.

In 1946 the Chamber began to call for a loyalty purge. Its new report has shifted the attack to the loyalty boards themselves. "The greatest weakness in our loyalty program," the new report says, "lies in the departmental and agency loyalty boards," and says that "Communists or doubtfully loyal persons may be coddled at the very time that other officials, in the tax or money-lending fields, are summarily dismissed for questionable associations."

In the field of labor the Chamber asks amendment of the Taft-Hartley Law to tighten up the anti-Communist provisions, and prosecutions for perjury where affidavits have been filed. "Since the proof that even one national officer perjured himself," the report says, "would debar all locals from NLRB facilities, it should not be too difficult for the Department of Justice to prove that any purported resignation [from the Communist Party] was not bona fide."

In the field of free speech for workers the Chamber makes two proposals. One is "a collective bargaining clause" in union contracts which would permit "the discharge of any worker who is a Communist or who continues to join in pro-Communist activities." The other is an amendment to the Taft-Hartley Act "to permit a union to expel and demand the discharge of a Communist member under a union-shop contract." The Chamber of Commerce complains that at present employers "are bound by contract to submit protested discharge cases to grievance procedure." It says, "Unions have sometimes defended discharged Communists and arbitrators have upheld the claim."

In the field of opinion-making professions, the Chamber gave the cue long ago to the Peglers and McCarthys. Thus the 1946 report said "a prominent and highly regarded metropolitan newspaper has followed the Communist line in its reporting and editorials on foreign affairs." The Right's lunatic fringe attacked the *New York Herald Tribune* as the "uptown *Daily Worker*."

The attack on Little, Brown which led to the discharge of Angus Cameron was foreshadowed in that same report, which took sideswipes at "a well-known conservative magazine from a conservative city, and a book firm in the same city . . ." The 1948 report also gave the cue to similar attacks on the literary pages. It said public libraries were in danger not so much from the librarians themselves as from "the fact that many of their important book review sources are infiltrated by Communists or sympathizers." This was later widely amplified by the spokesmen for the China Lobby.

The Chamber of Commerce and its allies are out to surpass the success achieved by Big Business after World War I, when anti-Red hysteria enabled it to establish its "American Plan" open-shop philosophy in industry and to control all the agencies of American public opinion, restricting dissent largely to peripheral and precarious publications.

This time the campaign must contend with a more powerful labor movement, but is helped by big-power rivalry between the United States and the USSR.

Another new factor is the new political power of the Catholic Church and Catholic parties in Western Europe and the United States. The chairman of the Chamber's Committee on Communism from 1941 to 1950, the chairman of the committee which prepared the first four postwar reports on Communism, was Francis P. Matthews, a papal chamberlain and former head of the Knights of Columbus, a man who lost his job in the Truman cabinet as Secretary of the Navy because he took MacArthur's side against Truman and publicly advocated preventive war against Russia in August, 1950.

The Chamber, representing most of America's richest banks and corporations, wields great power in Congress and seeks also to build a grass-roots community "anti-Communist" organization "among business, labor, service, veteran, patriotic and religious groups."

It advises its members to "be on the alert for Communist sympathizers in your community," to "find out from reputable sources such as *Counterattack, Alert* or the American Legion about Communist sympathizers in the entertainment field," to watch out for Communists "promoting appeasement in the name of peace," to "support patriotic ex-Communists who cooperate with the FBI," and to "identify public officials . . . displaying softness towards Communism."

This is a clear invitation to terrorize radicals and to make it unsafe to voice radical views. The Chamber is digging in well in advance to fight any new period of reform, even if it has to create an American variety of fascism to do it.

The Case of the Legless Veteran

Washington, October 22, 1948

The Case of the Legless Veteran is beginning to haunt the men in charge of the loyalty program. It is not merely the cruelty with which the government has treated a man who deserved consideration from his country. The circumstances provide a *reductio ad absurdum* for the syllogism of suspicion which has hitherto served as rationale for the purge.

Just as discussions of the race question in the South sooner or later come around to sex, so discussions of the purge always get back to the atom bomb. The clincher, the would-you-want-your-sister-to-marry argument, is whether you would place a Communist in charge of the secret of the atom bomb. The answer at the moment is, of course, obvious. This answer is triumphantly assumed to justify the discharge of a letter carrier for having once contributed $5 to the Joint Anti-Fascist Refugee Committee. Some people think the atom bomb more precious than the Constitution.

The Case of the Legless Veteran demonstrates that the loyalty purge goes beyond any supposed necessity for protecting secrets so vital they justify the abandonment of traditional liberties. The political views and the job involved show that the effect is to punish a man for his ideas, irrespective of his conduct or his record.

James Kutcher, who lost his legs to a German shell and his livelihood to American hysteria, is a member of the Socialist Workers Party, a Trotskyist group opposed to the Soviet regime. No one could suspect a Trotskyist of trying to steal the atom bomb and ship it to the Kremlin, except perhaps with mechanism attached to make it go off when Stalin turned the spigot on the office samovar.

No suspicion of divided allegiance is raised. The Trotskyists have been black-listed for their political ideas. Just what the government finds objectionable about their ideas is not clear. They are lumped with other radical parties, including the Communists, under the general heading of organizations which "seek to alter the form of government of the United States by unconstitutional means." That's as vague as it is broad.

No further explanation is given. The loyalty order does not require the Attorney General to give an accused organization either a hearing or an explanation. The loyalty board in turn is not required to determine whether the accused employee shares the ideas to which the government objects.

Membership in the black-listed party is enough for discharge, though the organization may be a legal political party, campaigning for public office. That this provides disturbing precedent for the future should be obvious. If Trotskyists can be proscribed, why not socialists? If socialists, why not New Dealers?

There is another aspect of the loyalty purge which the Kutcher case helps to clarify. There are "sensitive" government positions, and there are a few places in the government where political standards can reasonably be defended.

But Kutcher was a $42-a-week clerk in the Veterans Administration in Newark. Atom bombs are stored in less accessible places. There was no finding that his job was so "sensitive" that it would be dangerous to have a man with Kutcher's ideas or associations in that post. No such finding could have been made, for there is hardly a job in the whole federal service further removed from vital secrets.

Just what could a clerk in the Newark VA office do that would be disloyal? He could make it harder for veterans to get satisfaction in their grievances. But that's being done far better than Kutcher could do it by higher-ups in Washington and by groups like the real estate lobby. A man idealistic enough to belong to a radical party is more likely to get in wrong by trying to do too much rather than too little for veterans.

Basic political liberties and basic procedural safeguards are threatened by the standards of judgment and procedure applied in the Case of the Legless Veteran. These in turn are not the handiwork of that 80th Congress, but were established by the loyalty order. The order was Harry Truman's, and Harry Truman claims to be a friend of civil rights. More pitiable than a man without legs is a President without firm principles.

Red Channels: Liz Dilling Rides Again

New York, June 25, 1950

One of the weirdest passages in J. Edgar Hoover's testimony before the Senate Appropriations Committee dealt with the radio business. At a time when hardly a liberal voice is to be heard on the air, and there is an organized undercover campaign to frighten sponsors and stations, the FBI chieftain would have us believe that a Communist conspiracy may take over the business.

Anyone who knows how scared and sterile radio is must be startled to read in that testimony, "Many Communist fellow travelers and stooges have been able to secure positions enabling them to actually control personnel and production."

The liberals who have been driven off the air and the middle-of-the-roaders who still manage to hang on must rub their eyes when they read, "One front group boasts of having thousands of monitors in every section of the country who will take up a letter-writing campaign against any commentator who disagrees with what they advocate."

Unless the Communist underground is in cahoots with Fulton Lewis, Jr., it seems strange that the result of all this supposed activity is the increasing dominance of ultra-rightist commentators and the rapid disappearance of dissent.

One can only conclude that the forces Mr. Hoover serves will not be content until they have imposed utter conformity to rightist views on the air waves. It is in this light that one must consider the publication by the *Counterattack* group of a booklet, "Red Channels," which purports to fill out the details of Mr. Hoover's alleged conspiracy by naming names and citing cases.

To see this whole affair in perspective one must go back to Upton Sinclair's *Brass Check* and its story of how Big Business finally wiped out the "muck-rake" magazines whose exposés did so much to build up the progressive and socialist movement in this country before World War I.

When that campaign was over, the days when magazines like *Collier's*, the *Atlantic Monthly*, and *Munsey's* dared criticize Wall Street or the trusts were gone forever. So were the days when Hearst made circulation the same way and was himself assailed as a millionaire stooge of that "Red," Arthur Brisbane.

What we are seeing now is another organized campaign to use Cold War fears to drive out of the "opinion industries" any opposition to the preconceptions of the big money and the screwball fringe it mobilizes — "professional patriots" used to be the name for them.

Since the press, however conservative, is by tradition intensely wary of governmental interference, it is as yet passed over lightly, though Mr. Hoover included it specifically in his list of communications industries which "the Communist Party has, through its increased activities, endeavored to exploit." That Communist activities are "increasing" is another FBI "scoop."

The radio and the movies are easier prey because neither has anything like the tradition of public service which still has its effect

on the newspaper business. As Ed Sullivan wrote of the radio
business in an enthusiastic column Wednesday previewing the
radio red hunt, "Advertising agencies, held responsible by sponsors . . . , want no controversy of any kind."

In this atmosphere, Liz Dillingism can thrive. Elizabeth Dilling
was a bright Chicago girl who made a good living before World War
II reading the *Daily Worker* for nervous millionaires.

Every time she saw someone favorably mentioned or a record
of someone's affiliation with some organization or cause supported
by the Communists, down it went in her little book, *The Red Network*, which had a considerable sale.

Little has been heard of her since her trial with other rightists on
charges of pro-Axis seditious conspiracy during World War II,
but her spirit goes marching on in "Red Channels."

This book, published by "American Business Consultants,"
publishers of *Counterattack*, a red-hunt newsletter gotten out by
ex-FBI men, aims to be the *Red Network* of the radio business. It
is a compilation of names and affiliations through which any spon-
sor can tell whether any commentator, writer, or entertainer has
anything on his record which may stir "controversy."

This is flossier, cuter, and more cautious than Liz Dilling's compilation, partly to avoid libel and partly to carry on the pretense
that campaigns of this sort are not aimed at "honest liberals."

The purposes are announced as threefold: to show the extent of
Communist "infiltration," to indicate the extent to which prominent
artists "have been inveigled to lend their names to Communist
causes," and "to discourage actors and artists from naively lending their names to Communist organizations or causes in the
future."

This is a weapon of indirect censorship. One can only escape
"discouragement" by avoiding anything from revolution to Rice
Krispies which may also be favored by the Communists.

This covers practically every vital issue of our time. The introduction, in speaking of Communist methods, says "No cause which
seems calculated to arouse support among people in show business
is ignored: the overthrow of the Franco dictatorship, the fight

against anti-Semitism and Jim Crow, civil rights, world peace, the outlawing of the H-bomb, are all used."

How is one to prove that interest in these basic issues is politically pure? The only safe course is to avoid them. This is pointed up by the case of one radio writer here who has no "subversive" affiliations but is nevertheless listed for two reasons.

One is that he helped write a playlet, "Horror Bomb *v.* Humanity," put on at an H-bomb rally; the other is that he turned down an invitation from the American Legion to write a script on Communism in the schools and churches.

According to the "Red Channels" compilation, he had the temerity to write the Legionnaires, "after the rioting in Peekskill I would be glad to do a script on Fascism in the American Legion."

Like Liz Dilling's, this compilation relies heavily on Communist Party publications, and makes one wonder what these rightists would do for a living if the *Daily Worker* ever went out of business.

The listings go back as far as the late 1930s. To have been against the sale of scrap iron and oil to Japan figures as data on "subversion," as well of course as having been for aid to Spain. Ditto for work with the Hollywood Anti-Nazi League, and cooperation with Russian War Relief, though during the period when Russia was an ally.

One left-wing commentator long forced off the air is listed both as a Communist and a Titoist, while one radio reporter abroad is down for having "condemned proceedings in Polk murder trial in Greece."

To have been for Wallace gets on this unofficial black list. So does signing the petition to the Supreme Court for a review of the Hollywood Ten cases. A musician gets a black mark for attending the Peekskill rally and an actor for having eleven years ago opposed continuation of the Dies Committee.

Though the *Counterattack* group may pretend to monitor the air waves, an examination of the handbook shows that, like Lizzie before them, what they really monitor is the *Daily Worker*, and this none too accurately.

A striking example is provided by a well-known radio reporter and writer, one of the last American radio men abroad still unafraid. If he has been guilty of "subversion," even by screwball standards, it would be easy enough to document it from transcripts of his almost daily broadcasts over the last few years.

The compilers could find no "subversive" affiliations. All they could record were three items on opinions. But none of these was documented directly from his broadcasts, and there was of course no indication as to context.

The most heinous mark listed against him is that he once said of the Mindszenty trial, "There is absolutely no reason to believe the charges were false." The source given is the radio reporter of the *Daily Worker*.

In this instance the compilers gave the date and page of the *Daily Worker*. A check showed that the source was not the radio reporter of the *Worker* but a book reviewer. The quotation was not from a radio broadcast at all.

The reviewer, in discussing a book on the Mindszenty trial, quoted this sentence from a book the radio reporter wrote on Europe. It would be interesting to know the full context and what this radio reporter actually said on the air about the Mindszenty affair.

It is in the light of this kind of "investigation" work that one must read Ed Sullivan's picture of one of *Counterattack's* ex-FBI men at work.

Sullivan wrote that this vest-pocket Torquemada "has sat in my living room on several occasions and listened attentively to performers eager to secure a certification of loyalty. On some occasions, after interviewing them, he has given them the green light; on other occasions, he has told them, 'Veterans organizations will insist on further proof.'" Everybody knows what a stickler the Legion is for legal niceties.

Sullivan reported breathlessly that *Counterattack* is "tremendously important to the radio and TV area, because it is the only agency which will define a performer's loyalty status. Its reports are accepted as authoritative by religious publications, by agencies, and by sponsors."

The plug may be overstated but the trend is unmistakable.

The Shadow Cast at Foley Square

New York, October 14, 1949

Judge Medina was as composed as a law school professor addressing the final class of a term, just before examinations. Now that the nine months of trial were over, there seemed almost to be a tinge of regret to the conversational tone with which he read his seventy-page final charge to the jury in United States *v.* William Z. Foster *et al.* In the high, dark, and gloomy courtroom, with its four yellow lamps, the judge rocked back and forth in his leather-backed chair, pleasurably aware of the suspense centered upon him, expounding the law and summarizing the facts in the traditional ritual of trial. The case of the eleven Communists was drawing to its close at Foley Square.

The jurors and the three alternates, looking like any group of citified Americans in their best go-to-meeting clothes, listened with a mixture of awe and pride. The questions Judge Medina expounded with admirable clarity are among the subtlest of the law: the nature of conspiracy, the determination of intent. These are areas in which jurisprudence merges into metaphysics. Even in ordinary crime, where there is an overt act or a corpus delicti to provide some objective test, it is difficult to judge whether there was a conspiracy and what was the intent of those who took part in it.

Here a jury of ordinary folk were called upon to decide these extraordinarily subtle questions in a far more tenuous context. United States Attorney John F. X. McGohey cut through the incredibly voluminous record of this prolonged trial to its essence when he brushed aside the defense contention that no overt acts were alleged in the indictment. In his summation the day before, he had told the jury no overt acts were required by the statute. The Smith Act of 1940 is a sedition act, and the defendants were accused under it of seditious conspiracy. They were accused not of conspiring to commit acts aimed at the overthrow of the government but of conspiring to teach and advocate the doctrine of the overthrow of the government by force and violence.

Thus from first to last the government has not alleged or sought to prove that the defendants committed any act which was unlawful. They were not accused of trying to put a bomb under the Capitol or of inciting others to do so or of drilling a private armed force with which to march on Washington. They were accused of disseminating revolutionary ideas. There are revolutionary ideas in the Declaration of Independence and in Lincoln's First Inaugural; the right to overthrow a despotic government is basic in Anglo-American political thinking; the right to utter revolutionary ideas is protected by freedom of speech. The difficulty was recognized by the judge when he said, "I charge you that if the defendants did no more than pursue peaceful studies and discussions or advocacy in the realm of ideas, you must acquit them."

Where draw the line? This was a question for both judge and jury, one of those mixed questions of law and fact. Did the key lie in the judge's reference to "peaceful studies"? But if the studies were not "peaceful," where was evidence of overt acts breaching the peace? And can studies alone ever be nonpeaceful? In the absence of overt acts, the case dealt with the ideas in the heads of the defendants. The judge said it was not unlawful to study these ideas or to permit the books which teach them in public libraries. He was anxious to make this point clear, betraying his own point of view in his anxiety. "Do not be led astray," he told the jury, "by talk about thought control, or putting books on trial."

This only sharpened the dilemma. The classic liberal way to resolve it, the Holmes-Brandeis doctrine accepted since their time in the United States Supreme Court, is to say that the government has a right to step in at the point where advocacy of an idea threatens "a clear and present danger" that it will disturb the public peace. But the government shied away from the "clear and present danger" concept in this case, and the judge made no mention of it in his charge. For there was no evidence to show that after thirty years of legal existence the tiny Communist Party did in fact and in any way represent a "clear and present" danger of overthrowing the government.

This is the point at which the Smith Act, the first American sedition act since the disastrous Federalist experiment with repression in 1798, will be tested. Can there be such a thing as seditious conspiracy without an overt act or a clear and present danger? There is no doubt of the answer which precedent dictates to that question. The only doubt is as to how this present Supreme Court will stand up for basic tradition under current pressure.

Judge Medina avoided the "clear and present danger" concept by question-begging generalization. "No one could suppose, nor is it the law," he told the jury, "that any person has an absolute and unbridled right to say or to write and to publish whatever he chooses under any and all circumstances." From this he concluded that the Smith Act, which makes mere advocacy a crime, does not violate the First Amendment. But since the First Amendment says Congress may pass "no act" abridging freedom of speech, and offers no ifs or buts, the judge had to fall back on the legally shoddy device of finding justification for the Smith Act in the words of the Constitution's preamble about insuring "domestic tranquillity."

Intellectually, this was the low point of the charge. The fact that it was so is not Judge Medina's fault, for his is an able mind. The weakness of this formulation reflects the weakness of the case. If ideas are punishable apart from overt acts or some clear and present danger, then we are in an area of thought control, we are putting books on trial.

If Congress, despite the First Amendment, may seize on the general phrasing of the preamble to punish the dissemination of ideas it considers dangerous to "domestic tranquillity," if the prosecution need not prove definite connections between these ideas and disturbing acts or circumstances, then we have turned in new and alien directions. It will be safer not to express certain ideas. It will be more discreet not to have certain books in one's library. It will be necessary to watch what one says in the classroom.

There are subsidiary questions which need not be discussed at this time. As subtle and complex as the question of intent in the law is the question of revolution in the Marxist dialectic. This has become a quasi-theological problem, and the space given it by the judge in his charge lent the trial the flavor of a heresy inquiry. There is the legal question of whether the government succeeded in proving that the Communist Party did preach revolution after April, 1945, the effective date in the indictment; the evidence seems to rest on a thin thread leading from Communist Party study courses to earlier Marxist and Stalinist handbooks. These will be aired on appeal if the verdict is guilty.

The fundamental question is the effect of this trial not on the Communist Party but on freedom in America. If a guilty verdict is returned and stands on appeal, the Communist Party will have been made illegal. Then, as it dissolves or goes underground, the real panic, the real terror, will begin. Then it really will become dangerous to have Marx on one's bookshelf, to teach an objective course about the role of revolution in history, to declare oneself for socialism, or to be critical of capitalism.

Will these not be taken as possible evidence of secret Communist sympathy or underground affiliation? Will there not be a basis for inquiring further into a man's ideas and books as a means of rooting out the "menace" which will have been driven underground? Success in the Communist prosecution will provide the Right with a fulcrum for frightening America into an ideological goosestep, for heightening the hysteria with which to mobilize public sentiment for war abroad and reaction at home. This is its logic and this is what makes the trial an issue of first importance for thoughtful Americans, whatever they may think of the Communist Party.

Must Americans Become Informers?

New York, July 11, 1951

In a letter to the *Daily Compass* today, Arthur Garfield Hays agrees that the trustees of the Civil Rights Congress bail fund were morally right in refusing to give federal Judge Sylvester Ryan the names of those who contributed to that fund. "I am glad," Mr. Hays writes, "that Field refused to answer the questions put to him."

Mr. Hays says in effect that Judge Ryan and United States Attorney Saypol would have turned Frederick V. Field and his fellow trustees into a particularly despicable kind of "informer," since they would be informing — "a good deal like an agent provocateur," as Mr. Hays vividly expresses it — on the very people they had themselves urged to contribute to the bail fund.

Mr. Hays argues, however, that he would have more admiration for Mr. Field and his fellow trustees if, instead of asserting their rights against self-incrimination under the Fifth Amendment, they had simply refused to answer and taken the consequences. "Only when somebody takes a flat out-and-out position that Americans refuse to be informers on matters that they regard as confidential and are willing to take the consequences," Mr. Hays goes on to say, "can we arouse public opinion on the moral question."

Mr. Hays happens to be one of the few Americans left who have a right to ask people to go to jail for their principles. New York is full of lawyers, writers, and other intellectuals who are ready to chew your ear off on why Communists and other radicals ought to be bolder and braver. Most of these advocates of forthright revolutionary conduct are themselves hiding out in rabbit holes.

Mr. Hays, now a vigorous scrapper of seventy years, is still to be found fighting for freedom. He was a champion of civil liberties during the worst days of World War I and in its red-scare aftermath. He helped to defend Scopes. He helped to defend Sacco and Vanzetti. He helped to defend Dimitrov and his associates at Leipzig. He recently won a signal victory in the case of the Trenton Six. Of all the great civil libertarian lawyers of the past he is the biggest and best of the tiny handful who remain true to their beliefs. It gives one faith to come back from abroad and find Arthur Garfield Hays a kind of spiritual Gibraltar still standing where so many landmarks have been swept away.

On the law in this particular case of the Civil Rights Congress it is indeed, as Mr. Hays writes, "hard to understand how a man would be incriminated by naming persons who subscribe to a bail fund." It *is* hard to see the reliance on the Fifth Amendment as other than an evasion. But it would be unfair to Field, Dashiell Hammett, and W. Alphaeus Hunton to assume out of hand that there may not be other considerations in their minds which make their reliance on the constitutional protection against self-incrimination proper and in good faith.

They have a right to the benefit of the doubt. This doubt is strengthened by the circumstances of the Communist case. The government cannot have it both ways. It successfully contended in the courts that the Communist Party is an insidious conspiracy. Its Attorney General has listed the Civil Rights Congress as a subversive organization affiliated with the Communist Party. Under these circumstances, as I think Mr. Hays would agree, it becomes less difficult to see how a Civil Rights Congress bail fund trustee might reasonably think there was danger of self-incrimination in disclosing the contributors and other details of a bail fund available to Communists and their allies.

Under the circumstances, a lawyer might be foolhardy not to advise a client in the position of these bail fund trustees that (1) to answer any question at all about the bail fund might be held a waiver of their constitutional privilege under the Fifth Amendment, and (2) that perfectly innocent and lawful relationships might appear quite otherwise when looked at through the distorting lens of a "conspiracy" prosecution.

If I were a lawyer with a radical client these days I wouldn't let him assert under oath that he wasn't a two-headed calf. It is time to make the public realize that the Fifth Amendment is not merely a protection against "self-incrimination." The phrase does not appear in the Amendment. It says "No person . . . shall be compelled in any criminal case to be a witness against himself."

This may protect the wrongdoer but its purpose was to protect the innocent from being trapped, as victims once were by the shrewd casuists of the Inquisition, into statements or admissions which could be used against them. The purpose, as the Supreme Court said in one of the leading cases on the subject (Twining *v.* New Jersey, 211 U.S. 91), was as "a safeguard against heedless, unfounded or tyrannical prosecutions."

The real problem today is that touched upon by Mr. Hays in the final paragraph of his letter. Under the law as it stands a Communist is in a better position than a non-Communist not only to utilize the Fifth Amendment for his own protection but as a means of preventing the government from forcing him to inform on his fellows. A Communist can plead the privilege against self-incrimination. The non-Communist must either falsely pretend to be a Communist or go to jail, committing contempt of court rather than be an informer.

The dirtiest and most disgraceful aspect of the current repressionist trend, as evidenced in these cases and in the McCarran Act, is the tendency to turn a whole generation of Americans into stool-pigeons. The government has a right to a man's cooperation in dealing with ordinary crime. It has no such right in dealing with political prosecutions. The law of other free societies has long recognized the difference between crime and political cases.

Political prosecutions deal with men's thoughts. Such prosecutions violate the oldest traditions and arouse the deepest misgivings of free society. A man may disagree with another's thinking; he may abhor its assumptions and hate its tendencies. Yet he may, and if a true libertarian he will, fear the greater danger in allowing the state to police men's thoughts. To inform under such circumstances is as much a violation of conscience and moral obligation as it once was to return an escaped slave to his master. The task of tracking radicals is for dogs, not men.

The Tactics of the Crawl

Washington, March 23, 1950

To sit in on the Jessup hearing was to feel pity for America, a deep sense of sorrow for something beloved that was passing away.

There, under the familiar klieg lights, with the movie cameras whirring, before inquisitors in the high marble-walled Senate caucus room, a thin, graying, sharp-nosed man was saying in a strong voice with the flattish accent of the Northeastern American small town:

"An inquiry into my background would have shown that my ancestors came to this country from England in the seventeenth century and settled on Long Island and in Pennsylvania and New England. My great-grandfather, Judge William Jessup of Montrose, Pennsylvania, was a delegate to the Republican convention of 1860 which nominated Abraham Lincoln for the Presidency. He was chairman of the committee which drafted the platform upon which Lincoln was elected. . . . My father was a lawyer in New York City and a lay leader in the Presbyterian Church. . . . In July, 1921, I married Lois Walcott Kellogg, whose ancestors were also of English and Dutch pioneer stock and whose mother was a sister of the late Frederick C. Walcott, United States Senator from Connecticut."

This newspaperman, sitting there, a Jew, a second-generation American, whose parents were born in Russia, felt ashamed that our common country had drifted to the point where a man of Jessup's high character, a lifelong scholar, an authority on international law, should be forced to cite his ancestry, to indicate his religion, and to touch on the social standing of his family connections, as if to say, "You see, I am a real American, how can I be suspected of subversion?"

I hate anti-Semitism but I would have found it less painful to hear an American of my own "stock" and more recent standing attacked. Contempt provides ample fortification against the Jew-baiter, but there are no defenses for the feeling I had as I listened to Jessup.

I grew up in a small town founded by Quakers in the seventeenth century, with local relics which were vivid reminders of a precious heritage and the price paid for it. Washington and his ragged regiments retreated from Philadelphia along our "King's Highway," under its selfsame buttonwood trees, on their way to that terrible winter in Valley Forge.

My best friend bore the name, and was the direct descendant, of a famous general in the French and Indian Wars. I suppose that subconsciously I still have the little boy's awe for those who could sing in school the line "Land where my fathers died" without feeling awkward about it.

I apologize for intruding these personal recollections. I set them down to make understandable what I mean when I say that to hear Jessup say what he felt forced to say was a humiliation no Rankin could ever make me feel.

There was an abjectness about other parts of the Jessup statement which bodes ill for the future. Ambassador Jessup has been for a quarter century a teacher of international law. He was a protégé of Elihu Root. He first served in the State Department under Calvin Coolidge. He is on leave from a Hamilton Fish professorship of international law and diplomacy at Columbia.

The government and people of the United States have been fortunate to obtain the services of so able and thoughtful a man to represent them in the United Nations and abroad. He did not seek public service. It is costing him heartaches calculated to frighten from public office all but the politically illiterate and the unimpeachably narrow-minded. He did not need to be so defensive.

"One hears in these days," one was forced to sit there and hear him say, "that some individuals have been misled during their college years to espouse radical doctrines, including the Communist philosophy. If I had developed any radical tendencies in that period they presumably would have been revealed in my immediately subsequent activities."

"Actually," the ambassador felt it necessary to continue, "on leaving college I took a position as assistant to the president of the First National Bank of Utica, New York. I remained with the bank for two years, subsequently becoming assistant cashier. During those two years in Utica I was also superintendent of the Sunday school of the First Presbyterian Church and commander of a local post of the American Legion. I am still a member of the American Legion."

In what other Western democratic country would an ambassador under attack have cited his superintendency of a small-town Sunday school while omitting, as Jessup did, any reference to the authoritative books he had written on international law, to his past editorship of so distinguished and useful a series of scholarly monographs as the Columbia University *Studies in History, Economics, and Public Law* (1929-1933), or to his editorship of the *American Journal of International Law*?

This reflection of a need to curry favor with the prevailing Babbittry of Congress makes one blush for the cultural level of American politics. There are countries in which the ignorant have respect for learning. This is not one of them.

In a period in which loyalty probers check as a matter of course whenever they can on the content of a government employee's library, it is a hazard to possess books, much less to write them. It will grow more hazardous if men of learning, especially those who can afford to do so, lack the spirit to counterattack.

I am sorry that I must include Jessup among this number. Except for the statement that he did not believe in guilt by association, he nowhere did what it was his moral duty to do as a scholar and his political duty to do as an American. He did not assert the fundamental principles of fair procedure menaced by Senator McCarthy's skulking innuendoes. He did not touch on the menace which "investigations" of this kind represent to efficient government, and to government workers more defenseless than himself, and to the maintenance of a free society.

The high point of the hearing for me, as for many of the government employees in that tense and crowded hearing room, came when elderly, bowed, and self-effacing little Senator Green of Rhode Island spoke up in his cultured New England accent and said in a voice of deep emotion, "How fortunate you are to be able to answer these charges from so high a level and with such influential friends. What would have happened if you were some obscure government employee?"

The question, which opened an opportunity to strike a blow for the less fortunate, was passed over in a silence more discreet than valorous. The man who came armed with testimonials from Marshall and Eisenhower did not qualify his politically expedient "I wholly support" for the loyalty program.

The men to whom this country owes its freedom may have been of the same "stock" but they showed a different mettle. Whether from personal choice or under State Department direction, Jessup ended by pandering to the paranoia of which he was himself the victim. To crawl is typical of the State Department. But one can crawl only to defeat, never to victory.

The Right to Travel: The ACLU's Split Personality

New York, February 22, 1952

The split personality of the American Civil Liberties Union is evident in its report on denial of passports by the State Department. On the one hand, it is concerned with putting some check on the arbitrary and autocratic powers exercised by the Passport Division. On the other hand, it is equally concerned to lay down a series of propositions which would permit the very practices to which it objects.

It is almost as if the report were a compromise between its two general counsels, whose point of view, originally the same, has drawn widely apart with the years. Arthur Garfield Hays remains the consistent libertarian, while Morris L. Ernst manages at one and the same time to advise the Civil Liberties Union and J. Edgar Hoover.

The tendency to take away with the ACLU's right hand what has just been granted to its left may be seen at work on the first page of the report. Paragraph No. 1 climbs arduously up the libertarian hill, asserting the right to travel. Paragraph No. 2 climbs quickly down again, asserting "it is equally important to recognize that the right of free travel must be subject to limitations — on the basis of a preponderance of the public over the private interest."

The Bill of Rights would have evaporated a long time ago if it had been written in this way, balancing off each declaration of fundamental liberties with the specious formula that it was "equally important" to recognize the need for limiting them.

Dictatorships provide themselves with legal rationale in just this way, by embodying the exceptional in a general rule and then operating on it. Ernst and Hoover here agree with the Soviet constitution, and Andrei Vishinsky's authoritative exposition of it — that all the basic freedoms are there granted, except to those who might endanger the safety of the Soviet state.

"It will hardly be disputed," it is argued by the ACLU, "that a nation may properly deny the right of free travel when its exercise would endanger the safety of the nation." This is the law and logic of the Iron Curtain.

Once such question-begging premises are accepted, as they are in the ACLU's report, the battle is lost before it has begun.

On the one hand, the ACLU recommends that free speech for American citizens should be "as untrammeled abroad as at home."

"On the other hand," the ACLU says, "it believes that if the State Department has sufficient evidence from which it can reasonably infer that the passport will not be used merely for the purpose of exercising free speech, but, instead of or in addition, for the purpose of engaging in conspiratorial activities against the peace and security of the United States, a refusal of a passport would be proper."

This formula is·tailor-made for the Passport Division. It is wide enough to cover all the abuses of which the ACLU complains. This business of making inferences about future conduct is just the kind of clairvoyance and political psychoanalysis in which the Passport Division has been engaged all along.

How easy to infer that a critic of the Truman-Acheson "get tough" policy might "engage in conspiratorial activities" against "the peace and security of the United States." How difficult to furnish proof that such inferences are incorrect.

After this recommendation it is no longer surprising to find another which would allow the Passport Division to deny a passport "if there is a reasonable possibility of a citizen's being kidnapped abroad because of his possession of classified military information." This melodramatic standard is enough to restrict the movements of most American scientists today. Again it allows the Passport Division to use a crystal ball.

What is the good of talking about the establishment of hearing procedures, as the report does, when at the same time one sets up standards of judgment not susceptible of objective proof, dependent on uncertain forecasts of future behavior and necessarily based in large part on secret police reports? Here again, as in the loyalty program and in the detention camp provisions of the McCarran Act, J. Edgar Hoover's favorite excuse for star chamber proceedings pops up in the ACLU's recommendations.

Where "espionage or sabotage" is suspected, the ACLU recommends that the evidence be withheld from the passport applicant if a court can be shown "that the disclosure . . . might impede counter-intelligence."

This is the oldest horse chestnut of regimes which rest on a secret political police, and its acceptance by the ACLU will not alienate J. Edgar Hoover's affections. Neither will the "recommendation" which gives the ACLU's blessings to the denial of a special passport to Paul Robeson in the case of the genocide petition, and the revocation of William Patterson's for having presented that document to the United Nations General Assembly.

The report at some points verges on comic parody in its anxiety to help the Passport Division find legal fig leaves for its naked exercise of power. Recommendation No. 2 not only recognizes the power to protect the nation against any "clear and present danger," but adds a parenthesis which would have delighted Mark Twain and made Max Beerbohm envious. The parenthesis adds breathlessly "(and under present circumstances perhaps also against dangers which are neither wholly clear nor demonstrably present)."

Is this defending civil liberties or doing psychic research?

The CIO Purges Labor's Own Liberties

Washington, December 22, 1949

I understand the rancors built up in the labor movement by past Communist tactics and I think it idiocy to tie American trade unionism to the erratic zigzags of party line, but the more I see of the consequences flowing from the CIO's Red purge the more strongly I feel that it will end by seriously damaging the labor movement and stinking up the whole fight for civil liberties on which labor's own future depends.

Lack of principle and the easy logic of civil war within labor's own ranks are leading the anti-Reds into alliance with men and forces that are deeply anti-labor, like NLRB Counsel Robert Denham and the House Un-American Activities Committee, and committing the CIO more closely than ever to the Cold War policies of the White House and the ambition of the Jesuits to control the labor movement. Both the Cold War and the clerical influence are bad medicine for labor.

The whole issue is simplified if looked at in terms of the crucial struggle which finally led to the purge. Secretary-Treasurer James B. Carey of the CIO failed after many years of trying by democratic means to oust the present leadership in the United Electrical Workers. If he couldn't do it fairly, by ballots, why should he be allowed to do it unfairly by the purge, at the cost of wasting labor's substance on a long series of jurisdictional strikes and legal actions?

In the process, substantive guarantees and procedural safeguards important to all of us, and especially to the labor movement, are being undermined. All the methods being used against those unions which are under Communist-influenced leadership can as easily be turned against other militants by bureaucratic pork-choppers or by the employers themselves. The fact that Communists have never been disposed to give their opponents a fair break on civil liberties in the trade union movement or elsewhere is no excuse for the use of similar methods by those who claim to be the champions of "democracy" against "totalitarianism."

Only hysterics with short memories would overlook the dangers, for example, of utilizing House Un-American Activities Committee hearings as a weapon of warfare by Careyites and their clerical allies against the Fitzgerald-Emspak leadership of the UE. The clerics know what they are doing, but do the Careyites believe the House probes are actuated by anything but hostile feelings toward the entire labor movement and its liberties?

A similar question is raised by the linkage between this union battle and Robert N. Denham, general counsel of the National Labor Relations Board, a pet of the Taft-Hartleyites and a long-time target of the labor movement. Denham was forced by a UE suit to withdraw secret and highhanded instructions for hearing procedures which would have helped the Careyites now but established a most dangerous precedent for the future.

Out in Chicago, the once open-shop Stewart-Warner Corporation, which has been trying to break the UE at its plant in favor of the AFL International Brotherhood of Electrical Workers, is trying a new tack. Its director of industrial relations says "persons suspected of Communist leanings" in its employ will be asked to take non-Communist oaths or lose their jobs. The excuse is a farfetched interpretation of a War Department order on classified work. The sinister possibilities for union-smashing and the perjury frame-up of militants are obvious. The atmosphere being generated by the CIO purge encourages the use of such devices, which are a danger to all trade unionism.

It becomes difficult to fight devices of this kind when the CIO by its own behavior sets so bad an example. No one claims that the overwhelming majority of the membership in the purged unions are Communists; it is clear that most of them are ordinary American workers in their political beliefs. They elected the leaders to whom the CIO objects. Have they no right to pick the leaders they want? Why should they be penalized by expulsion from the CIO they helped to build? Why should their unions be weakened or destroyed in jurisdictional fights with new unions representing minority elements unable to win their votes in the past? Is this democracy? Or a device for minority rule-or-ruin tactics?

There are able and honorable labor leaders on both sides in this struggle, but men like Harry Bridges, Albert Fitzgerald, Julius Emspak, and Ben Gold are not men whose records for faithful service to American workers can be denied, or easily matched. If their rank and file is too devoted to them to be shaken in open democratic conflict, there is reason for that devotion. And if their opponents cannot win against them by democratic means, why should they undercut the desperate struggle for civil liberty in America by adopting undemocratic means and procedures?

The loyalty test for Communists set up by the CIO convention cannot be limited to party members alone. If a man's position on the Cold War or the last election can be made the measure of his right to stay in the CIO, labor bosses can become the political dictators of their membership. This is a serious matter when closed shops and union shops are widespread and the loss of a union card can mean the loss of a man's job.

As dangerous is the procedure of the purge. The kangaroo courts set up to "hear" the unions to be purged, the secrecy in which the hearings are being held, the denial of right of counsel, the refusal to let outside organizations argue the basic issues involved, and the openly expressed determination of the "judges" to find them guilty, make this worse than a farce. It sets an example the Right will be encouraged to imitate.

In the injunction action brought by the UOPWA, it is asserted that the purge and its procedure violate the basic rights of the union members. I have not had time to examine the case fully but I note that in the answering brief filed today by the CIO the main answer advanced is that constitutional guarantees are irrelevant to the case and provide no safeguard against private action. "The Bill of Rights and the Fourteenth Amendment," says the brief, do not apply. This argument summarizes better than anything I could say the mentality and method of the self-destructive course on which the CIO leadership has embarked.

Free Speech Is Worth the Risk

Washington, May 18, 1949

In principle, the majority and the minority of the United States Supreme Court were separated by a mere hair's breadth in deciding the successful appeal of the Jew-baiting suspended priest, Terminiello, against a $100 fine for breach of the peace.

The majority left untouched an earlier decision which permits local authorities to punish when hatemongers use so-called "fighting words" — derisive racial or religious epithets likely to precipitate a rumpus. The minority agreed that free speech protects advocacy of "fascism or communism" and allows speakers to "go far" in expressing sentiments hostile to Jews, Negroes, Catholics, or other minority groups.

It was in deciding where the line shall be drawn between the permitted and the prohibited in this area that the Court nicely illustrated Mr. Justice Holmes' astringent dictum, "General propositions do not decide concrete cases."

The majority, through Justice Douglas, reversed Terminiello's conviction on the ground that the Illinois trial judge went too far in ruling that "breach of the peace" was broad enough to allow the prosecution of any speech which "stirs the public to anger . . . dispute . . . unrest."

The decision is given unusual interest because Justice Jackson, with his experience at the Nuremberg trials fresh in mind, protested bitterly for the minority that "if the court does not temper its doctrinaire logic with a little practical wisdom, it will convert the Constitutional Bill of Rights into a suicide pact."

In the Terminiello case, as in most questions of law, the Court had to choose between two dangers. Justice Jackson and the minority are impressed with the danger that fascist or revolutionary movements may utilize the basic freedoms of the Constitution to destroy it. Chief Justice Vinson, though dissenting, did not take a position on the merits. But Justices Jackson, Burton, and Frankfurter obviously prefer the risk of some infringement on basic liberties to the risk of permitting antidemocratic movements to get out of hand. The majority, Justices Douglas, Black, Murphy, Rutledge, and Reed, are more fearful of the risk that officials will abuse this power and limit the open discussion which is the foundation of a free society.

Justice Jackson's distillations from German experience do not impress me; they embody commonly current misconceptions. The German people did not succumb to Hitlerism because there was too much freedom in their laws but because there was too little freedom in their hearts. The Weimar Republic could be energetic enough in dealing with the Left. There as elsewhere it was demonstrated that it is the Left rather than the Right which ultimately bears the impact of these shoddy rationalizations about turning the Bill of Rights into a suicide pact. This is the panic of faltering spirits.

The choice the Court had to make was difficult because the dangers either way are real enough. But you cannot have freedom without the risk of its abuse. The men who wrote the Bill of Rights were willing to take their chances on freedom. This willingness to take risk, whether in theology, science, or monetary investment, is the prime characteristic of the whole period of human history which encompasses the Reformation, capitalism, and rationalism in one great burst of human energy. The world has seen any number of closed systems, from the ancient Roman Catholic to the modern Communist, which sought to eliminate risk by relying on revelation of one kind or another, and on this basis justified inquisition and purge. But everything we know from the past teaches us that suppression in the long run provides an illusory security, and this is why, though a socialist, I am also a libertarian.

Almost every generation in American history has had to face what appeared to be a menace of so frightening an order as to justify the limitation of basic liberties — the Francophiles in the days of the Alien and Sedition Laws, the abolitionists, the anarchists, the Socialists in the days of Debs; fascists, anti-Semites, and Communists in our own time. Each for various people seemed to provide compelling arguments for suppression, but we managed to get through before and will, I hope, again without abandoning basic freedoms. To do so would be to create for ourselves the very conditions we fear.

I am, I suppose, exactly what Terminiello in his harangues meant by an "atheistic, communistic, zionistic Jew." I would not demean myself or my people by denying him the right to say it. I do not hold the liberties I enjoy as an American in so little esteem that I am prepared to run from them like a rabbit because someone else uses them to say what I suppose ought to disturb me deeply. It does not disturb me.

I do not think the danger from fascist ideas on the Right can be met by imprisonment any more than can the danger from revolutionary ideas on the Left. All history testifies to the contrary. The judges of the minority who would have permitted some measure of suppression in my protection are not men whose championship I care to have. In too many recent cases I have seen how current anti-Red hysteria has kept them from doing the humane, the just and rightful thing.

I learned in Israel what men here once learned at Lexington — not to scare easily. If there is a growth of unemployment and mass misery, it will be exploited by the Right as well as the Left, and anti-Semitism will grow like any other fungus on the muck of despair. This gutter paranoia can only be prevented by fighting the conditions in which it can breed, and for that fight we need more and not less freedom of discussion, even though it be at the price of a few Terminiellos.

Satiric Summation: Session in a Booby Hatch

Washington, August 9, 1948

Paranoia is a mental disease difficult to cope with. The facts of the patient's world are the facts of ours. The illness lies in the pattern created from these facts.

Because the facts are real, and the patient logical, it is almost impossible to convince him that the conclusions drawn are fantastic.

The paranoid lives in a world bent on persecuting him. Everywhere there are plots to destroy him. Secret machinations aim at his undoing. He suspects everybody, most of all his physicians. They foolishly insist on ignoring the significant little fellow over there in the corner.

This disease bears a resemblance to the phobia about Reds. The facts with which the phobia is concerned are indubitably facts.

There is a Communist Party, partly open and partly underground. It is part of a world-wide movement whose base is in the Soviet Union. Its members are disciplined and devoted. There have been and are such people in the government.

This creates problems to which there are no easy answers in a free society, except that like any other revolutionary movement Communism can make no substantial headway so long as the system it opposes operates with reasonable satisfaction.

But for those who lack confidence in their own society, it is but a step from these facts to panic, the kind of panic Freemasons, Jesuits, abolitionists, and anarchists inspired in other times and other countries. And, from panic, it is but a step to something else.

Naturally those who take part in conspiracies hide their identities. Communists engaged in secret missions of course deny they are Communists. Thus a denial is not conclusive.

Conservative notables come forward to attest a suspect's loyalty. That may only prove how clever he is at deception. The suspect brilliantly expounds his devotion to capitalism. That may only demonstrate the diabolic ability of the comrades; a J. P. Morgan, under the same circumstances, might have harumphed helplessly.

In this state of mind the wilder the charge the more eagerly it is heard, for truth may lie in what the heedless world dismisses. The phobiac feels he must beware most of gentle attempts to explain and tender efforts to persuade, for the satanic powers are subtle in their efforts to disarm. They penetrate everywhere.

One must be very clever to outwit the dark powers. Three years of investigation by the FBI and eighteen months of inquiry by a grand jury failed to result in any indictments? That may only prove how all-pervading is the sinister conspiracy; its tentacles may be in the Department of Justice; it may have hidden allies among ostensibly respectable businessmen on grand juries.

Trust becomes folly. What of the FBI, you ask? It is hamstrung by crypto-Communists in the Justice Department. You don't suspect that stalwart Texan, Tom Clark? There are Communists in Texas; Texans are not immune to Communism. You say the FBI has smeared anti-Communists like Dave Saposs and held up security clearance on anti-Communists like Arthur Schlesinger, Jr.? That's interesting; maybe the Communists have their agents in the FBI.

You think that is nonsense, Doctor? Read the history of the relations between the czar's secret police and the revolutionaries in Russia, and then tell me who's crazy. Where could Communists operate more safely, where would they be better situated to trip up the government, than within the FBI itself?

How would they get in? By pretending to turn stool pigeon, but confessing in such a way as so to confuse truth with falsehood, innocent with guilty, as to make prosecution hopeless and to discredit investigation. How does it happen that inquiries like the House Un-American Activities Committee turn at the crucial moment into circuses, with foolish slip-ups on Shirley Temples? Maybe the Reds are smart enough to pull strings everywhere.

You don't suspect J. Parnell Thomas, do you? No . . . but you never can be sure. There's a man in the next ward who swears that one night he met a fat, bald-headed man coming out of the Workers' Bookshop with three volumes of *Das Kapital* under his arm. The bald-headed man broke down and cried when asked point-blank whether his name wasn't J. Parnell Thomas. Of course Thomas would deny it on the witness stand. What do you expect him to do, confess?

12 | CAN WE HAVE PROSPERITY WITHOUT WAR?

New York, June 24, 1952

Can the United States keep its economy going without war alarums, war orders, and war?

If the United States cannot prosper without war, then the rest does not matter. It does not matter whether Russia is Communist or capitalist. It does not matter whether Stalin is intransigent or conciliatory. It does not matter whether Russian power retreats to its old borders or remains on the Elbe and the Danube. It does not matter whether China remains Communist or Mao Tse-tung invites Chiang Kai-shek to come back and take over.

If the United States cannot prosper without war, then new excuses for war fevers will be manufactured as the old ones disappear, just as at Panmunjom new obstacles to agreement have been found when older ones were cleared away.

This does not mean that American disagreements with Russia are not real, or that American leaders are "insincere" when they claim to want peace, or that there are not genuine difficulties in the way of reaching a settlement. But nations, like men, cannot be judged merely by what they say.

Anxieties, lines of least resistance, unconscious convictions too fearful to be faced in the full daylight of the mind, affect the conduct of nations as well as men. It is said to be Communist propaganda that America fears peace. But no one can read the commercial and financial journals of this country with any regularity without seeing the extent to which business is haunted by a fear of what will happen if the armament boom falls off.

These anxieties cannot be attributed to something that businessmen read in *Pravda*, or hear about on Radio Moscow.

The problem is muddied because people often confuse two closely related but different questions. One question is: Can America prosper without war? To this the answer is Yes.

We had prosperity without war in the '20s. We had recovery without war in the '30s. We learned from both experiences. It would be defeatist in the struggle for peace, and it would be untrue from the standpoint of logic and economics, to say that America cannot prosper without war alarums, war orders, and war.

The other question, however, is a harder one. Can the American people and the American government muster the will, the intelligence, and the sense of common purpose to solve their economic problems without war?

The United States has been on an inflationary binge. The main component in the drink which has kept its economy "high" is preparation for a new war. It would be wrong to say that the

United States cannot possibly pull itself together. But it would also be wrong not to see that it is a lot easier for that rosy gent at the bar to go on drinking himself to death.

The United States can prosper without war alarums, war orders, and war, but only at the cost of some painful adjustments. It is the painfulness of these adjustments which makes the outlook for peace so precarious.

In a sense it might be said that we need to allow more free enterprise in our foreign trade while accustoming ourself to less in our domestic economy. The non-Communist world cannot go on forever living on the handouts which war alarums extort from Congress. Ultimately, in peacetime, it can be a stable market for American goods only if permitted to earn dollars in return by trading more freely in the American market. Lower tariffs are essential to a prosperous peacetime America, but American business is even now asking greater restrictions against foreign imports.

The non-Communist world cannot prosper unless the United States government, working with, through, and on occasion against, private business, keeps the American economy at a high level of activity. This, like the lowering of tariff barriers, can only be achieved by overriding private interests. There's the rub.

In last Sunday's *New York Times*, Professor J. K. Galbraith wrote an article which purported to answer "the Communist argument that we fear peace would bring on depression." Professor Galbraith said that if peace broke out we could promote prosperity by such measures as "a vigorous housing and public works program." He said, "The Missouri, as we have recently been reminded, is still untamed." More untamed than the Missouri are the private interests which block such alternatives to war orders.

Professor Galbraith "proves" that fear of peace is a Communist lie by saying that government-directed spending to raise living standards at home and abroad could take the place of war orders and war alarums. So they could.

But it is a lot easier to make faces at Stalin than at the power trust. It is a lot easier to get appropriations out of Congress to contain Communism than to contain the Missouri and the St. Lawrence.

American productivity has grown terrifying in its enormity. Where war would ruin America, peace would now make possible within our lifetimes the complete eradication of poverty in our own land and much alleviation of misery elsewhere. But this is where Roosevelt came in and Wallace went out. This is the old New Deal program long ago hooted down as "communistic."

To replace war orders at anywhere near the present level would require far more than marginal public works. Either we create new slums in war or wipe out the old ones in peace. The magnitude of spending and planning necessary is enough to make any politician falter. Taft himself was called a Red for a very minor housing program. Who today would dare talk of the domestic improvements necessary to replace the billions being spent on armament?

It is not difficult to plot on paper the economic measures necessary for prosperity in a peaceful world. It is difficult to muster the political resolution to make those measures feasible. The Cold War has created an atmosphere which makes it more comfortable to drift on to catastrophe. Here lies the main roadblock to peace.

13 | SOME STRANGE USES FOR RELIGION AND LEARNING

Einstein: The Need for Relativity in Politics

Washington, October 31, 1949

Perhaps it only proves the danger of giving a Belgian work horse of a newspaperman a week off. I feel a little like a character in science fiction. I stayed at home, not venturing beyond the library, but I could not have traveled farther, and I am still giddy with the vast spaces covered. It started quite by accident Sunday night a week ago after the front office said I could have a week off. I bought a 25-cent copy of Whitehead's *Science and the Modern*

World in the railroad station and began to read it on the way home.

I know of nothing so exhilarating as the discovery of one's own ignorance; the horizons widen and the stars recede. Halfway through Whitehead, I felt myself by far the most ignorant man I have ever encountered. For I know almost nothing of science and mathematics. I flunked Trig three times. A full-time newspaper job while going to college forced me to avoid science, lest the long laboratory hours cut into my working day. There are areas of knowledge in which I am as illiterate as an aborigine or a congressman.

Whitehead was both entrancing and repelling. The repellent were long passages of what seemed verbalistic gibberish — a metaphysician's melancholy effort to build a new home in a universe turned topsy-turvy by Einstein and Planck. The glimpses of this new universe itself were entrancing. Halfway through Whitehead, I realized I had better catch up on my education before I went further.

I read myself bleary; I didn't touch a newspaper or listen to a radio all week. I went from Whitehead to books on the theory of relativity to non-Euclidean geometry. In the Library of Congress I found a translation of those few dazzling utterly incomprehensible (to ignorant me) pages with which Lobachevski a century ago began man's greatest adventure into space and time. At home, still catching up, I had a good look at that mysterious Fifth Postulate of Euclid in my daughter's elementary high school geometry textbook, and found that entrancing too.

The combination of the lucid and the elusive, of the precise and the enigmatic, made geometry suddenly seem quite different from what I remembered of it at school. I remembered also that Spinoza had tried to build a philosophy as Euclid built a geometry, and the *Ethics* tackled from this fresh vantage point no longer seemed an aridly eccentric collection of definitions, axioms, and propositions but a harmonic unfolding as majestic as Beethoven's. One new ignorance led to another and I tried to answer a lot of elementary questions for myself among the library stacks, in textbooks of physics and with vivid popularizations like Kasner and Newman's elegant and witty *Mathematics and the Imagination*. A bit of Poincaré's *Foundations of Science* and a brilliant essay by Felix Cohen on "systemic relativity" helped to chart the bearings of this kaleidoscopic journey, now ended with a bump in the return to work.

For a few days readers must forgive my newly discovered truisms; I operate a six-day-a-week mill and all must be grist for it. A poor reporter, accustomed to deal with the stereotypes, wishful thinking, and mildewed concepts of politics, could not but be impressed like a gawking yokel by the quite different *modus operandi* of this new world of science into which he had blundered.

The passionate concern with getting the facts, the endless skepticism in re-examining the concepts which give these facts meaning, the splendid bravery in challenging the tyranny of common sense — Washington was never like this (except for a few pages of Holmes and Brandeis). There are no Galileos here to disprove what every respectable idiot takes for granted.

In trying to cram modern physics and mathematics in a few ill-chewed hasty gulps, I was getting a glimpse of the new world which produced the atom bomb. I began to understand that fatal equation with which Einstein in 1905 opened the way to Hiroshima.

I admit that the contrast between the methods of science and the methods of politics is obvious — as "obvious," and as full of unplumbed meaning, as the fall of an apple before Newton. Less obvious is the contrast I want to develop for whatever therapeutic value it may have in treating minds frozen with the fevers of the Cold War — the contrast between the spirit from which that equation grew and the spirit in which its poisonous fruit is being utilized.

The incredible equation which said, a generation before it could be tested, that the energy hidden in matter was equal to its mass multiplied by the square of the velocity of light (186,000 miles per second) grew out of a new vision of the universe. This new vision has led to a lot of moaning and groaning by folk who want the security of dogma. But for those who are unafraid there are noble ethical implications in the world of Einstein; his labyrinthine equations distill meanings of more human import.

The new world opened up in the half century since the discovery of the X ray was a world in which the absolute had been dethroned at last. It was not merely that Einstein made time and space relative matters. The special and the general theories of Einstein alike seem to have been developed in the atmosphere of a readiness to accept an even broader relativity in thinking.

In the past, one basic theory seemed to demolish its predecessor; one was flaming truth and the other was proven falsehood. This was how Newton demolished Aristotle. But Einstein did not demolish Newton in this sense; Newtonian mechanics is as serviceable and "true" as ever for most purposes, and its equations are not disproved but embraced in the broader equations of Einstein, which prove more serviceable for the vaster spaces and the vaster velocities. Here Einstein found the "imaginary" geometries of the non-Euclideans more useful than those of Euclid, but that does not prove Euclid "false."

It only shows that the world is too immense to be encompassed by any one theory; that different theories provide different spectacles for different purposes; that each may contribute to that whole truth which is the unattainable total of an endlessly differentiating series of new analyses and new wonders. This is the essence of the new relativity, and the essence of this old wisdom in a new form is humility. Science has grown too wise for absolutes.

This is not the same as tolerance. Tolerance is weak beside it. Who can tolerate falsehood who knows the truth? This relativity is more than tolerance. It springs from laboratory observations and mathematical calculations which indicate that no one "truth" is big enough and good enough for every purpose, that different situations can be understood only in the light of different "truths" equally valid in different circumstances, no longer mutually exclusive. This is no stranger than the enormous concrete fact which grew from these same observations and calculations — the atom bomb.

Nothing better illustrates the relativity of time and space than the contrast between the mentalities which made the bomb possible and the mentalities which are brandishing it as a weapon. In one sense, Einstein and Truman are contemporary. In another, they are centuries apart. The political leadership of our time is aware of the philosophic implications of the new world, but basically — and this applies to Moscow as much as to Washington — it is rallying mankind for a new war on the basis of absolutes as spurious as those of the holy wars of the past. As pictured in the propaganda of both sides, "capitalism" and "Communism" are naively and dangerously simplistic concepts, incommensurable and irreconcilable, therefore mutually mysterious and fear-inspiring. Peace must be precarious in this framework of bogeyman-thinking. It is to dispel these deadly fallacies that we need to extend relativity to politics.

H-Bomb and the Moral Duty of the Scientists

Washington, February 2, 1950

I do not understand what has come over the good people of America. The same people and the same papers who have been endlessly debating the right to put a suffering incurable out of his misery take for granted the development of a new weapon of mass destruction.

The decision to make what the headlines cheerfully call "the hell bomb" is the culmination of many months of matter-of-fact speculation by officials and experts about our prospective targets in Russia, a country with which we are still at peace. This speculation has fostered an atmosphere of moral imbecility.

Few stop to think that there are realities behind these speculations. One might think this concerned a kind of cosmic pinball game, with big bombs setting off bright lights when a hit was made.

The hits will be made upon cities. The cities contain men and women not so different from ourselves. These people aspire, struggle, rise to work in the morning a little weary. At night, after dinner, Papa takes his shoes off to rest his feet in Smolensk as in Sioux City, under Communism as under capitalism.

We discuss plans to kill on an enormous scale without stopping to consider that what we propose to kill are people, that they have children as dear to them as our own, that we are supposed to believe that all men are brothers, and that we were taught that to kill is wrong. Remember? It is the vacant-mindedness of what is happening that is so horrible.

A nation is like a man. It must strive to be true to itself or decay. How long can a nation call itself Christian and teach its people to take mass slaughter for granted? Shall it be said that America believes man can live by bombs alone?

I remember the day the atom bomb was dropped on Hiroshima and the argument we had about it at the office. I felt then that what we did was wrong and that someday our own homes would suffer in retribution. I heard all the familiar and fallacious arguments. It would shorten the war. It was only a question of degree. Poison gas was just as bad.

The same arguments are being heard again. "Such hideous weapons as burning phosphorus," says the *New York Herald Tribune* brightly, ". . . are just as terrible." I suppose it is just as bad to burn a man to death as to blow him to pieces but I do not see that the equation justifies either.

Questions of degree are not to be dismissed. All war is horrible. Are we to put no limits on it? We cannot solve the problem of war overnight but we can try for some progress. The only progress we make is toward more terrible weapons. We move toward the point where we risk the total destruction of mankind.

I think the time has come when men of science must examine their consciences, and act on what they find there, or be drawn with irresistible momentum to a degradation worse than death, for every man must someday die but no man need do evil if he does not wish to do so.

The men who make the hydrogen bomb will be fashioning a more monstrous weapon than the world ever had before with which to kill people. To kill is wrong. The word for it is murder. The scientists who create the bomb will be guilty of murder.

It is the moral duty of the scientist to refuse to work on the hell bomb. The defense America needs is not a defense bigger bombs can supply. It needs defense against its own fears, fears being propagated by evil men and rationalized by weak ones.

I see America destroying itself out of fear, wasting its resources, betraying its past, moving toward a crime against humanity.

General Eisenhower Makes His Debut at Columbia

New York, July 9, 1948

The *New York Times*, in its account of Eisenhower's first address at Columbia University Wednesday, says:

"Laughter and groans greeted him when he said: 'Just as I am a student with you, so you are a soldier with me.' "

The *Times* report adds: "The general did not respond to the many smiles that his remark evoked."

Gerald Blank, who covered the address for the *Star*, reports that the groans were "typical GI" and "half-humorous." I can hear the boys saying, when Eisenhower came to that point in his address, "Whoa! Here it comes again. This is where we came in."

I'm sure no disrespect to the general was intended, and that with the student body at Columbia, as with the rest of us, Eisenhower is naturally popular. The incident is, however, disturbing.

The Eisenhower address was less than five hundred words long. The only point it made was a "plug" for the army. It might have been an address to a group of new draftees rather than a group of new students. It stressed the need, in Eisenhower's words, for "blood, sacrifice, and death." Unwittingly, perhaps, it made war seem the main instrument of national policy.

"If we are to have better homes, better working conditions, better anything, then each of us," Eisenhower said, "has the responsibility to defend with his life the liberty and the rights that have brought all this about."

Though war has its advantages for slum clearance, this is the first time I ever heard it prescribed for better housing.

The general dipped into the current cant with which public opinion is being warmed up.

"In doing so," Eisenhower continued, "we recognize our kinship with all people throughout the world who recognize the dignity of man, the invaluable character of the human soul, and who conduct government in that concept." In this category with us, he said, are "the other governments of America and of Western Europe and everywhere who follow this concept."

Now this, to be blunt about it, is the kind of hooey apt to evoke Bronx cheers from fresh young minds. One has to stretch a point to regard Chiang Kai-shek or Tsaldaris' regime in Greece or the smart babies raking it in behind the de Gasperi government or the semi-dictatorships of Turkey, Brazil, and Argentina — or the majority in the 80th Congress — as being especially concerned about "the dignity of man" or the "invaluable character of the human soul."

I'm sure that General Eisenhower did not intend to imply, as he did, that better housing and better working conditions and "better anything" depends on the readiness of youth for another round of "blood, sacrifice, and death."

The first time the new prexy drops in on an economics class during a tour of inspection he will find that the obstacle to better housing and better working conditions and "better anything" at this moment is the inflationary spiral being given new momentum by war preparations.

Of course, men must fight for their country and be prepared to die for it. What they need to learn in universities is that it is as important to think for your country as to fight for it.

The fight for liberty is not waged on the battlefields alone, nor does it consist only in war against a foreign foe. It is also a war against ignorance and prejudice and troublemakers in high office who drift into the easy task of making war rather than persevere in the harder task of making peace.

I am sorry that in his first talk at Columbia General Eisenhower slipped into the lingo of blood and guts. It is not for lack of either that the world today is less than inspiring for freshman classes everywhere.

John Foster Dulles: In the Image of Sullivan & Cromwell

New York, August 27, 1948

In the days before the Second World War, John Foster Dulles was content to be a humble worker in the vineyard of corporation law. About the middle of the war, he seems to have felt an urge to be numbered among the prophets. Ever since, he has paraded as a Christian with a capital C, ostentatious in his piety, like those of whom Jesus said, "all their works they do for to be seen of men."

In the days before the Second World War, Dulles and his firm, Sullivan & Cromwell, numbered among their clients some of the leading German cartels Hitler used in his attempt at world conquest. I find no record of any speeches in those days by John Foster Dulles denouncing totalitarianism. He did not attack Nazi paganism nor reject retainers in protest against concentration camps.

Certain aspects of the Dulles conversion seem odd, if coincidental. It was at the moment when the fortunes of war had turned definitely against the Axis that Dulles raised the slogan of "a Christian peace." He who had never risen to plead for the victims asked mercy in defeat for the oppressors.

The bipartisan foreign policy of which Dulles was an architect is calculated to aid the return to power of the cartels he served as counsel. This time again (as in Goebbels' day) the plea is that they are needed as arsenals of Europe against the Menace in the East.

The Menace in the East is Dulles' constant theme. His speech at the first World Council of Churches in Amsterdam made one feel that, for Dulles, Christ was a symbol to be drafted in the Cold War. The speech was a smoothy, but its message was clear.

The churches must expose the futility of war. But — "at times, war may have to be risked as the lesser of two evils." The problem cannot be solved by "trying to crush Communism by force." But "collective action" may be necessary "at times — pursuant to the United Nations Charter."

Even as he spoke, those early Christians, the editors of the Hearst and Scripps-Howard papers, had seized their cue. The latter's editorial juxtaposed "Christianity and Communism." The *Mirror*, its eyes heavenward, discovered from the Dulles address that "our difficulties with Russia are not basically political or economic; they arise from the Marxian opposition to the spiritual nature of man." Thus room is made for the soul of man beside Miss Far Rockaway in tights. And the Prince of Peace is to be put through basic training again.

Those who never heard a Park Avenue sermon might take the Amsterdam speech for the address of a liberal. The warmongering is neatly packaged with pale pink ribbons. We must translate "faith into works." Dulles was incautious only in citing examples.

"Social security," Dulles said, "has expanded rapidly — works of public utility have come to be owned or regulated in the general interest." But Dulles was very much in opposition when FDR was translating faith into old age pensions and the Public Utility Holding Company Act. And if Dulles has changed his mind since, why is he campaigning for a party which hopes to undo what FDR accomplished? For this I suggest as text Matthew 7: 15-16.

His is the kind of cant which has robbed Christianity of vitality. I do not want to hear Dulles say at Amsterdam that man is created in the image of God. I want to hear him say it in Atlanta, Georgia, when one of those images, done in charcoal, has been strung up to a tree. I do not want to hear him deplore materialism as long as he devotes his life as a lawyer to defending the rights of a few to monopolize its blessings. The man who keeps Mammon for a client shouldn't talk so much about God.

If Jesus had been as this man, He would not have struck out on the path of sorrow. He would have opened a law office in Jerusalem, catering to the wealthiest of the Pharisees. He would have spread calumny ever so meekly about the Gentiles, preaching only peace of course, except for those occasions when war becomes the lesser evil.

14 | THE BLACK MAN'S BURDEN

The South: An Old Testament Story

Washington, June 5, 1950

The South is a story a white man must write in Old Testament terms; only God and the Negro have a right to be forgiving about it. The observer of that explosive caldron of humanity below the Mason-Dixon line is lost if he does not hold firmly to simple conceptions of right and wrong.

There are always excuses. The oppressed always have bad table manners and the oppressors always have their rationalizations. This is the kind of story on which a man must decide first where he stands, and the decision is not one he can make by looking up the facts in the *World Almanac*.

When I say the story of the South must be approached in terms of right and wrong, this is what I mean. It is wrong to treat another human being as a "nigger." It is a crime far greater than any lynching to put a cancer in another man's heart, to treat him and his children in such a way as to make them feel like "niggers."

This is the wrong done in the South, and the retribution for it lies like a curse upon the land, visible in its poverty, its ignorance, the low level of its culture and politics, its one-party system, its restricted electorate. The white man has degraded himself by degrading the black. The handcuffs of hatred hold both, the jailer and the jailed.

126

The Negro is a first-class citizen nowhere in these United States. The Negro ghettos of the North merely hide the problem better from the observer. White and black mix only on the edges in the North, and the self-righteous Northerner has a weaker plea for Judgment Day than the poor Southern white man, who was never brought up to know any better.

The Negro is inescapable in the South. His humiliation is visible in the streets and offices, as is the colossal racial conceit of the white man. The more ignorant the white man the more inflated the arrogance which reflects itself in his very slouch and drawl. No people ever prided themselves so much on so little as the common white man of the South.

There are moments when one feels physically sick. The Southern white man in that softly benevolent and courteous manner of his can make the most ordinary and ostensibly friendly remark subtly and poisonously insulting.

The "Hiya, boy . . . how you doing?" with which White Man Big Shot hails the poor "nigra" on the street or in the hallway is sometimes genuinely kind but more often manages to sound like "Say 'Yassuh, fine, boss,' and roll those eyes, you black bastard, or you know what I can do to you any time I want to."

There is a certain look which goes with it, a look I suppose only a Negro can fully savor — under its surface of geniality, thin enough to be transparent, is the shadow of contempt, hate, and murder. When you catch a glimpse of this, you want to puke. I have to write it just that way.

To watch the slow agonies of the South, white and black, as it gropes for self-emancipation out of the muck of racial hatred, is to peer into man's heart and destiny at depths vaster than those to be found anywhere else in the country.

The sickness of the South has old and complex roots. Slavery is only one of the more obvious devices by which every society appropriates one man's labor for another man's benefit. The slave has always been despised, even when he was of higher cultural status than his enslaver. One can see this in the literature of Rome, which enslaved Greeks and used slaves as teachers and government administrators.

There is something of this in the poor Southern white man's attitude to the Negro who was but recently his slave, though the white man is supposedly a Christian, and the cross was a symbol of the slave's ultimate degradation in the ancient world.

There is also reflected in white man's hate of black the natural fear of the free farmer confronted by a slave labor economy. Slave labor in Rome pushed the small farmer off the land and turned him into lumpenproletarian, as slave labor pushed the poor Southern white man up into the poor land of the hill country, stunting his development for generations.

The slave here was of a different race and color, so that even freed he remained recognizable in the general mass. The slave developed the slave's virtues — what Nietzsche called the slave ethic of Christianity — that is, humility, abnegation, subordination, a willingness to wait for pie in the sky; the slave's wisdom, which is to bow before the storm. All these — and so much more — are woven into the South's misery.

Had the North insisted on the complete transformation of the South after the Civil War, the division of the land, the re-education of poor white and black, it might have become in a generation one of the richest and happiest parts of the Union. As it is, an alliance of the defeated planter and the victorious Northern capitalist took over, exploiting the old racial hates for their own purposes, establishing a regime not so different from the semidictatorships of Latin America and the prewar Balkans.

I know of nowhere else to study more deeply the fundamental questions of politics — and of morality, for these are ultimately the same. I met a lot of people to whom I felt drawn in friendship. What could I say to the questions they raised? If the good people, white and black, leave the South, how can it be changed? If they stay, how can they be effective without compromising with local racial mores?

I do not know the answers but I am fascinated by the magnitude of the questions. The easy answer begs them. The easy answer is that history, change, or progress require many different kinds of instruments. Great movements are not born of compromise but of fierce affirmations made in the face of overwhelming unpopularity. There must be John Browns and William Lloyd Garrisons to anger and prod men into change. There must also be Lincolns, to "trim" and compromise but finally to bring forth the future.

But the realm of compromise is treacherous, for in it men may easily lose their moral bearings, especially when they share the fruits of the evil they wish to eradicate, as do the good white men of the South. For the Negro is poorly paid and easily cheated under existing conditions.

How much compromise? How gradual must be gradualism? How easily this may degenerate into the cheapest opportunism! How easy to deceive oneself! How easy to end in the muck of acquiescence in cruelty, injustice, and wrong!

Men are limited. Nobody feels the cut in somebody else's skin. There were times when I found the rationalizations of so-called Southern liberals harder to bear than the subhuman savagery of the Negro-hater. If the Negro waits for his emancipation on the white people of the South, he will have to wait until after the Second Coming.

The Negro must free the white man, and the Negro can only do so if he fights for himself, and if we support him.

The Negro is America's No. 1 moral problem. If we succeed in solving it, no section will flower so magnificently as the South, for misery and suffering fertilize the human spirit. The heavy hand of the same alliance which rules the South also lies on Congress. The struggle for the South is a struggle for America.

Under the surface of the South lies as great a potentiality for evil as for good. Out of this section can come an outbreak of savagery and inhumanity and fascism as ugly and terrible as the worst which came out of Germany; the storm-troop material and the sadists are on every street corner, and in every poolroom.

The nostril grown sensitive descries a faint odor, in the breeze over Birmingham, as if of distant Buchenwald. The joke about whether they are having white meat or dark this week on execution day at Kilby prison outside Montgomery is a joke that leads in the direction of Maidanek. All this is as yet ever so tenuous, though unmistakable; not necessarily the shadow of things to come, but a warning which may still be heeded.

In the Realm of Jim Crow

New York, August 23, 1948

I take my hat off today to Ray Sprigle of the Pittsburgh *Post-Gazette* for his series, "In the Land of Jim Crow." His was one of those rare adventures in service which still make it worth while to be a newspaperman. He acquitted himself in it as a true reporter should: noting what he saw as truthfully as he could but without that anemic "impartiality" between wronged and wrongdoer which passes as objectivity.

It misses the point to say that neither the device Sprigle used nor the discovery he made was new. The device was that utilized to explore anti-Semitism in the novel, *Gentleman's Agreement*. Sprigle had to disguise himself as a Negro to get at the truth of life in the black South. Those with whom he talked would not have talked freely to a white man. It is to his honor that what began as subterfuge ended in identification. By the time he finished he was speaking of "us."

The discovery he made was that the Southern Negro exists in a twilight between slavery and freedom. This is important because it is not "news." We know that fact so well that we stowed it away long ago on the back shelves of our minds, with that comfortable absent-mindedness which converts bystanders into accomplices. Sprigle jogs our elbow and says, "Look—"

By descending himself into the Negro inferno, Sprigle enables us to understand what it means to be a "nigger," to sit apart, to use the separate entrance, to do the dirty work of a society and sup off bones. He gives us a moment's shivering plunge into a way of life in which one is compelled to put the branding iron to one's

own children by teaching them early that they are "niggers" too —
lest some white man teach it to them first.

There are people here not easily forgotten: Mrs. Gilbert, whose
deacon husband was beaten to death in a weird tangle of white
man's justice. "Twenty-two years we were married before the
white folks killed him." Private Snipes, who came back from the
war to pay with his life for being the first Negro to vote in Rupert,
Taylor County, Georgia. White supremacy hounded him even in
death. "You try to bury that nigger," the undertaker was told, "and
you better have another grave ready for yourself."

An omnipresent terror, which may make death the price of
"talking back" to a white man, pays off in the bookkeeping of the
South. Negro sharecroppers accept without question what "the
man" says is their share. The Negro is no longer a slave. He can
leave. But he'd better tiptoe out. "Best way," one Mississippi delta
Negro told Sprigle, "is to leave quiet at night. That way there just
can't be any trouble."

Those not content to pass this spectacle by with a sniffle must
go into harsh questions for man, white and black. The circumstances which turn fourteen million Americans into "niggers" are
a source of profit and should be a cause of shame to every white
man. There is not one of us who does not in some way benefit from
the cheap labor made available by the second-class character of
black citizenship.

It was once said that this nation could not endure half slave,
half free; it may prove as true that it cannot endure half equalitar-
ian, half "master race." Those who cling passionately to the system
which degrades the black would extend it to the white rather than
give it up. It is no accident that the first shadows of fascism in
America are cast by men like Rankin, the "nigger-hater" of
Mississippi's "white man's country."

The Negro himself, if we are to be honest, is not exempt from
painful question. History teaches some bitter lessons. The docile
forever wear the collar of any tyrant ready to crack a whip over
them. Only those obtain freedom who want it badly enough to

pay its price, and only those pay its price for whom death is preferable to bondage.

If the Negro continues to get off the sidewalk, he can never expect to stand upon it as an equal. The Negro himself will determine just how long he is going to go on being treated as a "nigger." I apologize for saying what a white man has no right to say, and I know I will offend those who prefer liberal platitudes, but this is the truth. Men ultimately determine their own fate by their choice.

Mein Kampf with the (Lily-White) National Press Club

Washington, December 20, 1948

I wanted to talk to a man on a story. I called up and asked him to lunch. But lunch was a problem. Where in Washington could I take him? This man was a Negro, and there are, as you know from the vivid report made by the National Committee on Segregation in the nation's capital, few places outside our Negro ghetto which will feed a colored man.

I invited him to lunch at my club, after asking him whether he minded the risk of possible embarrassment. I didn't think the embarrassment would amount to more than a few glares from some mossbacks, since this was the National Press Club, and one expects newspapermen to be above that sort of thing.

My companion had just resigned as civilian aide to the Secretary of War. He was then dean of the Howard University law school and had been the first Negro to sit (though in the distant Virgin Islands) as a judge on the United States federal bench. My companion, William H. Hastie, has since been appointed governor of the Virgin Islands by President Truman.

We managed to get as far as a table by the window when a waiter came over and told me I was wanted on the phone. The manager was waiting for me outside the door. "Is that a colored man with you?" he asked. When I confessed it was, he told me that he would not be served. I replied that as a member I insisted on service for my guest and returned to the table. The insistence didn't do much good. We sat for an hour talking, but not a glass of water was served us.

I tried to make a formal protest but could not get the twenty-five signatures required to call a special meeting. Only ten of my fellow newspapermen were willing to sign. I resigned from the club.

Now I'm a great believer in the moral value of gestures. With public attention focused on the antisegregation report, I challenge the National Press Club to make a gesture. I challenge it to make the gesture of changing the unwritten rule which keeps Negroes from being either guests or members.

Only a few weeks ago, thanks to Walter White's white skin, Ollie Pilat of the *New York Post* managed to get him into the Press Club dining room and served before Mike Straight of the *New Republic* unwittingly gave the game away by a hearty, "Hello, Walter White." By then it was too late; the deed, done.

All the fellows here write plenty about democracy. Will they demonstrate by this simple gesture that they believe in it? I now belong to the Capital Press Club, the Negro press club. Why not signalize a change in the rules by inviting us darkies to lunch?

How many Washington correspondents are willing to lift the National Press Club color bar as their contribution to the fight against Jim Crowism in the nation's capital?

The Voice of America Falters

New York, February 8, 1951

PARIS — *Scene: the office of Voice of America; an imaginary interview.*

Q. Are you in charge of European broadcasts?

A. I am.

Q. I was wondering how you were going to handle two criminal cases involving American policy which attracted a great deal of attention in Europe during the past few days.

A. What cases do you mean?

Q. One was the reprieve of twenty-one Nazis sentenced to death for war crimes, and the release of Krupp and other prisoners condemned to long terms in jail. The other was the execution of seven Martinsville, Virginia, Negroes.

A. I don't see any connection between them.

Q. Clemency was granted in one case and not the other.

A. Yes, but what's the execution of some Negroes for rape in Virginia got to do with the reprieve of some Nazis at Landsberg?

Q. It will be said that American policy is more tender with Nazi war criminals than with American Negroes.

A. That's just Communist propaganda.

Q. But I thought it was the job of the Voice of America to counter Communist propaganda? How are you going to do it in this instance?

A. We're going to let people know the truth. Those boys in Martinsville had their day in court. They were found guilty. They had their full right of appeal. The case showed that today even in the South and even for the crime of rape Negroes can get a fair trial. We'll present the facts as they are — a triumph of American justice.

Q. The Nuremberg trials were also a triumph of American justice. The Nazis also had their day in court. They were found guilty, and the review board in recommending the reprieves reasserted the justice of the convictions but advised clemency.

A. I still don't get what you're driving at.

Q. Well, how are you going to answer when people ask why Nazis guilty of heinous crimes against humanity were considered worthy of clemency while Negroes found guilty of rape are considered unworthy, although no white man has ever been given the death penalty for rape in Virginia, and there are doubts both about the fairness of the trial and the actual role of the poor half-witted woman in the case.

A. Look, I'm on to newspapermen like you. We're engaged in

the opening maneuvers of a vast war against the totalitarian evil you pinks help to cover up. I don't like those Nazis any more than you do and I wish to God they had freed those Negro boys. It makes my job a lot harder. But we've got to have the Germans on our side in the scrap that's coming, and we can't infuriate the South by reprieving some Negro boys who have had a fair trial instead of just being strung up as they might so easily have been. We can't change the South overnight and we need national unity more than ever.

Q. Then you think war against Communism so necessary and inevitable as to excuse clemency for Nazis and denial of clemency for American Negroes?

A. I certainly do.

Q. Why?

A. Because we're up against an immoral force which believes the end justifies the means, and will distort and pervert any and every human ideal to get its way.

Q. But didn't you just finish telling me that you were ready to excuse the Nazi pardons and the Negro executions, much as you regretted both, because you felt the end — war against Communism — justified the means? Aren't you condoning mass extermination of peoples and the ugliest side of "white supremacy" in the South because you think these immoral means justify the end — war against Communism? Where, then, does your kind of thinking differ from that you impute to the Communists? Where does it differ from those who supported Hitlerism on the same grounds, that objectionable as its methods might be, they were necessary for war against Communism?

A. Get the hell out of my office, you dirty R - d.

EASY, ONE HAND: COLLIER'S
WIPES OUT RUSSIA

The Marines to the Rescue in the Urals

New York, October 23, 1951

The old-fashioned movie melodrama had an easy way out of its dramatic difficulties. It could always arrange to have the heroine rescued at the last moment in a surprise landing by the United States Marines. *Collier's* seems to have borrowed the technique in its current issue, which is devoted entirely to a preview of World War III. The war between the United States and the USSR is shortened and victory for the United States assured when "Task Force Victory" drops parachutists into the enemy's underground A-bomb vault in the Urals and destroys all of Stalin's atom bombs.

This sort of thing was sure-fire stuff in the days of the nickelodeon and would still — indeed, probably will — make a dramatic end to a forthcoming Hollywood movie depicting a future Soviet-American conflict. It is not as satisfactory in a composite "expert" symposium which asks to be taken seriously and aims "to demonstrate that if The War We Do Not Want is forced upon us, we will win."

The Urals cover a lot of territory, about as much as our Rockies. Suppose the parachutists don't find the exact spot? Suppose they are overwhelmed by guards? Suppose not all the Russian atom bombs are in that one place? Suppose they are not in the Urals at all?

Or suppose Stalin, on reading this issue of *Collier's* (it is intended as a warning to the Kremlin), at once orders his atom bombs taken out of the Urals and distributed among scattered hiding places in Siberia and the Russian Arctic, even placing a few spares for emergency under Molotov's bed? What, then, happens to the course of the war?

Were this a piece of science fiction no one could reasonably object to the episode. But the success of this exploit is the most important single assumption in a forecast which sets out to demonstrate that the United States can not only win this war but can win it in three years.

Collier's insists that this is a sober document. It claims that this special issue is the result of many months spent in "study and consultation with top political, military and economic thinkers — including high-level Washington officials . . ." The editors explain that this "authoritative research" resulted in a 60,000-word outline which became "the blueprint of the project."

This blueprint was made available to all the contributors. The story of "Task Force Victory" is thus told from varying viewpoints by Robert E. Sherwood in his overall picture of the war, by Hanson W. Baldwin in his military survey, and by Lowell Thomas in his "eyewitness" account which is, of course, headed, "I Saw Them Chute into the Urals."

The course of the war hangs on the success of an exploit which depends, as Sherwood tells it, on the transport of 10,000 British and American paratroopers by air to the right spot from Middle Eastern bases "1,800 to 2,000 miles from the target." Much of the flight would be over Russian territory, but in the movie version, of course, the intercepter planes will be shot down and the flak brushed off.

After that, Sherwood writes, "there was no more atomic bombing by the Reds in World War III . . ." and so things could be cleared up in short order. But what if somewhere along this chain of slaphappy assumptions something goes wrong and the exploit fails? What if Stalin keeps his atom bombs and can go on retaliating on American cities for American raids on Russian cities? What then?

The editors of *Collier's* called the preparation of this issue "Operation Eggnog." If it were not for the effect at home and abroad of this widely advertised and sensational issue, the whole affair could be passed off with the surmise that they used too little egg and too much whiskey.

But this is, in fact, whatever the intentions of the editors and writers, an evil journalistic exploit. Whether those "high-level Washington officials" intended it as such or not, it not only prepares the public mind for what would be the most dreadful war in all history but encourages the most giddy kind of complacency about it.

Collier's says, in effect, "Well, now, an atomic war wouldn't be so terrible. Of course, there'd be some — even dramatic — damage to a couple of American cities, but it wouldn't last long. We'd be sure to win, and then everything would be hunky-dory."

This is war propaganda of the most wicked sort.

Shall We Take the Gamble Hitler Lost?

New York, October 25, 1951

In the first days of the Nazi attack upon the Soviet Union, when General George C. Marshall himself thought the USSR might collapse within a few weeks, *Time* magazine spoke of the "pathetic fallacy" that Hitler could be stopped by the same defense-in-depth and scorched-earth tactics which defeated Napoleon.

Events proved this was no fallacy. The pathetic spectacle was the hitherto unbeatable Wehrmacht after two winters on the vast frozen Russian plain. The experts who drew up the blueprint for *Collier's* special issue on "Russia's Defeat and Occupation" did take note of Napoleon's defeat and Hitler's, but only to fall into as serious an error.

They realize that an invasion of Russia has proved fatal on three occasions. Napoleon, Wilhelm II, and Hitler alike were fatally enfeebled by their attempts to invade Russia. To meet this problem — quite a problem — *Collier's* assumes that Russia can be defeated without being invaded!

This needs to be read to be believed. Hanson W. Baldwin in his contribution, "How The War Was Fought," says, "No deep land penetration of Russia was ever attempted — or indeed ever seriously contemplated."

The main drive eastward halts at the Pripet marshes, i.e. on the ancient natural border dividing Russia from the Western lands. "Spearheads" move into Finland and the Baltic states and establish advanced air bases. A southern drive through Turkey ends "in a lodgment in the Crimea, where the last formal battles" are fought.

"In the meantime," Baldwin explains, "as the Red armies fell apart in the West, Siberia, and Red China, . . . limited amphibious operations, many of them made against little opposition, put United States and allied troops ashore in Korea, Manchuria and China."

As easy as that!

This picture of the Red armies falling apart and of the Moscow regime collapsing is based on the notion that the Russians are a kind of faceless enslaved mass of what Robert E. Sherwood calls "docile flesh and blood."

The impression *Collier's* creates is that Russia is one vast slave labor camp where we need only shoot the guards and wreck the gates to be hailed as liberators. The Communist regime, as Arthur Koestler explains in his contribution, "was simply a rule of terror."

Millions of lives have twice been staked — and lost — on Koestler's view that the Soviet dictatorship is "simply a rule of terror." The first time was in the years of armed intervention which followed the Revolution. The second time was when Hitler attacked the Soviet Union.

The same factors on which our anti-Soviet experts rely today — hatred of the secret police, the harshness of the Bolsheviks in dealing with dissident elements, dissatisfaction among the Ukrainians and other non-Russian peoples, "religious longings," etc. — also figured in the earlier calculations.

Twice the collapse failed to occur, though Russia was invaded and large portions occupied. *Collier's* would have us believe that this time a collapse would occur without an invasion. This is quite a gamble.

A great deal is being written in the American press about the danger of some "miscalculation" in a Kremlin blinded by its own propaganda. There is at least as great a danger of a miscalculation in a Washington blinded by *its* own propaganda.

Much that is being culled from Soviet newspapers and Soviet refugees is undoubtedly true, as much is true that can be culled about American weaknesses from the American press and American radicals who have gone abroad. But in neither case is this likely to be the whole truth.

A Russian whose head was full of stories about American lynchings and slums — both realities — might well imagine that at the approach of Soviet armies to our shores the Negroes would revolt and the American workers would hail their liberating brothers. An American whose head is full of stories about forced labor camps and secret police — both realities — can well imagine, as the contributors to *Collier's* imagine, a fervent welcome for the Western armies in the Soviet Union.

There is wishful thinking on both sides, and a fear on both sides of becoming politically suspect if one dwells on the sources of strength in the other country. Even amid the hostile propaganda here, there are glimpses which explain Soviet capacity to survive and which warn against reliance on theories of easy collapse.

Margaret Mead in her new book on *Soviet Attitudes Toward Authority*, a study financed by Cold War funds, speaks of "the reserves of zest and energy which the present population [of the Soviet Union] displays." A nation of cowed slave laborers does not show "zest and energy."

Ambassador Alan G. Kirk, just back from two years in Moscow, spoke here October 18 of a trip he made across the Soviet Union. He pictured "imagination and driving force at work" in Siberia. He spoke of the Soviet peoples as "a young race, virile and vigorous, with imagination and inspiration."

Regimentation is undeniable but "despite regimentation the individual is made to feel that he is a contributing member of society — a feeling that adds purpose and happiness to life." The quotation is not from the Dean of Canterbury. It is from the book written by the wartime director of American lend-lease in Moscow, General John R. Deane's *The Strange Alliance*.

Collier's blueprint calls for round-the-clock bombing but assumes we can fight Russia's masters without fighting her people. There is no way to bomb with such pinpoint accuracy as to hit only card-carrying Communists. There is no way to wage a war of liberation with atom bombs. History shows foreign attack tends to solidify Russians against the invader rather than against their rulers, whether czars or commissars.

Let us listen to a bitterly anti-Communist writer, who himself advocates American aid to counter-revolutionary movements within the Soviet Union. "If," Boris Shub writes in his book *The Choice*, "through the continued absence of a positive American peace program toward Russia, the Kremlin does convince the majority that we intend to wage genocidal war, they will have to rally behind Stalin as the lesser evil."

"For no matter how much they hate the police state," Shub continues, "they cannot welcome mass extermination by American hydrogen bombs." War against the Soviet regime would inescapably be war against the Soviet peoples and their allies in China and Eastern Europe. That is a lot of people, about three quarters of a billion of them. It will take the lives of a good many American boys to subdue them, if instead of collapsing (as in the *Collier's* blueprint) they resist.

Russian Hopes and American Delusions

New York, October 28, 1951

It is a pity. If I were asked I would have said: "One system! Two systems! There have been all sorts of systems on Earth, but, nevertheless, people used to live somehow, got adjusted, came to some understanding between themselves."

He raised his voice: "There should be no more war. You under-
stand? There should be none. It has no right to be by whatever
price. I shall tell you, a system might be good, but I shan't need it
when I shall be dead."

"Why do you look at me?" he shouted provokingly at Basargin.
"Do you think that I dare say this only to you? Even if Stalin
would have been sitting here facing me I would have said to him
the same thing, looking straight into his eyes."
            —Konstantin Simonov, *The Smoke of the Fatherland*

This passage from a popular postwar Soviet novel is taken
from a United States document, "Tensions Within the Soviet
Union," prepared by researchers at the Library of Congress. The
passage was cited in the pamphlet as evidence of the deep fear
of war in the USSR. The implication of the dialogue is that the
coexistence of capitalism and Communism is not only possible but
necessary. The implication of the sensational issue *Collier's* has
devoted to "Russia's Defeat and Occupation" is the contrary.
Collier's says in its foreword, "The Soviet Union must change its
outlook and its policies" or face the prospect of an atomic attack.

Why this haste and hatred? When the State Department recently
released the full text of that famous round-table conference Harold
E. Stassen attended in 1949, the transcript revealed that George
F. Kennan, then chief of the department's policy planning staff,
said he did not think Russia would attack the West. When the
United Press asked him a few days ago whether he was still of this
opinion, Kennan said he still did not believe that the Russians had
"the intention or expectation or desire" to launch such an attack.
On this the experts are generally agreed.

Ernest T. Weir, the steelmaster, pleading for "positive and constructive" leadership toward peace in a speech here last June, said
his observations abroad led him to believe that Russia would not
attack the West. For one thing, Weir said, "the central belief of
Communist doctrine" is that Communism will eventually prevail
anyway "because capitalism will fall of its own weight. . . . Russia,
therefore can afford to wait." Shall it be said that our dominant
leaders, unlike Weir, are afraid to wait, have lost faith in them-

selves and our society, feel that socialism must be smashed and smashed quickly before it is too late?

Weir expressed the view that peace and coexistence would be preferable "to a war which would destroy Western civilization and plunge the world into an era more terrible than the dark ages." *Collier's* attempts to combat this argument by building up a fantasy-picture of a relatively short war and easy victory. It is significant that, amid the experts that *Collier's* marshaled to discuss various aspects of this imaginary war, there was none to discuss (1) its impact on the American economy, and (2) its impact on freedom in America. Perhaps it was felt that in these spheres silence was best.

The defeat of the Axis increased the public debt of the United States from 40 billion to 270 billion dollars. The dollar today is worth not much more than half its value before the war. How much does *Collier's* think it will cost to defeat the Soviet bloc? The area of the Axis powers was less than 900,000 square miles and their combined population less than 200 million. The area of the Soviet bloc today is more than 13,000,000 square miles and includes some 750 million people.

The weapons of war have grown vastly more complex and expensive. The average plane in use at the peak of World War II cost about $160,000; the average plane being built today costs $800,-000 or $900,000. The strictest kind of controls over the economy will be necessary to cope with destruction and panic at home while spreading them abroad. One atom bombing of New York alone might do damage amounting to billions of dollars.

The last two world wars have been accompanied abroad by shrinkage of capital, impoverishment of the middle classes, the rise of revolutionary movements of the Right and Left, a vast expansion of statism, the weakening of capitalism everywhere except in the United States. War might destroy Communism in Russia and China, but the price may well be the end of the free enterprise system in America.

Collier's does not touch on these costs in money, nor does it try to lift the curtain on the terrible hysteria and Red-phobia which would accompany such a war once bombs began to fall on our own soil. In the ensuing atmosphere of frantic suspicion, the concentration camps would fill up, the slightest dissent would be crushed, disloyalty would be suspected behind the most respectable façades. What would be left of capitalism and freedom in America while we were trying to export them to Russia?

And what of Russia when the war was over? Can capitalism and political freedom be exported? "Of one thing we may be sure," George Kennan wrote in *Foreign Affairs* last April. "No great and enduring change in the spirit and practice of government in Russia will ever come about primarily through foreign inspiration and advice." The most important influence we can bring to bear, Kennan wrote, "will continue to be the influence of example."

What kind of an example is Cold War America already setting, an America in which a whole generation is growing up to "accept, as an accustomed thing, the detailed control over their private lives by a powerful central government"? The description is Weir's in the same speech from which we have already quoted. America is in danger of becoming a counter-revolutionary police state in its struggle against a revolutionary police state.

Russia — Communist or not — would still be Russia. The real but delicate problems of reconciling its natural aspirations with those of its neighbors cannot be solved by war, or by a change of regime. Kipling's menace, the bear that walks like a man, was the Holy Russia of the czars. Kerensky's Russia was as patriotically intent on control of the Ukraine and access to warm water at the Straits. Russian liberals like Herzen became as contemptuous of Western individualism as the Bolsheviks. Anti-Westernism and the Iron Curtain antedate the October Revolution.

Collier's warns that, after victory, "We should not expect from Russia a carbon copy of American democracy or American economy." We should not force either upon her. What, then, was the ultimatum and the shooting all about? Why risk all that America holds dear on a war that cannot attain its objective? Why invite the hatred of all mankind to loose destruction — when the selfsame problem would face up to us once the smoke cleared from the ruins?

16 | POLITICAL SCIENTISTS AT WORK AND PLAY

It May Be Political — But Is It Science?

New York, December 29, 1949

This is the season when the learned societies gather for their annual meetings. The *Daily Compass* brought me up from Washington to cover the one being held by the American Political Science Association at the Hotel Roosevelt. These scholarly gatherings, for all their diversity, have one point in common. Their principal purpose seems to be the cultivation of the science which found its Aristotle in Dale Carnegie. They combine Christmastime conviviality with the business of making "contacts," the American way of "getting ahead," whether in soap or science. In this, as in the name badges pinned to their lapels, the savants crowding the lobbies of the Roosevelt are not outwardly distinguishable from Rotarians or morticians.

The big men of these associations take advantage of the visit to cultivate those bright lights of Wall Street who like to think of themselves as serious thinkers and can often be induced by reverent listening to endow periodicals and "chairs." The younger men take advantage of the occasion to meet the older men, and do their best to make an impression which will be remembered when a vacancy occurs. In this businesslike atmosphere there is little room for any but solid opinions, though even here a few ne'er-do-wells may be encountered, like the assistant professor of

145

political science at a large university (both shall be nameless) who flippantly accosted your correspondent in the lobby and wanted to know for what sin in what previous existence I was doing penance by attending the sessions.

The festive atmosphere of back-scratching, the hallways crowded with the textbook displays of publishers, and the hot and smoke-filled little "seminars" were the same as ever. In these separate discussion groups, fledgling juniors were reading the usual "papers," trying out safe platitudes with an air of discovery and eager emphatic motions of the head, like the "pecks" of jitterbugs. I heard one of them intrepidly suggest at a conference on "Liberty vs. Authority in the Age of Revolutionary Change" that the Foley Square sedition prosecution was "probably" not in accordance with American tradition.

Though this was said in passing, and with many ifs, buts, and howevers fore and aft, it was enough to make him seem danger-ously Tom Paineish to the others on the panel, who promptly put him on the defensive. The star performer on that panel was quite a card in his remarks at the expense of libertarian Supreme Court Justices from Holmes downward, but wanted it understood that he did not approve of the Alien and Sedition Laws (1798). Any angry Federalist who wants to know who this radical is can obtain his name by sending a stamped self-addressed envelope to the *Daily Compass*.

The American Political Science Association has never been an ultraradical organization, though in the years of the New Deal it once listened to Henry Wallace. The keynote speakers of this year's session were guarantees of propriety. The opening address was made by John Foster Dulles and the first luncheon speaker was a general, complete with war maps.

The general was to have been Walter Bedell Smith, but at the last moment his place was taken by Lieutenant General Alfred M. Gruenther, deputy chief of staff, United States Army. General Gruenther thoughtfully supplied the press with a three-page single-space biography back to his birth in LaPlatte, Nebraska, and down to his various medals and citations for "keen judgment," "outstanding diplomacy," and "exceptional administrative ability." But his aide announced that he would speak off the record and only if the press were barred from the luncheon.

Later he relented and allowed the press to sit in but still off the record. Since I was already eating at the nearest Horn & Hardart, I can reveal without breach of confidence that his speech dealt (you say you already guessed it?) with that "hypothetical" war with Russia. One map showed all the places the Russians could hit in this country, but whether with atom bombs or rocket warheads stuffed with poisonous blintzes I was unable to ascertain.

How this came under the heading of political science was not made clear. The Dulles keynote address was also something of a puzzle on this and other scores. The program listed Dulles as chairman of an opening general session on "The Current Status of International Cooperation," with the main speeches to be given by James T. Shotwell of Columbia and William Y. Elliott of Harvard, but signals must have been crossed. The session opened in the robin's-egg blue grand ballroom with an address by Dulles on "The Blessings of Liberty," which sounded suspiciously as if it were a leftover from his late unfortunate campaign for Senator. Only the lead appeared to be new. After referring to the welfare state, Dulles said "No doubt, this issue will be finally resolved in the heat of political campaigns."

Perhaps it was the recollection that the issue had just been resolved against him which led him to add sadly, "But the voters are more apt to decide rightly if, in cooler intervals, political scientists like yourselves work on the problem."

This melancholy introduction made the speech sound like an appeal from the electorate of New York to the membership of the American Political Science Association.

Dulles read his speech, not very eloquently except for a slight tremolo in a passage on high taxes, and then picked up his brief case and left. The audience was restless and the applause was perfunctory, but the address made it pretty clear just what the boys who know on which side their professorships are buttered will be expected to do.

This keynote address ("penetrating and challenging analysis," Shotwell hastened to call it) was about equally divided between attacks on federal aid to education, the Brannan Plan, "socialized medicine," British socialism and (of course) Red Russia, and appeals for a return to "God." Dulles made one feel that if only people would worry less about material comforts like better schools and better medical care and pay more attention to the "spiritual" life, taxes could be "substantially reduced so as to give those who produce greater incentive." Nobody rose to ask Dulles why his wealthy corporate clients couldn't be "spiritual" enough to produce without the incentive of lower taxes and higher profits.

Dulles spoke on "The Blessings of Liberty," but if by liberty he meant free self-government he seemed to be talking about its disadvantages and dangers. Dulles thinks "Already, in this country, steeply graduated income and estate taxes bring society close to the professed Communist goal. . . ." Ever since 1932 the voters have been voting consistently for the welfare measures he stigmatizes in his attack on "the welfare state." Under the circumstances, it would not be surprising if Dulles' devotion to democratic processes was somewhat shaken.

Perhaps this is what he meant when he told the assembled political scientists, "Another danger sign is the increasing political attention paid to the assumed views of what the Communists contemptuously refer to as 'masses.' " Dulles seems to share the view he attributes to the Communists. Otherwise he would hardly consider increased political attention to the "masses" as "another danger sign."

Was this a slip of the tongue? Did he mean fascists, not Communists? Was he thinking of the Axis states which ignored the masses? Of those unhappily vanished societies he praised in 1939 as "dynamic," comparing them unfavorably with the "static" democracies? Was Dulles unable to speak frankly in striking the keynote for the political scientists? Was he trying to say that democracy was an expensive nuisance?

Dampening Freedom's Spirit with Holy Water

New York, December 30, 1949

Of the many issues being discussed at the forty-fifth annual meeting of the American Political Science Association, the most important is the one which is the theme of a series of conferences under the general title of "Liberty vs. Authority in the Age of Revolutionary Change."

It is in this series, which deals with the central problems of government in all times and places, that one becomes aware of the extent to which political science in America is beginning, slowly but unmistakably, to subordinate itself to theology.

The tendency was obvious in yesterday's luncheon, the second of this series, at which both speakers dealt with "A Re-Thinking of the Relationships Between Religion and Democracy."

One was the eminent Roman Catholic philosopher, Jacques Maritain; the other was a leading Protestant layman, Charles P. Taft, brother of the Senator and formerly head of the Federal Council of Churches of Christ in America.

I was told by several members of the association that this is the first time that the religious issue has been brought into its annual discussion of political science.

It may seem symbolic that the chairman was an official of the ECA, the able Donald C. Stone, a minor New Dealer in the '30s. For, except in staunchly Protestant England, everywhere in Western Europe the ECA has allied itself with the Catholic parties of the Right or Center and sought to entrench them in power, supposedly as our most reliable mainstay in the fight for freedom, but actually as a means of splitting and checking the socialist parties.

The horrid meaning of this is simple and I am going to say it out loud. Just as the forces of feudalism tried to make a comeback after the French Revolution in alliance with the Vatican, so American capitalism — for all its robust secular, Protestant, and individualist origins — is trying in alliance with the Vatican to stem the world march to socialism.

Every pill needs sugar-coating, and no doubt yesterday's two luncheon speakers, Maritain and Taft, were chosen to make the growing dosage of clericalism more palatable.

The saintly if extraordinarily confused and confusing Jacques Maritain provides the most attractive window-dressing for the clerical forces. The Gospel, as he propounds it, is seen through the eyes of 1789, a Revolution the Church has not forgiven but which no Frenchmen, right or left, can quite escape.

His are heresies the Church is temporarily willing to overlook because of their usefulness in bringing new business into the Church. Once inside we shall hear no more nonsense about loving-kindness but only fire and sword for the infidel.

The gifted M. Maritain's position in the Church is much like Charles Taft's position in the Republican Party. Both may be useful fronts but neither will be trusted with power for both are too truly Christian in spirit, and Christianity — if practiced — is a subversive force leading in much the same direction as socialism and communism, which the first disciples were indeed indiscreet enough to practice.

As a Protestant, Taft was somewhat on the defensive. For Protestantism, liberalism, individualism, and capitalism all grew out of the same context. These are all, in their various spheres, philosophies of risk. Capitalism in its decline is now as unwilling to risk its soul on the individual conscience as it is to risk its money on individual free enterprise. It must reject Protestantism and crawl back to the Canossa of dogma for comfort.

Taft's speech was far and away the best address the association has heard or is likely to at this meeting. His pragmatic discussion of what constitutes authority is the one discussion I have heard here that is worthy of the best in political science. But this and his genuinely Christian bias ("Jewish Christian" was his own way of phrasing it) led him toward the espousal of industrial democracy in a form that began to give vitality to an old catchword.

This, like his sideswipes at U.S. Steel and "anti-Red crusaders," explains why it is his brother Robert rather than Charles Taft who speaks for Ohio's capitalists in the Senate. They want theology only as an inexpensive insurance policy. To put it in old-fashioned evangelical terms, they are willing to let "God" serve them so long as they can go on serving Mammon.

A general loss of faith, a yearning for security, a desire for new motivations mark our time and are evident in the current meeting.

Those of us who believe that eighteenth-century liberal concepts are necessary ingredients in the society of the future, who believe that only a synthesis of freedom with socialism can build a good society, will not run with fools and fanatics in the current panic flight from freedom.

But if America, abandoning what it has to offer mankind, turns on its own heritage and offers only the decayed dogmatism of a closed medieval system, it may win for Moscow what Moscow cannot win for itself.

This is what a priest-ridden political science will never be able to see, yet it is toward clerical domination that America's political scientists seem slowly to be drifting.

Brass Hat and Clerical Collar

New York, January 1, 1950

The American Political Science Association ended its forty-fifth annual meeting at the Hotel Roosevelt on Friday. Of the many conferences in session, I picked the two which bore most closely on the Cold War, a morning seminar on "The Geographic Basis of the Strength of the Key Powers" presided over by Colonel Herman Beukema of West Point and an afternoon meeting on "Democratic Motivations in the Cold War" of which Father Edmund A. Walsh, S.J., of Georgetown, was chairman.

Either too much or too little may be read into the symbolism of the brass hat and the clerical collar on closing day. Too much, if it led one to conjure up a picture of America's political scientists goose-stepping to war. Too little, if the juxtaposition at these closing sessions were dismissed as accidental.

From the keynote address by Dulles on Wednesday and the off-the-record opening luncheon speech by General Gruenther, the meeting seems to have been planned for the emotional mobilization of the political scientists. But the plan was far from successful. To move about was to encounter a stimulating and quite unstuffy group of younger men, and to see — like relics out of a glorious past — grand old-timers like the revered and loved Thomas Reed Powell of Harvard Law School, whose wit and good sense are undimmed by the years. Neither martial music nor holy water have yet swamped the association, though both are rising.

This was evident in the small attendance drawn by the two meetings I attended. Colonel Beukema's meeting was held in the grand ballroom, but the meeting opened with an audience of less than two dozen, and there were hardly three dozen when it was over. Father Walsh's meeting was crowded, but only because it was in a small room on the mezzanine floor, which held not much more than fifty people.

At the morning session one had the illusion of attending a freshman class at West Point. Colonel Beukema introduced Colonel G. A. Lincoln, professor of social science at West Point, who gave an elementary but intelligent and quite unhysterical talk on "The Position of Soviet Russia and the United States in Terms of Military Geography." This ended with an unexpected, astringent, and dryly humorous warning that "learned" analyses by military experts of what could be expected in another war had proven to be poor guesses before 1914 and again before 1939. Colonel Lincoln impressed one as no fool.

The next speaker, however, seemed to have a weakness for melodrama. He was introduced as Colonel Sidman Poole, professor of geography at the University of Virginia and a wartime officer in G-2, military intelligence. He made one feel he would make a first-rate narrator for the Lone Ranger program.

With a series of maps covering the periphery of the Soviet Union, Colonel Poole pictured the Russian leaders "tingling with excitement" as they pressed closer to the Atlantic north of Finland and prepared forward bases all around the globe. The colonel, who can tingle with the Kremlin's best, is a hop-skip-and-jump man. The Russians in Poland need only hop to reach the Rhineland and skip into France to jump the English Channel; from the Albanian coast they can hop to Rome; they are within skipping distance of the Straits; and further east only a bare six miles separates them from Pakistan, whence they can soon be in the "warm waters of southeast Asia."

Colonel Poole seems obsessed with the warm water menace all around the globe; he talks mysteriously of geopolitics, heartlands, and rimlands, Haushofer style, but seems to take his geography flat. Those six miles between the USSR and Pakistan, for example, are part of some of the most rugged and highest country in the world, not easily to be crossed even by a corps of mountain goats.

Judging from Colonel Poole's exciting sketch of the fearful possibilities, the Himalayas must still be a secret to military intelligence. A tired, bored, and unusually bright Air Force officer, on the program as a "discussant," pointed out that in skipping lightly over mountain, desert, and jungle barriers, it was easy to forget that the warm waters and countries of southeast Asia were more accessible to the United States by water than to the Soviet Union by land, so long as our Navy kept the sea lanes open. This plug for the Navy by an Air Force man was also unusual.

The other speaker on the morning panel was Professor Arnold Wolfers of Yale, who spoke on "The Geopolitical Character of the United States Containment Policy." He is also a great heartland-and-rimland man, but the measures of his political insight may be taken by his summation of the Tito break. He said Tito wanted to set up a "second Holy Fatherland of Communism."

The geopolitical morning session may be summed up by saying that it demonstrated that the Soviet Union occupies a great deal of area in the heartland of Eurasia, that we have to help our friends in the rimlands, that there are large bodies of water surrounding North America, that in a war between the United States and the USSR the two combatants will be a long way from each other, and that both will therefore require forward bases in order to "project their military power beyond their national borders." Thus military science marches on.

On the politico-ecclesiastical front, however, our forces seem to be split and marching forward rapidly in opposite directions.

According to Leo Pasvolsky, Kerensky's gift to American foreign policy and political science, the Soviet regime is "completely bankrupt," has made no contribution to government or economics in its thirty years of existence, and is run by "very stupid people we take too seriously." They have no political theory, and Lenin's *State and Revolution* is, according to Pasvolsky's considered judgment, "the bunk."

On the other hand, according to Father Walsh, the Russian Revolution owes its dynamism to a completely worked out system of metaphysics, which explains its "quantitative success." Father Walsh contrasted their dogma and "faith" with our own compromises, and called Lenin's *State and Revolution* a complete handbook of revolution.

The gray-haired elegant Father Walsh, gracefully waving his small delicate hands in the air as if physically fashioning the course of his argument, seemed to have a medieval schoolman's admiration for Communist metaphysics and a Jesuit respect for Communist single-mindedness and discipline. He expressed the view that the Russians took advantage of the American dislike for abstract thinking, and left one with the impression that only a battery of philosophers could put down the menace.

Thus at the closing session of the American Political Science Association two savants who had observed the Russian Revolution for more than thirty years from near and far offered their conclusions on the character of its leadership. One may now say definitely that the leaders are either (1) very stupid, or (2) extraordinarily clever. It is good to have these questions settled scientifically.

Academic One-Party State

New York, January 2, 1950

May I put down a few final observations on last week's annual meeting of the American Political Science Association?

(1) It was curious to see how much attention was paid to the

problem of setting some limit on freedom of expression as a safe-guard against subversive ideas. If one looks at contemporary American politics objectively it is clear that America is suffering not from too many radical ideas but from too few. The danger lies in the tidal wave of conformity engulfing the country. Writers, teachers, and journalists who dissent from dominant attitudes have rarely been in a more precarious situation. The process of free debate grows more theoretical than real. There is a profitable market, of course, for new political concepts which will make it seem respectable to preach freedom and repress radicalism at the same time. But what America needs today is protection from con-formity, not from dissent.

(2) A science which is afraid to test different ideas and hear different viewpoints is not a science. There are still a few men in the academic world who differ with the ideas which dominated last week's conference, but they had little if any place on the program. Those who still believe in the possibilities of peace, secularism, and civilian control of policy were heard interstitially, if at all. The program was pretty well rigged by the Cold War crowd, with its clerical and military allies.

(3) Indicative was the award given Leo Pasvolsky, director of international studies at Brookings Institution, for his leadership in the preparation of the series Brookings has been issuing in monthly and annual form on major problems of United States foreign policy. These are being widely used. They reflect an ultra-right point of view.

"Suppose we roll the Russians back?" Pasvolsky asked at a final conference, "We still have to contend in each country with a fer-ment that is not merely communistic. We are confronted with a conflict between two basic ideas of the role of the state."

What this means in practical terms may be seen by the record of Brookings, which fought the New Deal from the beginning and operated as a pseudo-scientific sounding board for the American Liberty League.

Today the same group is trying to utilize the momentum of the Cold War as a means of blocking social reform at home. This

means an attempt to fight revolutionary movements by fighting cor-
rection of the abuses which breed them. The experience of the last
two generations, from Nicholas II to Chiang Kai-shek, does not
recommend the idea. This is, however, the frame of reference in
which Pasvolsky and Brookings Institution are doing their running
survey of foreign policy.

(4) Though the American Political Science Association is
strongly democratic in theory, in practice it operates on different
lines. An inner clique seems to pick the programs and speakers,
and to decide the nominations for officers. Since these nominations
are hardly ever opposed from the floor, nomination is tantamount
to election, as the press room learned when Quincy Wright's "inaugural" address as president was distributed several hours before
he was "elected." A behaviorist might say that the association re-
sembled a one-party state, governed by a hidden politburo, alert
to exclude the unorthodox. A revolt from below on the part of the
younger men would do a lot to revitalize the association, but any
young men trying to organize an opposition party would antagonize
the older men who control the faculty appointments. The academic
world seems to have its slave laborers, too.

17 | "PROGRESSIVE CAPITALISM" AND THIRD-PARTY TACTICS

Wallace Moves Right

Chicago, February 27, 1950

Emerging onto the icy streets last night from Ashland Auditorium, after sitting in on the most conservative third-party convention America has ever witnessed, I was cheered to pick up a
copy of the *Chicago Tribune* and read blazoned at the top of page
one, "NEW DEAL OUT, BUT WALL ST. STILL 'IN,'" followed by a

three-column exposé of bankers in government jobs. It is good to know that, however respectable the Progressive Party may become, good old Comrade "Bertie" McCormick is still in there pitching.

The Progressive Party convention disappointed its enemies and troubled its friends. When Henry A. Wallace in December, 1947, announced the launching of the party, he said with Gideon, "Let those who are fearful and trembling depart." Enemies of the party came hoping to see a fearful Gideon himself depart trembling. Friends of the party were sorry to see him falter just when events have begun to prove how wisely Henry A. Wallace's lonely crusade for peace has served his country.

Gideon never had a more devoted band than the thousand or more delegates who turned out in cold, shabby, historic Ashland Auditorium this weekend, and sang "Glory, Glory Hallelujah" with prayer-meeting fervor Friday night when Wallace arrived on the platform. It takes spunk of a high order to turn out in these frightened days for a Progressive Party convention, and the meeting was worth while if only to make the few radical stalwarts still holding out around the country feel that they were not alone.

But the Henry Wallace who spoke challengingly in 1947 of a Gideon's band, "small in number, powerful in conviction, ready for action," called this time for a new Progressive Party, "not the Progressive Party of today, with its narrow range of support." That last phrase did not sound like the old Henry Wallace. It was chilling to hear him say, after drawing a line between himself and the Communists, "We will not attempt the purge of any individual because of past or present beliefs."

If Wallace ever launches a purge of Reds from the Progressive Party he will do something more serious than wreck the party. He will fatally compromise the whole fight for civil liberties in this country. He will throw to the wolves not only the Reds but many non-Communists who cut themselves off from respectability to support him in 1948 because they believed (1) in peace, (2) in Henry Wallace, and (3) in Left unity against fascism.

Wallace's personal sacrifices are understood and appreciated. A man of wealth, never a radical, but with an instinctive and truly

Christian outlook, he has been isolated in a terrible period of re-action by his own devotion to peace and the ideals of the New Deal.

"I know what it is to work closely with labor," he said in anguish, "but since the death of Roosevelt, the labor leaders have changed — not I." He spoke of the "foul printer's ink" with which he has been bespattered, of the millions of friends he has won abroad and the millions he has "temporarily" lost at home.

"Both the psychic rewards and the psychic costs have been high," Wallace said. That one sentence was a glimpse into a troubled and aching heart. It has not been pleasant for a Wallace of Iowa to be called a Red dupe and to be accused of betraying atomic secrets to the Russians.

A sentence interpolated in his prepared speech Friday night is indicative. "Certainly England," said the text, "gives more freedom of expression than the United States."

Wallace added at that point, "Churchill wasn't afraid to speak for peace there." It is painful to see others applauded for saying what Wallace was slandered for saying only a few years ago. "PRAISE DELUGES MCMAHON OVER PLAN FOR PEACE," declares a headline in today's Sun-Times. Wallace could say with justice, "I had put up essentially the same proposal myself in France three years ago but I had hooked my fifty-billion-dollar approach to general disarmament, not to the adoption of the Baruch Plan." Wallace feels himself among the expended.

Seeing others reap where he sowed, Wallace is human enough to be bitter. He hankers for his lost respectability, and the Reds who sat in the auditorium and dutifully applauded his own attacks upon them understood this and forgave him. The party faithful in the lobbies spoke with averted faces, unwilling to speak frankly with the heathen.

Wallace likes Gospel; and he needs to be reminded how often Jesus was reviled for consorting with publicans and sinners. Those who dare to advance new truths and to preach peace rarely enjoy respectable company and always end on one Calvary or another. The heavy task Henry Wallace took up in religious fervor he can no longer lay down, if he is to live in peace with himself.

It would be a pity if Wallace began to weaken just at the threshold of a new period in which his foresight may at last win the general appreciation it deserves. If he can boast that "within the past two weeks there has been more open criticism of the cold war from every shade of opinion than during the previous two years . . . even such stalwarts of the cold war as Senators McMahon and Tydings question the policy of force" — if he can say "We predicted that the policy would fail, it is failing" — it is because two years ago Henry Wallace had the courage to venture.

It would be a pity if, just when serious problems loom in the field of full employment, which Wallace did so much to dramatize, he fell back into the role of a "me-too-er" with talk of "progressive capitalism" little different from Mr. Truman's. Boldness and vision would now perform an equal service on the home front but Wallace this weekend gave little indication of a readiness to supply them.

What of the Communists in the Progressive Party?

Chicago, February 28, 1950

What about the Communists in the Progressive Party? This is the question bothering Henry Wallace. It deserves an honest airing because the future of the Progressive Party depends on an adequate answer — and the Progressive Party, for all its shortcomings, is the only rallying point and instrument we have in any consistent fight for peace and freedom. So here goes:

(1) The less the Communist Party dominates the Progressive Party the better for the Progressive Party. There are several reasons for this. One is that the Communist Party in America has no leader intelligent enough and flexible enough to know how to run a popular front. The Communist Party oscillates between calling for a broad front against fascism and a "pure revolutionary" line, in accordance with what its leaders think is the wind blowing from Moscow. Except for Foster, who was at his best three decades ago, there is nobody of stature among them.

A second reason for keeping the Progressive Party as free as possible from Communist Party domination has to do with "party line." It is not that the Communists are too "radical." Most of the time they are not radical at all. The purpose of independence is to avoid the stultifications and idiocies, the splits and the heresy hunts, which make the Communists so ludicrous a spectacle half the time.

A third reason is that the Communist Party is concerned primarily with the defense of the Soviet Union as the stronghold of the world movement. This leads them to fight for peace, and peace is in the best interest of America too, but it may also lead them into such fantastic positions as those taken by the British Communist Party, which preached a phony pacifism while England was fighting alone for its life. The recollection of this is one reason for the party's weakness in Britain.

(2) The Communists have been the dominant influence in the Progressive Party. In justice to them it must be said that if it had not been for the Communists there would have been no Progressive Party, and if they are ever purged the Progressive Party will disappear.

This is not because the Communists are a majority in the Progressive Party. They are distinctly a minority. But they are fanatics, and they have the virtues which go with the defects of fanaticism. For them politics is their life. They work hard. They bring the Progressive Party a devotion, an earnestness, a drive no other group can supply. The debt owed them cannot justly be forgotten in the midst of the criticism.

Whatever may be thought of their leadership and however repellent their fanaticism can sometimes be, it would be ungenerous not to recognize what they bring the tiny remains of the Left in America. I see no way to wage an effective and principled fight without fighting for their rights and with their help. Everywhere in Western Europe we see that when the non-Communist Left is split, reaction takes power. In saying this I do not absolve the Communists and Moscow for their large share of blame in creating this split.

To those who honestly disagree with this popular front point of view I would only say this: Whether those who feel as I do are right or wrong, it is undeniable that these are the front line trenches.

When the Communists go under, the popular fronters will follow, and, when we have been taken, the ADA-ers and the liberals will be next in line of fire. The difficulties through which the Progressive Party is passing are no cause for jubilation anywhere left of Center. Its collapse would be a calamity for the whole sector.

(3) Now I want to come to the heart of the immediate problem. The Communists have been dominant in the Progressive Party because Henry A. Wallace has failed to provide real leadership. They have filled a vacuum he created. I love him. I revere him. I am grateful to him. But he has not done his job.

Wallace is a big man: the heir to Roosevelt, a giant in the pygmy world of the Left, a man with international prestige. Whether he likes it or not, he is the leader of the Progressive Party. It does no good to proclaim that it is "an independent indigenous American party" and to disown the Reds. Independence is proved by day-to-day action, not by frantic, intermittent verbal efforts at disentanglement.

If Wallace had done the hard work of hammering out party policy, the policy would be independent. So long as that policy opposed the Cold War and accepted left unity against fascism, the Communists would have followed him and they will follow him. He can be the dominant influence any time he is willing to make the effort necessary.

Wallace said in his speech at this convention that the Progressive Party made a mistake in turning down the non-party-line Vermont resolution at its first convention. It certainly did. But the responsibility for this mistake rests primarily on Wallace himself. He was there. He could see the sectarian idiocy which balked at the innocuous statement in the Vermont resolution that "it is not our intention to give blanket endorsement to the foreign policy of any nation."

It was his job to take the floor then, at the very beginning, and take the party-line curse off the Progressive Party by explaining and fighting for this resolution. There is no doubt whatever that he would have won.

This is not past history. It continues. Wallace arrived Friday night, made a speech intended to clear the party of the red smear, and then left that same night for Des Moines.

It would not have hurt him to stay and mingle with the delegates and by his personal influence help establish the independence he wants the party to have. He could not have mingled with a grander bunch of people than these devoted leftovers from half a dozen American radical movements.

Suppose there had been a revolt from the floor against those few items in the policy statement and among the resolutions which reflected the insistence for ideological independence in the resolutions committee?

All the fuss made from the floor about the obvious and pallid statement that "both" the United States and the USSR have "made mistakes in foreign policy" shows how strong is inflexible sectarian thinking among the Communist Party faithful.

All the fuss made within the resolutions committee about a statement on civil liberty which implies support of the Communist bête noire, the Trotskyites, showed the same spirit. It is to the credit of the Communist Party leadership at the convention that both statements were accepted and their rank and file held in line.

But what if matters had turned out differently? If Wallace wants the party independent, he ought to be present at the crucial times when its policy is decided. His influence is great. His views are respected. This is the job of leadership and Wallace owes all of us who have supported him the moral obligation to learn how to do that job.

A brave elderly lady stood up on the floor Saturday to object to the phrase in the statement of policy which says "we are not apologists for Russia." She objected quite rightly that in the fight for peace the friends of peace must to some degree be "apologists for Russia," since they must seek to improve understanding of Russia and sympathy with its problems. Peace cannot otherwise be attained.

But this cannot be done effectively unless it is as honest and objective as possible. To picture Russia as a democratic utopia is
only to store up explosively bitter disillusion. The line of sobriety
and kindly but adult good sense is the line which Wallace as the
party leader must work out in his own day-to-day action and
speeches.

Likewise it is not effective suddenly to term both the United
States and the USSR "the two big brutes of the world" to show
that one is not an apologist. The phraseology and the formulation
are alike unworthy a man of Wallace's intellectual capacity and
spiritual insight. That is not the way to say it, and the way one says
it is important.

(4) The red label cannot be avoided in these days of hysteria.
Pegler and the rightists have already turned their fire from the
Communists, whom they regard as dead pigeon, to the ADA and
Truman, and the *New York Herald Tribune* is being called the
"uptown edition of the *Daily Worker*." The red label is something
which can only be handled with a laugh and a "Nuts to you."

Political independence is to be sought not to get rid of the red
label but to do an effective job. A reputation for independence cannot be achieved by the push-button method of saying, "We are not
Reds." It can only be earned. Wallace has not earned it and therefore the Progressive Party does not have it. That is the unpleasant
truth, and the sooner he faces up to it the better for the future of
the progressive movement.

Wallace, Marx, and Keynes

Chicago, March 1, 1950

Henry Wallace said in his speech at the Progressive Party convention, "On the domestic economic scene the outstanding phenomenon of the past four years has been the postponement of the
depression by heavy cold war expenditures and high consumer
purchasing power. Year after year the economists have predicted

that depression was just around the corner. They were thinking in terms of Lord Keynes or Karl Marx and events have steadily proved them wrong. My personal belief is that the leaders of the capitalist system and of government have learned a lot about preventing a depression that they didn't know thirty years ago."

The passage quoted above is worth a careful examination because it brings us to the heart of the "progressive capitalism" line which is Wallace's contribution to leadership. To take this passage apart is to see that Wallace will have to do better than this if he is to build a third-party movement that can make a contribution to American political thinking.

The tactics lie in the slur at Karl Marx. This is intended to establish respectability. It illustrates the puerility of American politics that its foremost progressive leader feels it necessary to curry favor by a bit of political illiteracy for which a European conservative would blush. Marx was one of the seminal thinkers of the nineteenth century; he stands like Madison and Locke before him in the great tradition of English, not German materialist, political philosophy; he provides the most satisfactory frame of reference we possess for an understanding of history and social change; he inspired the dominant political movement of the twentieth century, and he has affected everyone's thinking, right or left, whether they know it or not. No movement can be progressive which does not take an adult view of Marx, and of socialism.

The reference to Marx was more understandable than the reference to Keynes. This was a novel note. It weirdly sought to disassociate Wallace from the economist who provided much of the basic philosophy of the New Deal and of Wallace himself. For while Wallace is not a Marxist he is certainly a Keynesian. Where Marx saw no solution for recurrent capitalist crises of "overproduction" except in socialism, Keynes sought a solution politically palatable to the middle class.

The idea of using government spending to correct "underconsumption" was given its most thorough and effective expression by the brilliant English economist. The New Deal concepts of "pump-priming," of government spending to maintain full employment by supplementing the deficiencies of private enterprise — these are derived from Keynes. Without them Wallace's own slogan about "progressive capitalism" loses any meaning that can command respect.

It is not true that "events have steadily proved them wrong." Marx and Keynes, a man of lesser stature who derives from him by illegitimate succession, share the basic assumption that the ups and downs of the business cycle are inherent in capitalism and can be corrected only by the action of society itself operating through government. That recurrent crises of "overproduction" are inescapable if capitalism is left to operate its own way is established by 150 years of modern history.

If, as Wallace says, "the leaders of the capitalist system and of government have learned a lot about preventing a depression that they didn't know thirty years ago," they learned it from the ideas of modern socialism and of "revisionist" theories like those of Keynes, percolating into politics through leaders like Roosevelt and Wallace himself. That "the leaders of the capitalist system and of government have learned a lot about preventing a depression" is, however, dubious.

Wallace says the "outstanding phenomenon of the past four years has been the postponement of the depression by heavy cold war expenditures and high consumer purchasing power." The latter is not an independent factor but is due to wartime saving, demand piled up by wartime shortages and cold war expenditures, i.e. by the stimulus of a war just past and a new war being prepared. What is so "outstanding" about this "phenomenon"?

The tendency of capitalism to find a way out of crisis by war has been clear for two generations. It is perhaps the main objection to capitalism itself. Far from learning, "the leaders of the capitalist system and of government" are forgetting what little they learned during the Roosevelt period. They have abandoned spending for peace and development and have reverted to spending for war and destruction. They have done so because the former cuts the rate of profit while the latter gives it inflationary stimulation.

The real lesson of the Roosevelt period was that the Keynesian approach is not enough, that compensatory spending and public works cannot maintain full employment, that measures of economic planning and in certain areas public ownership are minimum necessities for full employment. Mr. Truman and his Council of Economic Advisers have robbed the [Full] Employment Act of vitality by operating on the politically safe but economically disastrous assumption that somehow free enterprise can muddle through.

To spread this impression is to leave the American people disarmed to deal with depression when it comes. To disarm and confuse them is to leave them dependent on the crutch of cold war spending and then war itself. Wallace's unwillingness to speak frankly or inability to think clearly about the crucial deficiencies of so-called "free enterprise" are contributing to this confusion and compromising the fight for peace, since peace and prosperity are Siamese twins. Neither can survive without the other.

It is this which vitiates Wallace's ten-point program. This is not a program of political action or political education. It is a series of pious exclamations. They equate with the logical proposition that if wishes were horses beggars would ride. To say "Promote the maximum number of jobs" as does his Point 1 is to beg the question, "How?" To say, in Point 2, "Pay wages high enough, and farm income high enough, to give consumers the power to absorb an expanding flood of consumer products," is meaningless.

If Wallace were leader of the Democratic or Republican party, this kind of hortatory invocation of nonexisting motivations in an unreal world would be understandable. But he is the leader of a third party, and the function of third parties in the American two-party system has historically been to sell unpopular new and necessary ideas, to make them familiar and safe enough to be taken up by the conventional parties.

It is this function which the Progressive Party is not fulfilling. Its domestic program as developed at this convention differs in no essential from that of the Democrats and contains nothing the Republicans have not already accepted in theory.

If Wallace wants a progressive capitalism, this is not the way to get it.

You Can't Stem a Panic by Fleeing with the Mob

Chicago, March 2, 1950

"We believe," Henry Wallace said in his speech at the Progressive convention, "in progressive capitalism, not socialism." Who is "we"? It would be a safe guess that 95 percent of the delegates were people who do not believe in the possibility of a progressive capitalism and do believe in socialism.

Can capitalism be progressive? Yes. But only by progressing steadily toward socialism. A capitalist system in which democratic processes satisfy popular aspirations for economic security, in which monopolistic bottlenecks obstructing expansion are broken, and in which the government is strong enough to plan for full employment, would be progressive capitalism.

Is the achievement of such a system probable? No. Is it possible? Yes.

But the adaptation of business enterprise to social controls cannot be accomplished until some movement and some leader in America have the courage and the vision to speak in socialist terms, to say the horrid word "socialism" over and over again, until the fears which coagulate about it are overcome.

This semantic phobia has deprived the American people of their characteristic and pragmatic good sense in the one field of action in which they need it most.

The natural and instinctive American attitude is to tinker, to experiment, to try and see what happens, rather than to determine in advance by abstract reasoning whether success is possible or not.

Business enterprise, America's major career in the past, the magnet which has drawn to it the most vital resources of the American spirit, is a monument to the trial-and-error approach. For much that the great American business builders have accomplished looked impossible until tried.

But in dealing with the problems of economics and government, Americans have been dogmatic, unthinking, and scared stiff of certain words, especially the horrid word "socialism." The result has been to slow up necessary responses to changing conditions.

A pragmatic American approach to social problems would say, "This business is a racket whose fixed prices are exploiting the competitive industries. Antitrust enforcement has failed. We must try either to break the trust by a government yardstick plant or nationalize the industry. Since bureaucrats can get pretty stodgy, too, maybe it would be best to try the former and get some real competition, so long as the government plant has to operate on a basis fair to private operators in the same field."

A pragmatic approach would say of another industry, "It works well and gives good service. Let's leave well enough alone." It might say of a third, "Nothing's wrong with this industry. Both capital and labor are wedded to obsolete methods. Here's a businessman with a novel idea (let us say, for housing) but the banks are hostile or dubious. Let's provide him with government credit for his experiment."

Such practical methods for dealing case by case with economic problems are made impossible when political questions are seen through a bloodshot haze, in which the red tint creates taboos as irrational and disastrous as those of a primitive tribe facing novel conditions of life.

Capitalism can go on succeeding only if private business can be fitted into a system of social controls and planning effective enough to satisfy the demand for full employment without being so onerous as to crush genuine enterprise wherever it exists.

This pragmatic approach requires a different climate of opinion, not only to make experiment possible but also to understand what we need to do.

Only a socialist analysis can enable people to understand what capitalism can do and what it cannot do. Only so can we understand what government needs to do and what it need not do for an expanding economy and full employment.

A businessman may be the most liberal man in the world, he can be a convinced Marxist, yet in running his own business he must operate within certain limits fixed by the nature of a capitalist system.

He can operate, I suppose (if he is so lucky as to have a private income and no need for additional capital), without showing a profit. But he cannot long operate at a loss. He may believe in high wages and full employment but he cannot pay wages too high for profitable operation and he cannot produce goods without some assurance of a market in which to sell them.

If there is an ebb in demand, he must curtail his own production. If the ebb is serious, he may have to lay off workers and cut wages. He may regard the ebb as unfortunate but he cannot buck it without going broke. He cannot think in long-range overall terms. He must think in terms of his own business if he is to stay in business.

A capitalist, in other words, must abide by the economic law of a capitalist system. This is what made such nonsense of Herbert Hoover's belief in the early '30s that business could be improved by patting it on the back and saying "Have confidence." That is what makes nonsense of Harry Truman's belief that full employment can be obtained by "reassuring" business enterprise. It also makes nonsense of Henry Wallace's pious exhortation in his ten-point program to promote the maximum number of jobs, pay wages high enough to prevent overproduction and "cooperate wholeheartedly with government to prevent depression, not by an arms program but by a peace program." This is one problem evangelism cannot solve.

A businessman's power to make jobs and pay high wages is limited by a market over which he has no control. It is only action by government, including planning and some measures of public ownership, which can peacefully sustain the number of jobs and the level of wages by sustaining the market for the products of industry. This is a job too big for the wealth of a Rockefeller or the organizing genius of a Morgan.

The only alternative is a war program. To ask the businessman to "cooperate wholeheartedly" in a peace program instead is asking too much of human beings. The nature of the business system has made the businessman suspicious of government interference, not always without justification, either. To ask him to accept a peace instead of a war program is to ask him to give up the inflationary profits of an arms race for a system of planning for full output at home which would cut down his freedom of action and his rate of profit. There are Wallaceite businessmen, and my blessing is on them, but not enough to sell that kind of program to the business world. People are only confused by pretending otherwise.

If Wallace wants really to make the Progressive Party an instrument for the creation of a "progressive" capitalism, he must buck popular fears on the issue of maintaining full employment as he bucked popular fears on the issue of maintaining peace. In both cases, the fears which America has to fear center about the horrid word "socialism." This is the core of current political panic, and a panic is never stemmed by joining the frightened in their flight.

The Horrid Word "Socialism"

Chicago, March 3, 1950

The panic which is sweeping over the American people does not have its origin in atom bomb or H-bomb, though both have intensified it. The panic has its origin in fear of this new force let loose in the world called socialism. Until this fear is overcome, the chances of peace abroad and permanent prosperity at home are slight. It is the difficult, unpleasant, but necessary task of a third-party movement like the Progressives to tackle that fear.

In a two-party system, neither party willingly assumes the task of leadership. The Republicans try to rope in as many liberals as they can without antagonizing too many conservatives and the Democrats try to rope in as many conservatives as they can without antagonizing too many liberals. "Me-too-ism" is inseparable from two-party politics in normal times, as may be seen from the British election just over, in which the Tories outbid the Laborites in social welfare promises.

But a third party in a two-party system cannot hope to get anywhere as a "me-too" party. It must have the courage of its nonconformist convictions. It does no good to curry favor with the powers that be; they are too well served by the major parties. To the extent that the radical party rids itself of the radical label, it rids itself of the enthusiasm of the spark-plug minority which can alone give a third-party movement vitality. This is why flight from ticklish truths to comfortable fantasies can only divert the Progressives from the one essential task they might perform without bringing them any closer to power.

"The big job on the domestic front in the United States," Wallace told the Progressive Party convention, "is to convert our present reactionary capitalism into progressive capitalism which is willing to plan effectively with government to prevent depression by expanding the peacetime production and trade of the entire world — including Russia and the new China."

This is pure unadulterated pie-in-the-sky. Wallace could hold prayer meetings in every Chamber of Commerce in the United States without ever getting that kind of a conversion. If we wait for the conversion of "reactionary" capitalism into "progressive" capitalism, we shall wait a long time. It will not be brought about by exhortations from the Progressive Party, however respectable and politically antiseptic it may become.

The Chambers of Commerce are interested in peddling another kind of firewater. They stake their all on the bogeyman. They fight government planning and public ownership for full employment — by the scare-word of socialism. They fight trade with Russia and the new China — by the scare-word of Communism.

The Progressive Party has to destroy the bogeyman if it is to succeed. If it accepts the bogeyman, even by implication, it loses the fight before the fight has hardly begun.

Every speech on international affairs always contains the word "understanding." Without some understanding of the other fellow's way of life there can be no peace. Understanding is necessary. But almost no one takes the effort to create it, because this involves the risk of being smeared as a Red or pink. Someone has got to begin to tell the American people that Communism and socialism are in the world to stay, to help them understand how they arose and what needs they serve.

Until these seem reasonable responses to the conditions that evoked them they will appear so monstrous that any weapons seem justified against them. This task of education for peace cannot be performed until Americans look on socialism and Communism in an adult way, as part of the facts-of-life of our era.

The world has been moving toward socialism for two generations, and every form of society, whether revolutionary or democratic or counter-revolutionary, ends by increasing the power of the state over the economy at the expense of private rights in property. The more force is used to fight this trend, the more extreme becomes its final manifestation. Complex societies require complex controls. Traffic at 42nd Street and Broadway cannot be left at the mercy of the individual motorist's whims. The heavier traffic grows, the more the rules necessary to keep it moving smoothly.

There is no doubt that the movement toward statism involves genuine dangers. All change is dangerous. Only death is changeless. The task of wise leadership is, while moving with the tide, to seek to anticipate and avert these dangers. This can be done only by a calm acceptance of the trend; otherwise energies are wasted in combating the inevitable. This calm acceptance is not possible until more people have the courage to use the scare-word of socialism, to explain it, to preach it, to apply it, until its terrors are overcome. Fears can be vanquished only by facing them.

The Progressive Party under current conditions of hysteria can hardly elect a dogcatcher outside of New York. This weakness can be its strength. It has nothing to lose by being honest. It is down to bedrock. People who are still Progressives are too tough to be frightened off. Many of them are old-time Populists, wobblies, anarchists, Socialists, or Communists who know the score better than their leaders. Others are thinking youngsters more likely to be held and attracted by a vigorous radicalism than by phony talk about "progressive capitalism."

It is better to win a few people thoroughly to real understanding of present problems than to collect a dozen times that many so thoroughly confused by illusory slogans as to be disarmed for real attack on concrete problems. Thus I plead for a strong infusion of socialism into the anemic veins of the Progressives. They're not kidding anybody but themselves anyway.

18 INTERLUDE: THE CRUSADE AGAINST THE CALL GIRLS

New York, September 7, 1952

Before the affair of the call girls passes into history, I want to say a few words about it. Prosecutions of this kind are supposed to reflect the upsurge of an outraged morality, and it is the moral side which interests me.

I want to deal first with the morality of the newspapers. They went to town on the story, complete with pictures. No editor in town seems to have asked himself whether it was fair to shame a lot of girls in this way.

None of these girls had been found guilty of any offense. None of them had been indicted. The District Attorney's office had labeled them a bunch of whores, but the District Attorney's office might be wrong about some of them.

Yet the publicity, the pictures, were as bad a punishment for these girls, as ruinous for them, as any penalty likely to be imposed upon them if convicted. This is not the highest kind of morality in action.

Newspapers customarily interlard circuses of this kind with moral reflections on their editorial pages. They imply that they are performing some sort of public service in thus exposing wickedness.

The truth everybody knows but nobody admits. The newspapers expose this kind of wickedness for the same reason that Minsky's used to expose Gypsy Rose Lee. The public gets a big kick out of it. This is synthetic sin.

The difference between burlesque and the newspapers is that the former never pretended to be performing a public service by exposure. Minsky's sold tickets. Pimps sell girls for a fee. The newspapers sell them for circulation.

The call girl exposé was a useful way to pump up lagging August newspaper sales. The papers, in printing the names and pictures of the accused girls, were indifferent to the lives they might be wrecking. The morality of this is difficult to distinguish from that of the vermin who peddle women regularly for a living.

Just as exposés of "sin" are a cheap way of making circulation, so they are a cheap way of making reputations for ambitious district attorneys. The D.A.'s sell the girls, too, for publicity, and publicity — as every businessman knows — is the same as money. This is another form of pimping.

The morality of the situation would be different, of course, if the "exposers" were Savonarolas, so allergic to sin that they had to root it out with fury wherever they came upon it. Psychoanalysis (and, indeed, William Blake and Nietzsche long before Freud) provided less than flattering insights into such characters, but they at least have the excuse of their compulsions.

But I would guess that there is not a newspaperman, district attorney, or detective engaged in this noble work of righteousness who would not jump at the chance to go out on a whopping big party of just the kind they have been exposing — that is, if it could be done discreetly.

I have covered a good many police beats in my time and I have yet to come upon a crusading district attorney who was impelled by moral imperatives. On the other hand, I have known of a good many cases where the forces of righteousness, after a burst of crusading, went back to the more usual day-to-day practices whereby the magdalens paid the cops, and the cops divided with the higher-ups.

The worst offenders in this picture are the public. "Anglo-Saxon" countries have a gift for hypocrisy. Revivalists have drawn crowds for years as much by their vivid pictures of sin as by their denunciations. "Anglo-Saxons" not only wallow in it, but give themselves merit badges for high-mindedness while enjoying the pornography.

The Latins are franker and therefore more decent. Like our own Walt Whitman they refuse to regard what is natural as dirty. The dirt is in the dirty mind of the beholder.

The average reader (including me) of the call girl exposé was a little envious. The men wondered, at least for a fleeting moment, how one got invited to shindigs with such beautiful girls. The women, unless I misjudged them completely, wondered how it must feel to be so attractive that one can command $300 to $500 a night.

Very few turned, with hearts uplifted and souls purified, from the pictures in the *Evening Snooze* to the refreshment of the family Bible. I recall a passage there about an earlier call girl exposé, in which only those without sin were to cast a stone.

19 | CAN DIPLOMACY EVER BE "TOTAL"?

Acheson and the Bogeyman Theory of History

Washington, March 15, 1950

Budding intellectuals suspected by their schoolmates of such shameful vices as writing poetry often seek to prove themselves "regular fellows" by using obscene language and smoking cigar butts.

Mr. Acheson has adopted similar tactics. He is trying to be a Dead End Kid in diplomacy. Since becoming Secretary of State, he has so stooped to placate his Congressional critics that he is now half his normal size. The effort to ingratiate by simulating political illiteracy was evident in the theory of history implied by his "total diplomacy" speech last week at the White House.

It may seem pretentious to speak of a theory of history in a
capital where the screech of debate is more zoological than
ideological. But people operate on theories without being aware of
them, and they have their practical importance.

A man on the roof of a ten-story building who misunderstands
gravitation may commit an error hardly to be dismissed by his
widow as merely theoretical. A nation which operates on a wrong
theory of what brings about change in the history of society may
make as unfortunate a misstep.

The basic question of American foreign policy is: What causes
change? The stability and survival of a free society in America
depend on whether national leadership finds the right answer.

What undermines long-established societies? What leads to their
overthrow? How can revolutionary overturn, with its attendant cost
and chaos, be averted? These are the questions on which the future
of America depends. The answer which Mr. Acheson gave at the
White House last week was easy, politic, expedient, and wrong.

It was the bogeyman theory of history which Mr. Acheson expounded in his "total diplomacy" talk to the Advertising Council.
It was the theory that revolutions are brought about by conspiracies. He was so anxious to bring himself down to the level
of soap salesmanship that he threw overboard everything in the
science of politics from Aristotle to Marx to adopt the paranoid
delusion that has always served as the pseudopolitics of stupid
rulers and ruling classes.

The older imperialism, Mr. Acheson said, was "kid stuff to the
methods that we are up against." The world has never before seen
what the Soviet Union "has at its disposal" for expansion. "We
have seen it in China," Mr. Acheson went on. "The Communists
took over China at a ridiculously small cost." It was so simple, as
Mr. Acheson explained it.

"What they did," the Secretary of State told the Advertising
Council, which no doubt held its breath, "was to invite some Chinese leaders who were dissatisfied with the way things were going
in their country to come to Moscow. There they thoroughly in-

doctrinated them so that they returned to China prepared to resort to any means whatsoever to establish Communist control."

Back in China "these agents then mingled among the people and sold them on the personal material advantages of Communism. . . . They promised to turn over the land to them . . . but the Communists didn't only talk in terms of economic interest. We have all seen pictures from China of native dances out in the fields which were put on by the local Communist organization. In many cases they provided the only fun that these peasants had . . ."

This picture of a revolutionary movement as a combination of subversive buzz-buzz with free rumba lessons is a model of puerility. "No people, no age," the great English essayist Hazlitt wrote, rebutting similar views more than a century ago, "ever threw away the fruits of past wisdom, or the enjoyment of present blessings, for visionary schemes of ideal perfections. It is . . . the actual infliction of the present that has produced all changes . . . the intolerable pressure of long-established, notorious, aggravated and growing abuses."

The deposed President of China, Li Tsung-jen, only recently a guest at the White House, said the same thing in terms of his country's own experience when he told the Associated Press in an interview published last Sunday: "The Chinese Communists were able to come to power, not because of the merit of Communism, but because the regime of Generalissimo Chiang Kai-shek was rotten to the core."

Mr. Acheson knows this, as he himself admitted later in a weak aside when he said the Communists succeeded "because the Chinese people were not convinced that the National Government was concerned with their welfare." Mr. Acheson has grown fearful of touching on the implications. When he first launched the idea which became the Marshall Plan at Cleveland, Mississippi, four years ago, he spoke the language of Hazlitt, not Hearst. From Marshall Plan to military assistance program to total diplomacy he has undergone a steady degeneration.

The Marshall Plan as originally conceived was to avert revolution by feeding the discontented. The military assistance program was to avert it by shooting them.

This is the blunt meaning of arming governments against "internal aggression." "Total diplomacy" takes Mr. Acheson another step downward by making the bogeyman theory of revolution and history the first premise of foreign policy. This asserts that discontent is only the artificial fruit of diabolic whispers spread by the wicked. Mr. Acheson has retreated all the way from FDR to Metternich.

If revolutions are the fruit of social maladjustment, then a country which devotes its wealth and labor to its own development need have no fear of subversive pamphlets. But if revolutionary ideas are a kind of bacillus, if change is the result of conspiracy, if it is a Big Bogeyman in Moscow who threatens us, then the United States has no choice but to spend its substance on preparations for war against the ogre's stronghold.

If the former is true, leadership has the painful task of persuading the rich and powerful to social reform. But if the latter is the correct theory, leadership need only sit tight and hand out the arms orders, while expressing sentiments as impeccable as those of any D.A.R. dowager. The theory of revolution by bogeyman may prove catastrophic but it certainly is comfortable.

This theory serves to make Mr. Acheson appear to be "one of the boys" and it neatly fits Mr. Truman's needs — his reluctance to risk a new conference with Stalin, his preference for continuation of the Cold War as the line of least political resistance. For if we are confronted by monsters, there is no point in palaver.

Mr. Acheson revealed more than he intended when he told the Advertising Council, in discussing the demand for new peace talks, "It has been hard for us to convince ourselves that human nature is not pretty much the same the world over." It is always necessary, in building a war psychosis, to create the impression that those on the other side are not quite human. For a self-proclaimed Christian gentleman, Mr. Acheson is making rapid progress in strange directions.

Seven Points for War, Not Peace

Washington, March 20, 1950

Secretary of State Acheson's seven points are a program for war, not peace. They invite unconditional surrender, not negotiation.

The heart of the seven points is the demand that the Soviets "withdraw their military and police force" from their East European satellites and "refrain from using the shadow of that force" to maintain the present governments in power. This derives from Winston Churchill's speech at Llandudno on October 9, 1948.

At Llandudno, Mr. Churchill proposed that the West should "bring matters to a head" with the Russians while the United States still had a monopoly of the atomic bomb. Mr. Churchill proposed that the Russians be invited to retire to their old borders — or else. The "or else" has evaporated, now that the Russians (according to President Truman) also have the atomic bomb. The rehash of the Llandudno proposals when the assumptions on which they were based have disappeared gives Mr. Acheson's "total diplomacy" a somnambulistic flavor.

The idea of "pushing Russia back" to its old borders in Eastern Europe by threat and pressure is a pipe dream. The Russian response to the pressure which began with the Truman Doctrine has been to tighten the Soviet grip on the satellite states, not to loosen it. If the Russians had military missions and bases in Cuba and Colombia, as we do in Iran and Turkey, we would hardly loosen our grip on the Panama Canal or take any chance on hostile regimes in Mexico and Central America.

The Russians would be fools to give up their grip on the satellite area from which they have been twice invaded. This time they have created a *cordon sanitaire* in reverse. The phrase itself will recall enough history to weaken Mr. Acheson's dismissal of Russian fears about "a capitalist encirclement" as mere "morbid

fancies." Curzon was no hallucination, and Churchill is a remarkably robust phantom.

Morally, Mr. Acheson is on thin ground in his crusade to
"liberate" Eastern Europe. It is true that the Kremlin interpreted
the promise of free elections in its zone of Eastern Europe as
cynically as Mr. Churchill did in Greece. But history will see this
whole chapter in a broader perspective, and in that perspective it
would be better for the American people not to fall sucker for
the line of making Eastern Europe safe for democracy.

Western Europe wasn't safe for democracy until feudalism had
been cleared away and the masses raised from illiterate serfdom.
Russia in its own rough but effective way is doing that preliminary
job in Eastern Europe. Except for the Czechs, there is not a
people in the area which enjoyed free government before the war.
An illiterate peasantry worked an inefficient agriculture for an
incompetent ruling class, and in many places the Roman Catholic
Church we prize so highly as an ally bolstered this rotten system
and enjoyed its dubious profits.

To push the Russian power back to the old borders would be
to clear Eastern Europe again for German commercial exploitation
and imperialist domination in partnership with feudal and clerical elements, as before World Wars I and II.

No one would be more embarrassed than the American liberators by the consequences of the "liberation." We could get Cardinal Mindszenty out of jail, but what would we do when he demanded the return of the Church lands? He called the land reform
in Hungary "robbery." According to Emil Lengyel, no less than
145,000 peasants shared allotments of land taken from the Church.
What would we do when the cardinal demanded that these peasants
be dispossessed, their "stolen" land returned?

A preview of what the "liberation" would mean may be obtained
from a glimpse of the last "liberation" in that area — the Horthy
dictatorship which, with Western aid, overthrew the short-lived
Bela Kun Communist regime in Hungary after World War I.
I quote from a book published in London, in 1924, *Revolution
and Counter-Revolution in Hungary*, by Oscar Jaszi, Minister of

Nationalities in the Karolyi cabinet, who was himself forced to flee by the Reds.

"The grave errors, disappointments and the suffering of the Red dictatorship are forgotten," Jaszi wrote, "and there is a widespread feeling that, in comparison with the White terror, the Red terror was for the masses a time of freedom and dignity. Meanwhile the capitalist policy of the Entente is making general the conviction that the West is the chief protector of the Horthy system and that salvation can only come from the East."

It is not difficult to believe that the Russians may be far from popular in much of Eastern Europe. Tact, flexibility, and the light touch were never among their virtues. There is no reason to suspect that Americans coming as "liberators" with our current entourage and ideas would be more popular.

This area needs (1) land reform, (2) industrialization, and (3) the collectivization of agriculture. This is what the Russians are giving it, and history will decide that what the area is getting is worth the price being paid for it. The German-feudal-clerical yoke was worse, and gave nothing in return.

People here are kidding themselves if they think they could dress up John Foster Dulles as Thomas Jefferson and win an election with him in Eastern Europe. The combination of Wall Street with German apologetics and phony Christianity can no more be palmed off as "liberty" in Poland than it can in New York.

"In the beginning of the postwar period," Joseph C. Harsch of the *Christian Science Monitor* wrote after a visit to Eastern Europe last summer, "Western calculations were inclined to assume that the social revolutions imposed by the new Russian-sponsored governments were the greatest weakness of these governments. Events have proved this to be largely a false assumption . . . the real strength of the regimes actually lies in the social changes carried out since the war. Many of those changes are anathema to America, but acceptance of them is fairly general throughout Eastern Europe."

Restrictions on intellectual freedom may be irksome for the intellectuals in the area, and Russian suspicion no doubt makes life difficult for the local native Communists. But there is no doubt that for the masses in Eastern Europe the new regimes have brought benefits in the shape of education, land, and jobs.

German capitalism wants the area again as a source of cheap raw materials and cheap foodstuffs; these are obtainable only from an ignorant population. Soviet security requires the development of a working class in the area; this can be achieved only by industrialization and the collectivization of agriculture. The difference for the masses should be obvious, even in the State Department.

20 | STAR PERFORMERS IN THE NEW WITCH HUNT

Whittaker Chambers: Martyrdom Lavishly Buttered

New York, February 12, 1952

In *L'Esprit des Lois,* Montesquieu notes with contempt that the Roman Emperor Tiberius erected statues to informers and Nero bestowed triumphal honors upon them. The America of this generation seems to be taking over the degenerate habits of imperial Rome. American publications compete for the memoirs of informers, spies, and Communist renegades. Massachusetts has its "Philbrick Day." The *Saturday Evening Post* with fanfare begins to publish Whittaker Chambers' memoirs as "one of the great books of our time." NBC invites Chambers to read his "Letter to His Children" over a nationwide radio hookup at 9:30 P.M. on a Sunday night and then follow it up — as he did yesterday — on television.

The net effect of this outpouring is the opposite of its supposed intention. The effect is to make the Communist Party seem glamorous, awesome, and devilishly important. Philbrick pictures it as a conspiracy in which one meets attractive women, the elite of the intellectuals, and the very best people; to take his word for it, some of the most important businessmen and social leaders of Boston turned up in the meetings on which he spied.

Chambers dwells on Communist virtues with the unction of a bishop: "Communists," he writes in the *Saturday Evening Post*, "are that part of mankind which has recovered the power to live or die — to bear witness — for its faith." The *Daily Worker* itself would blush to put it so strongly. In this campaign against the Communists, Americans seem to have forgotten their favorite advertising adage, "Every knock's a boost." Chambers' memoirs indeed are more boost than knock.

This glorification of the Communists by spies and renegades from their ranks has a dual origin. Communism, like Roman Catholicism, is one of those total faiths which when really embraced leave an indelible mark on a man's mentality. The secret links and hidden longings for the old comfortable faith are reflected in a fierce hate and an unquenchable respect. The renegade is always more bitter than anyone else against the comrades he has abandoned; this bitterness is a form of self-hate. These twisted and ambivalent feelings hardly equip a man for objective observation.

The other reason for the glorification of the Communists by deserters and informers is that their own pride and livelihood depend on exaggerating the evils they claim to report and magnifying the dangers they are rewarded for exposing. This is a classic reason for taking the testimony of informers with more than a grain of salt.

A man who got up on the lecture platform and said, "I was a Communist but left the party out of sheer boredom," might well be telling the unvarnished truth, but he could hardly make that an exciting story. Bogeymen are more salable than the sober realities. If the Communist Party were one tenth as glamorous as renegades and FBI moochers make out, it might elect a candidate occasionally and be able to pay a living wage to the handful who put out the *Daily Worker*.

There are good and devoted people in the Communist Party but there is also a generous sprinkling of bores, bigots, and petty despots. The membership turnover is notoriously large, but the reasons would not make a Hollywood scenario. Some people can't take Communist discipline, and are unwilling to make the sacrifices entailed. Others leave from distaste for sectarianism, some from annoyance with the Popelets who dominate the intellectual life of the party, still others from disillusionment with the careerist opportunism to be found there as in any other political movement.

It is revealing that Chambers, writing in the *Saturday Evening Post* of such people, expresses the same contempt for them that Communists feel. "Nor, by ex-Communists," Chambers writes, "do I mean those thousands who continually drift into the Communist Party and out again. These are the spiritual vagrants of our time whose traditional faith has been leached out in the bland climate of rationalism." This, too, could appear without the change of a single word in the *Daily Worker*.

In a very real sense, both psychological and political, Chambers still believes in the party.

Chambers' fervor recalls certain periods in the Middle Ages when to doubt the power and potency of Satan was to expose oneself to a charge of heresy. The new orthodoxy growing up around us similarly requires belief in Christ and Antichrist. To disparage the importance of the Communist Party is to deny one of the elements in the new American credo. As the late Jo Davidson once said to me in Paris, "The Americans *must* believe in communism, otherwise they wouldn't be so excited about it."

With this glorification of the Communist Party by its "ex's" goes a self-glorification that is ludicrous. Chambers' "Letter to His Children" is a fantastic piece of self-advertisement. Its climax is a reference to the Cross which is blasphemous in its invitation to a comparison between Chambers and Jesus. The Hiss case becomes a framework for self-dramatization of megalomaniac proportions. "At issue . . . was the question," Chambers writes, "whether this sick society, which we call Western civilization, could in its extremity still cast up a man whose faith in it was so great that he would voluntarily abandon those things which men hold good, including life, to defend it."

According to this, his own account, all Western civilization depended "in its extremity" upon finding a man like Chambers. This is less than fair to the North Atlantic Pact and Eisenhower.

Chambers would have to admit that, whatever he abandoned, he hardly abandoned it "voluntarily." He was silent until subpoenaed by the House Un-American Activities Committee. He found safety by turning informer.

To say, as he does, that in deciding to testify he was "disregarding all risks, accepting all consequences" is certainly laying it on thick when the consequences included $75,000 from the *Saturday Evening Post* for the serial rights to his memoirs. No martyrdom was ever more lavishly buttered. This man so suffocatingly ostentatious in his new-found Christianity is the kind of martyr familiar in its early annals — the kind who threw others to the lions and retired to a villa.

From Anti-Marxism to Anti-rationalism

New York, February 13, 1952

Some years ago Whittaker Chambers wrote a rhapsodic piece for *Life* magazine about Satan. The first installment of his memoirs in the *Saturday Evening Post* is another rhapsody, this time about God. His break with Communism had its origin, he says, when he looked at his baby daughter's ears and decided, "No, those ears were not created by any chance coming together of atoms in nature (the Communist view). They could have been created only by immense design."

To call this the Communist view is to stigmatize as Communist something which is centuries older than Marx. The view of the universe as a mass of atoms in constant motion, without beginning or end, a purely materialist, rationalist, and nonsuperstitious view, began with the Greek philosopher Democritus four centuries before Christ, and lies at the very foundation of modern science.

Democritus, like all of science after him, presupposed not "any chance coming together of atoms" but a world operating according to natural laws discoverable by the mind of man. Chambers writes, "Communism is what happens when in the name of Mind, men free themselves from God." Men freed themselves from God in the name of Mind when they cast off the shackles of medieval dogma and laid the foundations of the modern world.

Implicit in Chambers' half-baked theorizing is an attack on all the pioneers of modern thought, on Galileo and Giordano Bruno and Copernicus and Newton: these were the men who first in modern times "freed themselves from God . . . in the name of Mind." Implicit in his attack on Communism is an attack on the whole rational, secular, and scientific tradition from which Marxism sprang.

In this, Chambers, whether he knows it or not, is much more a Roman Catholic than the Quaker he claims to be. He echoes familiar rightist Roman Catholic philosophy when he says, "The crisis of the modern world exists to the degree in which it is indifferent to God. Its crisis exists to the degree in which the Western world shares communism's materialist vision."

Chambers says the essence of Marx was in his remark, "Philosophers have explained the world; it is necessary to change the world." But this belief in man's capacity to improve the world is not a monopoly of the Marxists. It is not even the monopoly of philosophers or reformers. A whole line of fruitful practical minds in America — inventors, engineers, and businessmen — have lived by this faith. It was Edison's and it was Henry Ford's.

Chambers speaks of materialism as "an intensely practical vision," but says its tools are "science and technology, whose traditional method, *the rigorous exclusion of all supernatural factors in solving problems*, has contributed to the intellectual climate in which the vision flourishes, just as they have contributed to the crisis in which communism thrives." (My italics.)

The phrases are glib, but the message is weird. Business is engineering, and engineering is exact science. You cannot build an automobile without "the rigid exclusion of all supernatural factors." You cannot run a business in reliance on the supernatural. You cannot depend on prayer to sell washing machines, or on miracles to meet a payroll. This is as much an attack on American business as on Communism. It is fantastic that such warmed-over ideological obscurantism should be dished up as palpitating new truth in the pages of a magazine which lives on the advertising of automobiles and radios and television sets.

The businessmen who provide the revenues of the *Saturday Evening Post* and the readers they court with their advertising are certainly among those to whom Chambers refers when he says the materialist vision "is shared by millions who are not Communist." When Chambers goes on to say that these millions "are part of Communism's secret strength," he is saying that we must go back to a prescientific medievalism if we are to be safe from Communism.

To say, as Chambers does, that "Communism is what happens when in the name of Mind, men free themselves from God," is to brush aside several centuries in which what happened was the emancipation of mankind from priestly censor and superstitious fear, several centuries of the greatest material and intellectual and cultural progress the world has ever known.

"What happened," thanks to "the rigorous exclusion of all supernatural factors in solving problems," was rationalism and industrialism and capitalism and Protestantism and secularism and liberalism. Chambers echoes a rightist Roman Catholic philosophy which has never reconciled itself to any of these. It uses the war on Communism to make war on modernism. It seeks not to keep man free but to restore the rustiest of his chains.

Manichean Melodrama

New York, February 14, 1952

Whittaker Chambers sees politics as a kind of Manichean melodrama in which the Powers of Darkness continually conspire against the Powers of Light. His first installment in the *Saturday*

Evening Post declared that we were menaced by Communism because we had abandoned belief in God. His second begins by declaring that we are menaced because we have given up belief in the power and reality of diabolic conspiracy.

"One of the more attractive traits of the average American," he begins his second installment, "but one which for more than three decades has blinded him to a ruthless plot to destroy all that he values, is his contempt for conspiracy. . . . Even today, with Alger Hiss and others in prison, many good citizens retain a hunch that the whole affair was a mere political circus. . . . This incredulity was one of the biggest obstacles which I, as the ex-Communist witness, faced . . . when the Hiss case was getting under way and the Hiss forces . . . were suggesting that I was depraved and possibly insane."

So here we have sketched out Chambers' own answer to the crucial question he raised at the beginning of his memoirs. "How did it happen," he asked of Communism, "that this movement, once a mere muttering of political outcasts, became this immense force that now contests the mastery of mankind?" The phrasing is invidious — the political writings of Marx, Engels, and Lenin were no more "mere mutterings" than the political writings of Milton, Locke, and Jefferson — but the question is of transcendent importance.

How that question is answered may determine the moral climate of America for this generation, the survival of America's historic freedoms, the issue of war or peace in our time. The answer Chambers gives is not the traditional American answer, the libertarian and liberal answer. He does not say that the way to combat Communism or any other revolutionary creed is to meet it in open debate, and to correct by gradual and peaceful reform the social evils on which it focuses attention. Free expression, free thought, and free election — the creed of Milton and the creed of Jefferson — were not Chambers' creed as a Communist nor are they now his creed as an anti-Communist.

A haunted man living in a haunted world, Chambers would revive those "fantastic terrors of sect and schism" against which

Milton inveighed three centuries ago in pleading for the right to freedom of expression from political or clerical restraint. Chambers attacks not only Communism but the rationalist tradition from which it sprang. He blames the intellectual climate "in which communism thrives" on the scientific method and its "rigorous exclusion of all supernatural factors in solving problems." This is what Chambers means when he speaks of combating Communism by returning to "God." And with "God," in the guise of a new belief in the efficacy of conspiracy, he would restore his old *Life* magazine enthusiasm, the Devil.

The efficacy of these ideas, as contrasted with those traditional in Anglo-American politics, may easily be tested. Those "mere mutterings of political outcasts" to which Chambers traces the origins of Communism began in the middle of the nineteenth century. The principal "outcast" founders of the creed, Marx and Engels, were not only given asylum in England but allowed to write and publish their revolutionary views undisturbed. That same wholesome contempt and disregard for conspiracy which Chambers laments in the average American was shared by the average Englishman.

At the same time, on the other side of Europe, there was a regime which held fast to the Chambers formula. The czarist regime was based on a belief in "God" and the Devil. Heretic and dissenter were hounded, and the sharpest watch was kept on everything which might possibly be a political conspiracy. All writing was censored. The country swarmed with spies and counter-spies. Prison and exile were meted out wherever conspiracy was uncovered, and the czarist regime was as "prepared to kill" as Chambers says he is.

If a free intellectual climate and a contempt for conspiracy make a country fall victim to Communism, then England — by Chambers' standards — should be Communist today while Russia should still be "free." Yet we see that the land in which Marx was a forbidden book and Marxism a hounded creed was the first in the world to go Communist, while the land in which Marx and Engels were allowed to teach, preach, and "conspire" unmolested has today the smallest and least important Communist party in Western Europe. The czars are gone forever, despite their reliance on "God" and their ruthless suppression of all "conspiracy," while England remains a royal and a loyal kingdom.

This is all no accident. Nor is it an accident that the largest and most powerful Communist party in Western Europe is in Italy, despite a generation of rigid fascist thought control and a government of Roman Catholic principles. Nor is it an accident that in China the Communists came to power though Chiang Kai-shek, too, operated by these ancient and mangy priestly and despotic principles. If religious teaching, widespread espionage, and a readiness to kill were the answers to Communism, then Chiang Kai-shek's merciless 1927 massacre of the leftist intellectuals in Shanghai, his revival of Confucianism, his years of civil warfare against the Reds, his suppression of dangerous views, should have entrenched him in power.

It is shocking that in our time psychopathic personalities preaching views so fundamentally opposed to everything which lies at the very foundations of Americanism should be built up in the name of anti-Communism into popular heroes and seers. The truth is that Communism has become an immense force wherever and whenever the natural aspirations of human beings for a better life have been answered not by material improvement of their lot but by just this kind of pie-in-the-sky rubbish about "God," and by calling in policeman and priest.

Budenz: Portrait of a Christian Hero

Washington, April 23, 1950

The high-walled marble Senate caucus room was never so jammed as it was for the Budenz testimony on Lattimore. A half-hour before the hearing was scheduled to begin, the aisles were filled and the audience flowed in and around the press tables and behind the committee itself.

There was a sprinkling of priests, for whom obsequious attendants hastened to provide special chairs. Very important personages stopped to confer a handshake and a grave word on acquaintances in the front rows of the audience, who blushed with pleasure at being singled out from the anonymous herd. The women's hats were as refulgent as an Easter parade's. The klieg lights, the sense of good fortune in having been able to get in, built up the excited holiday atmosphere.

The Red hearing has become the American equivalent of the bullfight. This is how the crowd must feel in Mexico City or Madrid, waving to friends around the arena, tensely waiting for the bull to appear, the bright sand to be stained with gore.

In an earlier America, a man had to be born in a log cabin to make his mark politically; today he needs to have acquired a Communist Party card in his youth. The "ex's" are not merely used as informers but regarded as oracles; crowds shiver in expectation of their revelations. The longer they are out of the party the more they remember of frightful conspiracy and diabolic plot. Senators listen respectfully as they describe the innermost details of life inside the *Daily Worker* or on "the ninth floor," and the dubious hesitate to question them too sharply.

Budenz walked in alone at 10:30 sharp, well dressed and fatter than in his radical days. The flashlights went off. One saw his bald spot as he took the oath, behind him the strong face of Lattimore flanked by his attorneys, Thurman Arnold and Abe Fortas. Budenz launched into his familiar story of the Communist conspiracy with the glibness of a traveling evangelist describing the details of hell.

One could almost feel the delighted shivers of the visiting ladies from the D.A.R. convention as he took them into the intimate secrets of the "Politburo," rolling the word over his tongue like a lollypop and adding that it was "now known as the National Board," presumably to keep its true nature hidden. When Budenz came up to his first climax, with the charge that Lattimore had been in a red "cell" in the Institute of Pacific Relations, there was a rush from the press tables to the telephones outside.

Who says this is not still the land of opportunity? An obscure radical, not above borrowing two bits, is converted by confession into a respected member of society. His books are best sellers and lecture audiences clamor for him. High clerics consult him and the United States Senate hangs on his words. He gives an investigating committee to understand that he has been so busy that he has not yet been able to get around to the State Department. Hollywood and the "organs of public opinion" have had a prior claim on his attention, but the diplomatic service will not be neglected.

Should anyone have the temerity to wonder whether an ex-Communist is the best adviser on national policy, Budenz has an answer. He explained that many of the greatest saints in the Roman Catholic Church, to which he said he was proud to belong, have come over "from the other side." Budenz named St. Paul as an example, modestly disclaiming the comparison this invited.

The comparison would seem to be premature. The admissions wrung from Budenz by the flabby cross-examination — that he did not know Lattimore, that all he reported was hearsay, that he was not familiar with Lattimore's writings, and that he had never remembered to give this information to the FBI until a few days ago — would not have been so damaging to Budenz if stated frankly at the very beginning of his testimony.

In every case, however, he dodged the question like a casuist in a theological disputation, dragging in irrelevant if sensational charges about matters as distant as Hawaii, to avoid an answer. The questions had to be asked several times in several ways to elicit the truth. This is hardly the conduct of a God-fearing and Christian man. Brother Budenz is not quite ripe for canonization.

In a different atmosphere, one sentence in Budenz' testimony would have resounded. "They will lie for the cause," Budenz said of the Communists who were long his comrades. Men trained to lie for one cause may lie for another; in this respect Lenin can be matched by Loyola. No one dared press the obvious questions. Secularism is the ultimate target at which clerical influences aim in this ostensible crusade against Reds and pinks, but Protestant America has grown afraid.

In a court, in a sane and normal time, testimony like that Budenz gave against Lattimore would be stricken as incompetent; a man cannot be convicted on hearsay. Budenz himself told indignant Senator Green of Rhode Island he had been slow in getting up a list of Reds in the State Department because "I want to be very certain. . . . I don't want to base it on hearsay, in the sense of just an individual Communist telling me."

In a court, that contradiction would have opened Budenz to deadly cross-examination. His irrelevant but sly dragging in of Hiss on two occasions in unresponsive answers would have brought rebuke from the bench. His interminable evasiveness would not have been permitted. Here Budenz was respectfully allowed to rattle on, while counsel for Lattimore were treated as if they spoke for a culprit already convicted of a crime too contemptible to deserve defense.

The oafish Hickenlooper and the whited sepulcher Lodge did their best to prevent Brigadier General Thorpe, once MacArthur's counter-intelligence chief, from testifying in Lattimore's favor, and the committee refused to receive affidavits on Lattimore's behalf except in executive session. The Senators seemed in no mood to listen to anyone impious enough to answer our saintly Brother.

A Personal Note: Me and the Red Underground

New York, November 11, 1951

"SENATOR DUFF," said a headline over a report on one of the speeches at the recent Herald Tribune Forum, "DEPLORES TENDENCY TO SPREAD HATE BY INNUENDO AND FALSE REPORTS." A weekly column, "The Red Underground," signed by Ogden R. Reid, is spreading hate by innuendo and false reports in the *Herald Tribune* every Sunday.

The column is made up of three kinds of items. One covers public meetings on the Left. The second consists of "private eye" reports about private meetings. The third reprints alleged instructions to Communist Party members on how to commit sabotage and other crimes.

The "Red Underground" column has begun to expose the fact that I have been making speeches around the country against the Smith Act. I have heard of more sensational exposés. My views on the Smith Act are hardly a secret. I have written thousands of words about the Act in the last few years. I have made twelve speeches in nine cities against the Act since returning from abroad in June.

I have been fighting the Smith Act for a long time. The Act was passed late in 1940. The first indictment under it was returned on July 15, 1941. I attacked that indictment and the Smith Act in *The Nation* of July 26, 1941. That article, "The G-String Conspiracy," was reprinted by the defense committee. The defendants were then the Minneapolis Trotskyites. The Communist *Daily Worker* was blindly partisan enough to applaud the prosecutions, as were some of the Communists now themselves on trial.

Three of my meetings against the Smith Act have turned up in the "Red Underground" column. The places in which these meetings were held would hardly satisfy a Hollywood director casting a film about the underground. One was in the Bellevue-Stratford Hotel, Philadelphia, the second at the Boston Conservatory of Music, and the third at Chopin Hall in Chicago.

No attempt was made to hide the true character of these meetings. They were not advertised as violin recitals. I did not pretend to be a lecturer sent out by the National Geographic Society. I did not claim to be a card-carrying Republican. The meetings were open to the public. Except for a few jokes in Yiddish, they were carried on in the English language. It takes a rather overheated imagination to list these as "underground" meetings.

To put them in a column headed "Red Underground" is to smear all those who participated; to imply that they took part in something furtive, undercover, and sinister; to link them with activities the Department of Justice regards as criminal.

The Reid column in this way cast a slur on a respected member of the Philadelphia bar, Walter Longstreth, who was a fellow speaker at the Bellevue-Stratford meeting. Longstreth is a Quaker who has never been counsel for radicals but feels strongly that the Smith Act is unconstitutional. He landed in the "Red Underground" column, too.

In a febrile search for hurtful material, the column last Sunday came up with one isolated and garbled sentence from my Chicago speech. I was represented as saying that there was more freedom in the Soviet Union than in the United States. I consider a statement of that kind wholly untrue and politically idiotic. The very fact that I can speak and write as I do rebuts the statement attributed to me.

The name signed to the "Red Underground" column is that of Ogden R. Reid. The name of Ogden Reid is an honored one in American journalism.

Mr. and Mrs. Ogden Reid during the years they directed the *Herald Tribune* made a distinguished record for a kind of sober enlightened conservatism all too rare in American politics and journalism. Their editorial page was the first which had the nerve in the early '30s to attack Father Coughlin, years before the Church shut up that loose-mouthed cleric. Their record on civil liberties commanded respect. The *Herald Tribune* was, and in many ways remains, a conservative paper it is a pleasure to read, however one may disagree with its point of view.

A new generation of Reids has taken over. The younger Ogden Reid made his debut last November with a series on "The Threat of Red Sabotage" which was weirder than anything the Hearst press has published, complete with a four-column page-one cut of a sardine can in which Communists are alleged to have smuggled in sabotage manuals.

It seems that a sailor clearing spoiled canned goods from the hold of a ship making ready for sea in the harbor of Philadelphia opened a sardine can in which he found thirty-three tiny leaflets published in Spanish in 1946 and 1947 which purported to be sports handbooks but contained instructions on how to sabotage electric lines and other public utilities.

The can and its contents came into the hands of the FBI which "declined to elaborate" on the possibility that these Spanish leaflets were for some Spanish underground movement. But Reid asked excitedly, "To a nation exposed to military aggression all around its far-flung defense perimeter the sardine can rules for the sport of 'subversive' warfare pose a perplexing question, How secure is America?"

Every Sunday, Reid comes up with secret code words and instructions from the Red underground on how to commit sabotage, destroy bridges, slash tires, and cripple policemen's horses.

Now if this is meant seriously then either Reid is guilty of failing to pass information on to the authorities or the authorities are guilty of failing to use this information to enforce the laws.

It is a violation of the law to conspire to commit sabotage, to conspire to destroy public property, to conspire to interfere with the police. No question of civil liberties would be involved in such a prosecution.

The failure of such allegations to turn up in any case brought against the Communists provides its own commentary on these revelations.

The publication of such rubbish is unfair when radicals are on trial for sedition. It creates an atmosphere which makes fair trial impossible. The column runs counter to the *Herald Tribune's* own declared policies. How fight hysteria and McCarthyism and preserve free political discussion while adding to the barrage of wild and woozy charges which give American politics at the moment so demented an air?

I would not be too surprised to learn from some future Reid column that my real name was Israel Pegler, that I was smuggled in from Pinsk in a carton of blintzes, and that my hearing aid is a secret receiving set with which I keep in daily touch with the Kremlin. I do solemnly deny all these allegations in advance.

There is always a danger in fighting these witchcraft manias. Brooks Adams in his once famous *Emancipation of Massachusetts* wrote that the Reverend Increase Mather in defending belief in the existence of witches "took occasion to intimate his opinion that those who might doubt the truth of his revelations were probably themselves either heretics or wizards." So if you see a picture of me in "The Red Underground" lunching out of a subversive sardine can while riding a broomstick over Times Square, you'll know why.

21 | THE FALLACIES OF LIBERATION

All the Canutes Lost Their Crowns

New York, September 11, 1952

In the summer of 1920, after intervention against the Russian Revolution had failed, Walter Lippmann and Charles Merz published an historic exposé of the way news from Russia had been distorted by the *New York Times*, of which — it may be mentioned, incidentally — Merz is now the editor.

The purpose was to show how, even in one of America's greatest and most responsible newspapers, reporting of the facts had been so perverted as to make intelligent discussion and policy-making difficult.

The exposé was published in the *New Republic*, which Lippmann and Merz then helped to edit. The editorial in which their findings were applied to American-Russian relations (August 11, 1920) may be reread with profit today, when the Chinese Revolution has intensified the problem of whether to fight the revolution in one form or another or to seek a *modus vivendi* for coexistence.

In calling for recognition of the new regime and peace with Russia, Lippmann and Merz and their co-editors felt that "no constructive action would be possible until public opinion has been cleansed of fictions and bogies by therapeutic contact with honest and relevant fact."

It is not easy — as they recognized — to obtain "honest and relevant fact" on events and issues in which men's hopes, fears, and interests are deeply engaged. One of the obstacles which existed then and exists now was indicated in the advice given for future reporting on Russia. "Pretend," the editors of the *New Republic* said, "that you are reporting Russia to an adult people that does not need to be humored or protected. Therefore, you will not have to prove every day that you are not a Bolshevik. That will be taken for granted."

Unfortunately it was not taken for granted then and is not taken for granted now. Though the danger of mistaken policies is incomparably greater, it has grown more dangerous than ever to take an objective view of the revolution in Russia or China. Now, as then, the days of the first red scare, objective discussion is made hazardous because foreign policy is entangled with domestic issues by those who have a stake in panic and repression.

It is in this sense, and in this sense only, that it may honestly be said, as Governor Stevenson said in San Francisco, that "America is threatened as never before." The threat is from within.

Never has it been so hard to think straight and speak honestly of foreign policy. Yet never has a mistake been potentially more disastrous. War with Russia and China combined is not a war we can really win, even under the most favorable circumstances. Yet it is to such a war that we are drifting under the compulsion of forces which make that course the line of least resistance.

The most extraordinary aspect of Western relations with the revolution since 1917 is the willful blindness, the refusal to see the demonstrated facts. Intervention solidified the Bolshevik regime by giving it the support both of non-Communist Russian leftists who saw no other alternative to reaction and of Russian patriots who resented (as was predicted at the time) the obvious desire of the Japanese, British, and French to partition Russia under the guise of liberating it. The same process is at work in China today, for the alternative we offer is the same Chiang the Chinese drove out, and our ally is the same Japan from whose ambitions China has suffered so much.

"Containment" is not new. Neither is "liberation." The latter was tried from 1918 to 1920 at the cost of untold suffering to the Russian people and merely succeeded (as did the similar intervention against the French Revolution) in making the dictatorship more Draconian and more extremist than before.

"Containment" was the general policy of the '20s. Truman in 1947 merely picked up where the Wilson administration began. The trade war, the economic blockade, the hostile propaganda — all is a repetition of what was tried before. The only difference is that while we persist in not recognizing China we cannot quite bring ourselves to let the world see the full extent of our blind folly by withdrawing recognition of Russia.

We are in the grip of mythology, a mythology as dangerous to question as it was to question religious dogmas in an earlier age. Stevenson says: "We will not try to make their societies [Asia's] over in the image of our own." But that is just what we are doing in refusing to recognize the new China. "Land reform," the governor recognized, "is, of course, fundamental to the problem of Asia." But who dare admit that Communism has spread in China as it spread in Russia because the revolution alone really offered land reform? Certainly Chiang and the men around him do not offer it.

Governor Stevenson touched the heart of the matter with a characteristically swift stroke in saying: "When we think of communism, we think of what we are going to lose. When many of the Asiatics think of communism, they think of what they are going to win — especially if they believe they have nothing to lose."

Hunger, misery, poverty, foreign oppression weigh more heavily in the scales than all our talk of an "individualism" meaningless to the coolie and half fiction when applied to ourselves. The coolie may be ignorant, as the muzhik was ignorant, but not too ignorant to fight a "liberation" which would restore the freedom to go on being a slave in all but name.

None are so blind as those who will not see. The czarist armies had melted away in 1917, but Lenin and Trotsky raised 5,500,000 men to fight the first attempt at "liberation." The Germans and the

Japanese only recently finished a second attempt at "liberation," which ended by adding China and the old *cordon sanitaire* of Eastern Europe to the Soviet bloc. A third world war, and all Eurasia may be Communist. Each attempt to "liberate" has shown that the revolution commanded strong and deep popular support; "slaves" cannot be impressed as soldiers. But what respectable voice dare say it?

We must live with the revolution in peace or destroy our own society in a futile effort to smash it. Coexistence and the peaceful competition of diverse societies represent the only sane and humane solution, as Stevenson indeed seems to hint.

In such peaceful competition, the libertarian traditions of the West will command as much respect as the socialist achievements of the East; these are half-truths, neither of which alone can add up to the good society. But those most ready to take up arms are almost always those who care least about the freedom in whose name they speak, and the mere approach of war is already impairing at home the liberties we talk of spreading abroad.

"Containment" will not contain the revolution and "liberation" will only end by extending its boundaries. Titoism requires more finesse than we can muster. Communism is in the world to stay, and we must reconcile ourselves to it, as the crowned heads of Europe had to reconcile themselves to republicanism and democracy. The kings who survived were those who recognized the tide. The Canutes all lost their crowns.

22 | THE SCHOOLS BESIEGED

Devoted Teacher's Reward

New York, October 3, 1952

The Bedford-Stuyvesant area is the Harlem of Brooklyn. Its schools are dilapidated. The turnover of teachers is large. Few want to stay.

Mrs. Mildred Flacks proved one of the few. She went to Public School 35 as a substitute in 1931, more than twenty years ago, and has been there ever since. Until a few years ago, P. S. 35 was housed in one of the worst rat-traps in that slum area. Mrs. Flacks stayed on anyway.

Some people stay put through inertia. Mrs. Flacks stayed put from other motives, motives teachers and mothers will readily grasp. These were indicated by those who testified on her behalf before a special trial committee of the Board of Education this week. Two witnesses may be singled out, both named Coleman though they are not related and come from quite different walks of life.

The Rev. John M. Coleman, pastor of St. Philip's Protestant Episcopal Church, a member of the Bedford-Stuyvesant committee, startled his fellow "judges" by stepping off the bench to testify on behalf of Mrs. Flacks. Dr. Coleman testified that he had known her for fifteen or sixteen years, as the teacher of one of his own children, and as a fellow member of the P. S. 35 Parent-Teacher Association. Dr. Coleman testified to her good reputation and said, "I

201

have always been particularly appreciative of her great effort in community work."

The other witness, Mrs. Anna Dickerson Coleman, a housewife, who has lived eighteen years in the Bedford-Stuyvesant area, said her daughter was in Mrs. Flacks' class and that she saw the teacher "nearly every day" during that period, and later worked with Mrs. Flacks in the parent-teacher organization. "She had to deal with many problem children," Mrs. Coleman said, "but though they were problem children when they came to her they weren't when they left. . . . She is a person above reproach. . . . She is a good mother herself, and she looked on all those children in her class as a mother would. She loved every one of her children."

Why is a teacher with a reputation of this kind on trial? Mrs. Flacks is the first of eight teachers put on trial for refusing to answer questions about their political beliefs. She is one of those against whom the finger of suspicion is pointed in the current Red hunt in the schools. The *New York Times* says the "unregenerate" Communist teacher should not "be permitted to promote his conspiratorial philosophy in the classroom." The *World-Telegram and Sun* says parents have a right to be protected against teachers "whose continuing Communist allegiance permits them to find subtle ways of injecting Communist-influenced ideology even into classrooms."

Are the writers prepared honestly to look at the facts in these cases? Mrs. Flacks is a test. She has always taught first and second grade. Are there hysterics so idiotic they believe she managed to inject Marxism-Leninism into minds grappling with alphabet blocks and how-to-do-sums-without-fingers? Is there evidence that she taught her little ones that *D* stood for *Das Kapital* or that two plus two added up to surplus value?

The respectables pretend the only purpose of the Red hunt is to shield immature minds from dangerous ideas, from the abuse of power by "subversive" teachers. The principal of the school, Thomas F. Nevins, testified that an anonymous letter accused Mrs. Flacks of being a Communist. After that he watched her in the classroom "very carefully" for months. He saw no evidence that she was "subversive." He not only praised her work but said the school was injured by her suspension last year pending trial. An assistant superintendent of schools, a primary supervisor, and a former assistant principal also testified in her favor.

A postal employee — which means a man who works in the shadow of the loyalty program — had the courage to come forward and testify as an officer of the Bedford-Stuyvesant Neighborhood Council. He said among other things that despite the omnipresent poverty of the neighborhood Mrs. Flacks saw to it that the children in her classes were somehow decently clothed and shod. Maybe this is subversive.

Who were the witnesses against her? Only a secretary of the Board of Education. What did he testify? He testified only that the Board last December 6 adopted a statement declaring that superintendents had a right to question teachers about Communist Party membership. What was the charge against Mrs. Flacks? Insubordination. In this as in the other seven cases, there was no charge of impropriety or misconduct as a teacher, no charge of "indoctrination" in the classroom.

What is there left but interference with private political beliefs? What is there left but an attempt to coerce a teacher into disclosures which might subject her to prosecution in these days of sedition trials? Or into risking hopelessly one-sided battle against some pet perjurer? Or being asked to accept the moral degradation of turning informer? A letter read into the record from Superintendent of Schools Jansen said Mrs. Flacks was to be asked to name others if she admitted Communist Party membership past or present.

To the respectables who claim they believe in individual guilt and justice, there is a challenge in these cases. Are they willing to examine them one by one on the evidence? Are they prepared to apply the standard they claim to be applying — the right to prevent teachers from abusing their power in the classroom? Are they willing to give accused teachers some semblance of fair trial by requiring evidence of impropriety in the classroom? Or are teachers like Mrs. Flacks to be rewarded for a lifetime of devotion by discharge and disgrace?

If there is subversion here, it is subversion of faith in our society and its pretensions. The subverts sit on the Board of Education and turn to sham the very principles they are supposed to be protecting.

To Protect Immature Minds

Washington, December 13, 1949

A controversy has arisen on the local Board of Education over the banning of the *Soviet Information Bulletin* from the schools. The *Washington Post* is supporting the ban on the ground that while the *Bulletin* "makes amusing reading for adults . . . it is obviously not the right sort of fare for immature students."

Since immature students may, on hearing of the USSR, look up the *Bulletin* at the public library, its removal from the schools is not enough. Even the complete suppression of the *Bulletin* would be inadequate.

The problem must arise whenever students learn of the existence of a place called the Union of Soviet Socialist Republics. Some will inevitably be led into looking up the meaning of the words "Soviet" and "Socialist."

Mature Americans know the meaning of these terms — at least they know the terms stand for something bad. Immature minds, if they once hear the terms, may be led into exploring their meaning, and thence into reading literature of an improper kind like — [EDITOR'S NOTE: The examples which follow have been elided, since the *Daily Compass* is a family newspaper read by the young as well as the grownup.]

Thus such halfway measures as barring the *Soviet Information Bulletin* from school libraries are likely to prove unsatisfactory. The logical way to handle this problem so as to avoid the premature rousing of curiosity is indicated by the following dialogue:

PUPIL. "Why is our map blank all the way across from Poland to China?"

TEACHER (*firmly*). "I don't think we want to discuss that."

PUPIL. "But is there anything there?"

TEACHER. "Well, yes, there is."

PUPIL. "Well, is it a country?"

TEACHER. "Well, not exactly."

PUPIL. "Well, is it an ocean?"

TEACHER. "No, not exactly, but there are marshes there; the Pripet Marshes, they're called."

PUPIL. "Oh, so it's blank because it's all marshland and nobody lives there?"

TEACHER (*relieved*). "In a way, yes."

PUPIL. "Gee, so nobody lives between Poland and China?"

TEACHER (*blushing*). "Well, no. Some people live there."

PUPIL. "Well, what kind of people?"

TEACHER. "Oh, bad people."

PUPIL. "What do they do that is bad?"

TEACHER (*firmly*). "They're very bad and that's enough."

PUPIL. "You mean, like cannibals?"

TEACHER. "Oh, much worse."

PUPIL. "Well, doesn't the government stop them?"

TEACHER. "Their government's very bad, too."

PUPIL. "What's the name of that government?"

TEACHER. "Oh, why must you ask so many questions? The government is called the government."

PUPIL. "Well, what kind of a government is it?"

TEACHER. "I told you it's a very, very bad government."

PUPIL. "Is it run by Republicans or Democrats?"

TEACHER. "Something much worse."

PUPIL. "But what do they call the people that run that government?"

TEACHER. "It's not something that nice people talk about."

PUPIL. "You mean, like sex?"

TEACHER. "Only much worse."

PUPIL (*fascinated*). "Gee! Where could I get a book about that?"

TEACHER. "Little boys aren't supposed to read books like that."

PUPIL. "You mean, they have not-nice pictures?"

TEACHER. "Tommy, you are a horrid little boy."

PUPIL. "But if there are people there and a government, why is the space left blank on the map?"

TEACHER. "Because the Board of Education doesn't think it's a nice kind of place for little boys to know about."

It is by firm handling of this kind that the teacher may prevent the curiosity of the student about Russia and socialism from being prematurely aroused.

Patriotic Memo: The Training of Youthful Informers

New York, September 12, 1952

I do not wish to be critical of the McCarran Committee but the hearings with which it opened the school year here have added to the difficulties in detecting Communists and Communist sympathizers on our school faculties. Those who are left will become unusually careful in what they say, and it will rarely be possible any longer for the quick-witted student to sense a suspect teacher's true political views in some unguarded reply to a well-planted question.

We will no longer be able to depend on amateur volunteer informers among the students. It will require training to detect leftist opinion in the atmosphere which has been created in our schools. Radical teachers will hide their opinions and it will be harder than before to distinguish the loyal from the disloyal. Yet classroom surveillance will become more important, since few teachers if any will now venture to attend radical meetings, private or public, where their presence may be noted.

If the schools are to be policed adequately against subversive and dangerous thoughts, students will have to be given some formal teaching in the detection of radicals. Psychological as well as political conditioning will be required. Silly schoolboy prejudices against "snitchers" and "squealers" will have to be overcome.

Such psychological retraining will prove valuable in their later years, when they will be called upon to volunteer information about their friends to the FBI, military or naval intelligence, passport investigators, the red squad of the local police, and similar agencies which have been developed to keep America free.

At the risk of appearing to be in advance of my time, I would like to suggest that in the Americanism departments of our schools we begin to establish courses in informing. At the beginning, if local school boards are loath to appropriate the necessary funds, it may be possible to obtain contributions from public-spirited businessmen with the vision to see the value of having available graduates of such courses for their plant-protection and labor-spy services. It is even possible that the National Association of Manufacturers, which has begun to take considerable interest in our schools, would be willing to finance courses of this kind on a national basis.

The purpose would really be no different from that of courses in any other branch of technology. There is no more reason for the informer to start from scratch than the engineer. The techniques developed by earlier practitioners can be as useful to the one as to the other. But such courses should not be limited to technical matters. As in the newer teaching of mathematics, the student's interest should be stimulated by colorful stories about the famous figures of the craft in the past. Most important of all, in dealing with a profession which has until now operated under a social cloud, it is important to develop a certain pride in the business of informing, an *esprit de corps*. For this purpose the history of informing should be taught, though interpreted somewhat differently than before.

Even those great informers of the past who cannot be regarded wholly as heroes may sometimes be shown in a more favorable light if care is taken. The outstanding example, of course, in a Christian country, is Judas Iscariot. The thirty pieces of silver make it difficult to present him purely as a loyal Roman citizen working within a subversive movement for patriotic motives, though indeed the thirty pieces may only have been his expense account. But it is at least possible to explain that without Judas, the Saviour could not have achieved his mission. There would have been no crucifixion, no redemption, no resurrection had there been no Judas. His services to the faith have been too little appreciated.

I envision at the start two courses in informing, of one semester each. They might appear in the school catalogue as:

INFORMING I. HISTORY OF THE PROFESSION: Informing in ancient times. Informing in the Roman Empire. Its distortion in the one-sided works of Tacitus and Suetonius. The neglect of Judas in Christian theology. Informers who helped fellow Christians to achieve blessed martyrdom under Nero. Informing in the Spanish Inquisition. Informing against Dissenters in England. Informing against Roman Catholics — Titus Oates. Modern political informing, with guest lecturers during the term, to be chosen from among such distinguished contemporary informers as Louis Budenz and Whittaker Chambers.

INFORMING II. TECHNIQUES OF THE PROFESSION: The arts of disguise, simulation, entrapment, deception, and provocation, with some attention to the crafts of casuistry and cross-examination as practiced by the great inquisitors. How to appear to be a radical. How to draw others into political indiscretion by simulated sympathy. How to lead a conversation into dangerous ground. How to prove one's "loyalty" to the Left by recruiting relatives and friends. The importance of maintaining the appearance of strict Marxist orthodoxy and fiery leftism. How overt acts may be provoked. The collection of evidence, with guest lecturers from the FBI, the Passport Division of the State Department, and other agencies with specialized needs.

Informing has an advantage over most other branches of technology in that the student may obtain his practical experience while at school. Student informers should be encouraged to practice as much as possible on the faculty of the school in which they are enrolled, and their reports should be counted as part of the school-work in the course. In this way they will not only be preparing themselves for future usefulness but will, as I suggested at the beginning, help to keep the schools free from purveyors of dangerous ideas. In closing I would also recommend that those schools which combine Americanism exercises with Commencement may well consider the award of a prize to the best informer in each year's graduating class.

23 | HOME THOUGHTS FROM ABROAD

Bird's Eye View from the Eaves of Paris

Paris, October 1, 1950

I am writing this in a tiny hotel room high up among the eaves of Paris. From my window I can see the gardens of the Tuileries in all their eighteenth-century elegance. Outside it is raw, cold, and rainy, and were this any place but Paris I would describe the day as miserable.

I feel like a fugitive from a chain gang. As I sit down to report home I am trying to shake off the almost narcotic effect of all the beauty I have seen in the past few weeks: the Shah Jehan's palace in Delhi; Jerusalem from the high hill where David the King is said to be buried; *Aïda* sung under the stars in Rome among the vast ruins of the Baths of Caracalla; Giotto's lyrical bell tower in Florence and the grand simplicity of the Duomo; Fiesole perched high up on its hill above the Arno; Venice the incredible; and Paris, even after these still the most beautiful city of the world. I feel sorry for everyone who has not been in Notre Dame.

This is the time for all Americans who can manage it to travel abroad. One can still capture here those qualities so desperately needed at this moment in the history of mankind: an urbane detachment toward the idiotic clamor that precedes all wars; sophistication about the barbarous absolutes with which men customarily whip up their recurrent homicidal manias; a renewed sense of that common humanity being undermined by so-called ideological controversy; reverence for the treasures one generation must pass on to the next; and, above all, compassion.

It is difficult to write home because it is difficult to re-establish a common denominator with the mood in America. At this distance, in the quite different atmosphere abroad, America seems a kind of bad dream. To catch up a little with the American papers is to feel again that Mad Hatter quality of the USA in 1950, and to feel it more strongly than one did at home where the atmosphere infects everyone to some degree.

It does not make one homesick to read the summaries of the new McCarran-Mundt-Ferguson bill, or to get some echo of Mr. Wallace's latest statement: "This time Stalin has gone too far" — as if he were a character in a mid-Victorian novel. America seems to be making rapid strides toward fascism and folly, and Western Europe's atmosphere accentuates by contrast the febrile immaturity with which politics seem to be carried on back in the States.

Except among visiting Americans like myself I have yet to encounter abroad the atmosphere we know at home. The need for the dollar has cost the political leaders here their independence. The intellectuals everywhere feel the pull from Moscow and Washington for a choice between them. Korea is page-one news, but among ordinary people one feels that not only Korea but the whole affair of Russo-American rivalry is a distant contest in which they have no sense of participation and little interest. Since the people caught "in between" feel they cannot affect the outcome there is a general tendency to shrug one's shoulders and go about one's business. The characteristic comment in France is not fit for translation in a family newspaper.

In Italy and France the streets are gay, the cafés full, the summer resorts crowded. For all the poverty of the working class in both countries, they exhibit no such misery and filth as one can see in India or the Arab Middle East. Here one feels a cynical detachment about the Russians and the Americans. The Italians and the

French are old and civilized peoples who know how to enjoy life, and do enjoy it. They are enjoying it now. They are not letting the American mobilization interfere with the long lunch, the afternoon nap, and the late dinner hour.

This atmosphere, too, is infectious. In America there is a strong feeling that war is inevitable and the sooner we get it over with the better. In Western Europe one feels that war is not "inevitable," that American calculations are much too simplistic, that perhaps it may be avoided after all.

The European View of Push-button Politics

Paris, October 2, 1950

Americans, including yours truly, are too simple-minded in analyzing events abroad. We like drama. We were brought up on advertising slogans. We are conditioned to sensations. We are given to "either-or" thinking and, above all, we are a very impatient people. We have the push-button mentality.

One of the things that begins to dawn on an American abroad is that there are more things in heaven and earth than he ever dreamed of before, whether he is a man of the Right or Left. The deposits and mental habits of centuries cannot be changed in a day. Indeed they survive the greatest revolutions. Whether in Russia or France or India, the more one tries to understand the more one sees how fundamental an axiom of politics is that old French chestnut about the more it changes the more it remains the same. The tough persistence of national characteristics is a factor all of us have underestimated.

Neither Europe nor Asia can be remade in a day. They have been what they are for a long time and unless blown completely to pieces will stay that way a long time. The rise of capitalism and industrialism and Communism — they are parts of the same process — has created similar problems and similar conditions around the world and it has given rise to a new world movement with a common mentality, the Communist movement. But while this makes big headlines it can be overestimated and it is, every day, notably in Washington.

We have little history of our own in America and so we do not think in terms of history. But history is still important. Despite all the vast changes of modern times, the basic trends of French policy and British policy and Russian policy and German policy and Polish fate (for poor Poland rarely gets enough of a breather between partitions to have a policy) have not changed and will not be changed.

All this is blurred over at the moment by the American-Russian rivalry, the natural fruit of the mutual fears felt by the two great powers. But their effect on Europe and Asia derives as much from their similarities as from their differences. The Russians and the Americans, viewed from the vantage point of Western Europe, are much alike.

These are, from Western and Latin Europe's point of view, fresh barbarian peoples, vigorous, extroverted, naive, and slightly ludicrous in their passionate intensity. The Russians now as in the past speak of collectivity while the Americans preach individualism, but both are devotees of mass-production methods not only in manufactures but in mentalities. The Americans are as much the product of assembly-line methods as the Russians, and the Russians are as philistine as the American businessman. In painting, for example, Joseph Stalin and George Babbitt see eye to eye.

The Americans have never been very tolerant of differences and are becoming less so. In five years if not sooner there will be little difference between Washington and Moscow insofar as the right to dissent is concerned. Both countries export to their spheres of influence the primitive man's paranoid conception of a world in which one must constantly be on one's guard against mysterious portents and powers. The American obsession about Communism seems without parallel until one remembers how the Russians feel about that ill-defined virus they call Trotskyism.

Both the Americans and the Russians exercise a fascination because they offer means for accumulating capital. Both have shown great organizing capacity. The former have capital for export and the latter have a formula for raising capital. The dictatorship of the proletariat is from an economic point of view a method for facilitating compulsory savings, that is, compulsory accumulation of capital. Since this involves a great deal of suffering, those who can still get capital painlessly by mooching it from America will go on doing so as long as they can.

As seen from Washington — and, I am sure, from Moscow — it looks as if the powers in between must ultimately choose between these two methods of capital accumulation. But this is not a World Series in which either the Yanks or the Reds must win. What one begins to feel abroad is that the possibilities may prove more varied than the simplistic logic to which we are all addicted in America. It has been said of the law that its life is not logic but experience. This is not to postulate irrationality but to recognize the wonderful complexity and the many imponderables in every equation which deals with human beings. So it is with politics.

If this is wishful thinking, it is wishful thinking which reflects the mood of Western Europe. It may be that America and Russia will divide the world between them, and then destroy it in a catastrophic struggle. This would satisfy our American sense of history à la D. W. Griffith. We like our spectacles colossal.

But one thing seems certain. The longer war is delayed, the greater the recovery in Western Europe, the more likelihood there is of an independent policy and unexpected developments. These unexpected developments may also reinstate traditional patterns of national policy, especially with the projected rearmament of Germany.

Postscript by Aneurin Bevan

Paris, April 29, 1951

Two fundamental points, one bearing on domestic, the other on foreign policy, were made in Aneurin Bevan's brilliant speech explaining his resignation from the British cabinet. Both are inescapable for those who believe in democracy and socialism.

The domestic and, at the moment, lesser point was that a party which calls itself socialist cannot leave economic planning to a Chancellor of the Exchequer or Secretary of the Treasury. Modern planning cannot be done by financial means. As the witty Welsh rebel put it, "The great difficulty with the Treasury is that they think they move men about when they move pieces of paper about."

Even a capitalist economy, when really called upon to produce at top potentiality, must utilize direct orders and controls. Bevan was in a sense merely rephrasing for a socialist society what Baruch first demonstrated so incomparably for a capitalist society in the American industrial mobilization during World War I.

Bevan, in a proposal recalling one several times made by Walter Reuther in America, called for "a production department." The proposal is unlikely to get very far, given the British love of "muddling through" and the disinclination of such pallid socialists as Mr. Attlee and his colleagues to engage in any thoroughgoing kind of economic planning.

This disinclination, in a situation like the present, is of more than purely theoretical importance. The alternative is to let British industry go on enjoying an inflationary rearmament boom while cutting steadily into the social services and the living standards of the workers and the fixed-income middle classes.

Bevan's second and more important point grew out of the obvious fact that even if Britain were a fully and efficiently planned socialist society it could not carry the burden of the present rearmament program without so serious a derangement in living standards as to undermine faith in the possibilities of democratic socialism.

The budget against which Bevan revolted was a budget which did for the British ruling class what they could not do for themselves. It expanded the arms program. It began to cut social services. And it promises to make Labor and socialism take the blame for doing what they would have protested had they been in opposition.

From this point of view an election must seem of dubious benefit, for it would almost certainly provide a Conservative victory and make the Tories take the responsibility for this kind of a program.

Another coalition, with Gaitskell in Snowden's role and Attlee in MacDonald's, might be more to Tory taste.

Until recently, when the threat of charges for false teeth and spectacles broke the back of Bevan's patience, all seemed to be going beautifully for the Right. Bevan in taking the job of Minister of Labor seemed to have been successfully gelded. Labor's one dangerous potential rebel leader seemed safely installed in the invidious task of mobilizing British manpower for war.

Now Bevan has moved from protest against charges for false teeth and spectacles to a general onslaught against the rearmament program itself and beyond it against docile acquiescence in American diplomatic policy.

"This great nation," Bevan said, in a statement which all who still believe in democratic socialism will cheer, "has a message for the world which is distinct from that of America or that of the Soviet Union."

This was his second and major point and it is a point Western Europe will appreciate. Its great peoples ought not to have to choose between the gloomy thought controls of Russian Communism and that hysterical movement toward a police state which America calls "defending democracy," between the unwieldy centralization of Moscow and the quasi-monopolistic economic anarchy which passes for "free enterprise" in the USA.

But if Bevan is to carry on the promise of his revolt he must go a step farther. It is only in an atmosphere of peace and demobilization that democratic socialism in Britain or elsewhere stands a chance.

24 | SOME LONGER PERSPECTIVES

Revolutions Are Sometimes Necessary

New York, April 4, 1952

The basic principles of Communism are as "irreconcilable" with those of a free society as Justice Douglas said they were in his Occidental College speech which the *Compass* reprinted last Sunday. The dictatorship of the proletariat is not the same as a democracy. The "proletariat" is nowhere a majority. A dictatorship in its name by one party which becomes in practice a dictatorship by the leaders of that one party is a long way from a democratic society. The rigid party-line thought control of the Communist parties and Communist regimes can by no stretch of the imagination be equated with freedom of thought. Communists are neither Democrats nor democrats.

But all these inescapable truths can — and do — get themselves mixed up with a lot of inflammable rubbish in the atmosphere of the American Cold War. Justice Douglas waxed lyrical, for example, and said, "Man cannot be standardized like automobiles, or screws, or nails. God gave man the same amazing diversity that He gave the flowers in the mountain meadows." These pretty sentiments hide some dubious implications.

I, too, like to believe that in the long run man "cannot be standardized," but he does tend to be pretty well standardized whether in a primitive tribe or in a modern nation. Many Europeans believe, and I agree with them, that nowhere has a nation come closer to standardizing men "like automobiles, or screws, or nails," than in the United States.

We Americans like to think of ourselves as rootin' tootin' individualists, but in a huge country of 160,000,000 people we all awake to the language of the same alarm clocks, listen to the same radio programs, gobble the same breakfast food, wear the same clothes, read the same news-agency reports in the same kind of newspapers, take in the same ideas from the same big national magazines, and listen solemnly to the same platitudes from the two big — and very much the same — political parties. The American in a mass-production industrial society is not much less standardized than the Russian under Communism.

It is true that the American, unlike the Russian, can still buy a *Compass*, a *Nation* or a *New Republic*, or even a *Daily Worker*, but the small circulation of this nonstandardized opposition press speaks for itself, and many Americans are getting as nervous about buying a radical paper or magazine as a Russian is about being seen with a foreigner. "There is no room," Justice Douglas said of Russia, "for a crusading journalist." There is also very little room for a crusading journalist in America. On this, I can testify from experience. Five more years of the present trend and it will be as impossible for a dissident voice to be heard in Washington as it is in Moscow.

Justice Douglas' lyrical remark about God also deserves closer attention. To say in the context of an anti-Communist speech that "God gave man the same amazing diversity that He gave the flowers in the mountain meadows" is to link God not with botany but with the Cold War. It implies that "God" is for diversity as against Communist standardization. The remark may be classified in that large pigeonhole labeled "God Is On Our Side."

I don't know what "God" favors but I do know that a lot of people who favor God are as authoritarian in their beliefs as the Communist. God may have made man as diverse as mountain flowers but Roman Catholics are by no means the only believers who, when in power, try their best to make all God's creatures think exactly the same way. The Inquisition and the *Index Expur-*

gatorius were not invented by Stalin. The anti-Catholic Luther, like so many professional American anti-Catholics, was far from being a liberal. Most of the world's orthodox clergy, whether Greek, Roman, Lutheran, Moslem, or Jewish, tend to authoritarianism.

It would be best to leave "God" out of it. Too many throats have been cut in God's name through the ages, and God has been enlisted in too many wars. War for sport or plunder has never been as bad as war waged because one man's belief was theoretically "irreconcilable" with another. Theoretically, Roman Catholicism is "irreconcilable" with American democracy, but the most consistent libertarian on the United States Supreme Court in our time was a devout Roman Catholic, Frank Murphy. In practice American Catholics have proven as good democrats as anyone else, and certainly better democrats than the advocates of white Anglo-Saxon Protestant supremacy, with or without benefit of bedsheet.

Peace abroad as at home can only be achieved by reconciling the "irreconcilable," as in practice they have been reconciled for generations. The principles of Russian czarism were also "irreconcilable" with American principles. So are the principles of Franco or for that matter those of Chiang Kai-shek, a great believer in the one-party state, the secret police, terror, and enforced conformity in the name of reaction, as Justice Douglas would agree.

There is a third, more basic, and more important point to be made about this business of "irreconcilability." The Gospel says that in my Father's house are many mansions, a saying which I take to mean that "heaven" allows for at least as much diversity as there is on earth.

History teaches us that not all changes are brought about by counting ballots. History teaches us that sometimes revolutions are necessary. There will not be peace in the world until Americans are prepared to recognize this. (All of us who attended school before the era of the Feinberg Law recall that America itself once had a revolution.) There are times when force and violence can alone end abuses. There are times when revolutionary terror and the police state are necessary to remake an old and rotten society.

I am not advocating revolution or dictatorship. I hate cruelty and I love liberty. Nor am I palliating the crimes, stupidities, and evils which inevitably accompany revolutionary transformations of society. All I am saying is that in societies like czarist Russia and Kuomintang China which leave the people no other recourse this is what happens, and that the good outweighs the evil, as I believe the good outweighed the evil in all the great revolutions of modern times, from the English to the Chinese.

The best we can do when confronted by such convulsions is to set an example from which the new societies may learn and to create an atmosphere in which they may move back without fear of war or intervention to more normal and free standards. Indeed, this is the great contribution made in this period by Justices like Douglas who are seeking bravely to stem the tide which would turn America (in its fear of Communism) into a counter-revolutionary police state, borrowing Muscovite techniques of repression for Chamber of Commerce purposes.

History shows us that wars against revolutionary movements in major countries only push the revolutions to greater extremism while destroying liberty at home. To speak, as Justice Douglas did, in terms of a "world-wide struggle against Communism" is to speak in terms which lead to such wars. The real struggle is against war, and to preserve for the future those noble ideals of freedom unhappier peoples have never enjoyed.

We who were unable even to shape South Korea into the semblance of a democracy cannot hope to fashion the future of Russia and China with molds drawn from our own quite different and more fortunate experience. They must work out their destiny for themselves. The least the self-denominated "godly" can do when confronted by the "godless" is to exercise a little Christian charity, and look at the beam in their own eye.

With all this, of course, Justice Douglas has demonstrated his agreement, not least in courageously advocating recognition of Red China last fall. Such recognition and "coexistence," whether with Communist China or Communist Russia, is incompatible with the concept of a "world-wide struggle against Communism." If there is to be struggle, there cannot be recognition. This is the crossroads, where one makes the choice, whether to go toward war or peace.

Justice Douglas and the Peasant Revolution

New York, May 16, 1952

Mr. Justice Douglas' speech to the Amalgamated Clothing Workers Wednesday night amplified a theme he broached in April before a national conference on the Point Four program. He wants the United States to promote "peasant revolutions" in the under-developed areas of Asia and Africa.

The need for revolutionary change in the peasant areas is inescapable. Dr. Charles Malik, the Lebanese minister to this country, a man of learning and discernment, expressed the same idea at the same Point Four conference less provocatively. Dr. Malik said of the Point Four program, "in many cases it is hopeless to expect real development unless fundamental changes in the social structure are introduced."

What Dr. Malik meant was vividly expressed by Justice Douglas in his speech to the clothing workers. "You can move in to your agricultural areas of Asia and the Middle East with our wonderful Point Four program and increase the production of the land, but if the net return to the tenant is still only 5 percent," the Justice said, "all you are doing is making a few landlords richer."

The objection goes deeper than that. It is not merely that without a change in social structure the benefits of any program would go largely to the landlords. The social system is so hopelessly antiquated and cumbersome and inefficient that money invested in development pays off poorly from any point of view.

A society in which capital prefers the profits of usury and speculation to those of industry and development is a society which has a vested interest in maintaining the ignorance, the religious superstition, and the top-heavy land tenures which keep the peasant hopelessly impoverished and in debt. In such a context it is difficult to develop modern industry or agriculture as we know it in America. The masses are cattle to be milked, not customers to be served.

This description applies not only to India and Iran and the Arab countries of the Middle East but in large measure also to Greece, and Italy, and Spain. Presumably it is in such areas that Justice Douglas would have us promote "peasant revolutions." Now this makes good headlines, but it does not make political sense, and the subject is too serious for demagogy.

It is impossible, with the best intentions in the world, for the government of a stable capitalist and democratic society to bring about revolutionary change in backward areas. Let us begin with the land problem in a country like India. Here lease is piled on lease, and tenant lives off subtenant, in as crazy a pyramid as any that Insull built in the American utility industry.

The people at the bottom are so poor that they cannot afford to pay compensation for the land they need. The legal and ethical rights are entangled in a history of conquest and chicanery no court could unravel. The situation calls for the kind of clean sweep only a revolution can provide.

But could even the most enlightened capitalist be expected to invest money in a society undergoing such a convulsion? Who would trust his funds to a country in the midst of expropriating moneyed interests? What bank or insurance company would dare make capital available even indirectly for development in such a situation? Is it not a little silly to urge America to foster "peasant revolts" in the backward countries?

We have seen peasant revolutions in our time. "What was it that begot Communism in Russia?" Justice Douglas asked in his speech to the Amalgamated, and answered, "Feudalism." The same kind of "feudalism" is in process of being destroyed in Communist China and in Eastern Europe. These revolutionary changes all represent gigantic "Point Fours" for industrial development in backward areas.

The United States is opposed to all of them. Even Justice Doug-

las is forced to speak in terms of combating them. To ask the
United States to foment peasant revolution in India and the Middle
East when it is busy fighting to "contain" such revolutions in back-
ward areas elsewhere is to let rhetoric get out of hand.

An orderly society based on property rights cannot be expected
to encourage destruction of property rights elsewhere. It is no accident that the government has but to suggest the mere recognition
of Red China to find itself beaten over the head in Congress and
the press. America has much to sell the world, but it cannot export
revolution carefully confined, like tomato soup, in cans.

Justice Douglas becomes all the more confusing when he speaks
of fomenting peasant revolutions in order to "combat Communism" and to deal with what he calls Soviet Russia's "hungry appetite for imperialistic expansion" and "military threat." Once the
context of war, cold or hot, is accepted, the rest becomes wistful
window-dressing.

If we are going to talk in terms of war against the Soviet bloc,
whether metaphorical or real — and the two tend to merge — then
reforms must be subordinated to military necessity and the need
for strategic bases and alliances. You do not win allies by fomenting revolutions among their peoples, and when you begin to speak
of military necessities you speak a language that militates against
reform altogether.

The logic of war leads to acceptance of the status quo for the
sake of bases and alliances, whether this means alliance with
Franco, the pashas of Egypt, or the moneylender-landlords who
rule India. The first necessity for the development of backward
areas is peace between East and West, and the first way to help
the peasants of the Middle East is to make sure that neither side
atomizes them into a better world.

25 | EPILOGUE IN LIMBO

Dr. Einstein Takes the Problem up with God

New York, February 14, 1950

Far off, unbelievably far, beyond a distant star cluster, a delegation of elderly men trudges slowly through the Pearly Gates. They seem to be expected, and attendants take them at once to a huge reception hall where a majestic figure rises to receive them.

To the leader of the delegation He says, "Ah, dear Dr. Einstein." Dr. Einstein's eyes twinkle. "It looks as if theology has overcome the exact sciences, sir," he says. "How shall we address you?"

"Shall we say," is the answer, "that it would perhaps be easiest for such distinguished scientists to call me Mr. X?" He waves the delegation to chairs and the interview begins.

MR. X. I am told you and your colleagues wished to see me about the H-bomb, Dr. Einstein?

DR. EINSTEIN. In a sense, yes. In another sense, no. The H-bomb has created a new crisis. But the H with which we are concerned is not the H of hydrogen. We can handle that. It is the H of humanity that has driven us in despair to see you.

MR. X. But the H of humanity is an old story, Dr. Einstein.

DR. EINSTEIN. Forgive us, sir, but the more we examined the problem the more we began to see that the real destructive and explosive power lay not in the H of hydrogen, but in the H of humanity.

223

MR. X. Why did you come to me?

DR. EINSTEIN. Because this H is your creation, and we do not understand its operations.

MR. X. Please explain.

DR. EINSTEIN. In our studies and laboratories, when we seek to solve a problem we look for the missing element. When we find what is missing, we add it to complete our formula and the problem is solved.

MR. X. I understand. Go on.

DR. EINSTEIN. All war is hateful to those of us who are men of good will. The H-bomb intensified the necessity of solving the problem of peace. For by the bomb's use humanity may destroy itself.

MR. X. I am listening.

DR. EINSTEIN. So we put the problem to ourselves as we would have put any other scientific problem. "What can we do," we asked ourselves, "to bring about a peaceful coexistence and even loyal cooperation of the nations?"

MR. X. A very old question.

DR. EINSTEIN. But never more urgently in need of an answer. We decided that what was missing was mutual trust among the nations. We saw that in the relations of nations, as in the relations of individuals, government was necessary to create an atmosphere in which mutual trust might grow. For if every man were at the mercy of the strong and the unscrupulous, there would be no peace and security.

MR. X. So?

DR. EINSTEIN. So we had found the solution. We declared that mutual trust was the missing element, that a world government was necessary to foster it, that the new weapons were far too destructive to permit lawless anarchy among the nations.

MR. X. Well, what happened?

DR. EINSTEIN. Nothing. People listened and then brushed us aside.

MR. X. I still don't see why you came to me.

DR. EINSTEIN. Forgive our frankness, sir. You created this H of humanity. Its irrationality is appalling. Reason, logic, and the scientific method can do nothing with it. When we create a machine and it does not work right, we find what is wrong and change it. Our only hope is that you will change the nature of humanity. We fear that otherwise the earth is doomed.

MR. X. (*after a long pause*). Dear Dr. Einstein, you remind me of an old assistant of mine, dimly known on earth in the legend of Lucifer. He was proud while you are humble. But you make the same criticism. He could not stand the endless bloodshed, war, cruelty, and evil that man did on earth. He revolted, blaming me for man's irrationality, since man was my creation. Is that not your complaint also?

DR. EINSTEIN (*softly*). It would be untruthful to deny it. Yes, I blame you. If I create a formula or a machine which does not work well, the blame is mine. If humanity is obsessed with criminal and self-destructive folly, the blame is yours.

MR. X. Dr. Einstein, when you make a good machine, it works smoothly, doesn't it?

DR. EINSTEIN. It certainly does.

MR. X. Is a machine rational?

DR. EINSTEIN. It is built and operated on rational principles.

MR. X. Built by whom?

DR. EINSTEIN. By men.

MR. X. Could a machine have done the thinking of Euclid or Newton or Riemann or yourself?

DR. EINSTEIN. No.

MR. X. It is not rational then, as men can be?

DR. EINSTEIN. No.

MR. X. Would you like men to be as machines? To operate invariably and according to the strict logic of their mechanics? Could anything be expected of such creatures? Would they yearn for truths beyond their grasp, and create in their turn?

DR. EINSTEIN. I suppose not.

MR. X. I could not make man free to aspire without also making him free to destroy himself. He could only be truly rational if he were free to be irrational. Unlike your machines, he lives. And the essence of life is freedom. It escapes the subtlest formulas. It is powerful, explosive, and risky.

DR. EINSTEIN. Granted, but can't you intervene just this once to save your creation?

MR. X. I cannot. It is no longer mine. I provided the spark, but that was only the beginning. Man beyond that is his own creation. History is the record of his painful struggle to mold himself. The process is too much for formulas. In the struggle against evil, good was produced, and often in striving for good, man did evil. This is the counterpoint of his self-creation. Man cannot evade his freedom. If he fails its test, there are other beings, other worlds.

DR. EINSTEIN. Have you no pity? What purpose is served by so much agony?

MR. X. (*rising*). The violins in the orchestra do not understand their agony, either. . . .

The scene fades out.

INDEX

ABOUT THE AUTHOR

Born in 1907, I. F. Stone has been a working newspaperman since the age of fourteen when, during his sophomore year at a small-town high school, he launched a monthly, *The Progress*, which supported — among other causes — the League of Nations and Gandhi's first efforts at freedom for India.

While at school and college, he worked for daily newspapers in Camden, New Jersey, Philadelphia, and New York.

Since 1940 he has served in succession as a Washington correspondent and commentator for *The Nation*, the newspaper *PM*, the *New York Post*, and the *Daily Compass*. In 1953 he launched *I. F. Stone's Weekly*, a legendary venture in independent one-man journalism, which he edited and published for nineteen years. He has written extensively for the *New York Review of Books* and long served as a contributing editor. He writes a Washington column at irregular intervals for *The Nation* and for many daily papers at home and abroad, including the *Philadelphia Inquirer*, on which he worked while he was in college.

In semiretirement Mr. Stone returned to the philosophy and classical history he had studied in college. He taught himself ancient Greek and wrote *The Trial of Socrates*, a controversial probe of the most famous free-speech case of all time, widely acclaimed on publication in 1988.

Mr. Stone and his wife, Esther, live in Washington. They have three married children.